Lecture Notes in Computer Science   826

Edited by G. Goos and J. Hartmanis

Advisory Board: W. Brauer D. Gries J. Stoer

David S. Bowers (Ed.)

Directions in Databases

12th British National Conference on Databases,
BNCOD 12
Guildford, United Kingdom, July 6-8, 1994
Proceedings

Springer-Verlag
Berlin Heidelberg New York
London Paris Tokyo
Hong Kong Barcelona
Budapest

Series Editors

Gerhard Goos
Universität Karlsruhe
Postfach 69 80
Vincenz-Priessnitz-Straße 1
D-76131 Karlsruhe, Germany

Juris Hartmanis
Cornell University
Department of Computer Science
4130 Upson Hall
Ithaca, NY 14853, USA

Volume Editor

David S. Bowers
Department of Mathematical and Computing Sciences, University of Surrey
Guildford GU2 5XH, United Kingdom

CR Subject Classification (1991): H.2, H.4

ISBN 3-540-58235-5 Springer-Verlag Berlin Heidelberg New York
ISBN 0-387-58235-5 Springer-Verlag New York Berlin Heidelberg

CIP data applied for

This work is subject to copyright. All rights are reserved, whether the whole or part of the material is concerned, specifically the rights of translation, reprinting, re-use of illustrations, recitation, broadcasting, reproduction on microfilms or in any other way, and storage in data banks. Duplication of this publication or parts thereof is permitted only under the provisions of the German Copyright Law of September 9, 1965, in its current version, and permission for use must always be obtained from Springer-Verlag. Violations are liable for prosecution under the German Copyright Law.

© Springer-Verlag Berlin Heidelberg 1994
Printed in Germany

Typesetting: Camera-ready by author
SPIN: 10472592   45/3140-543210 - Printed on acid-free paper

Preface

This volume continues the theme established for the series of British National Conferences on Databases, and presents a number of papers which address current *Directions in Databases*. The papers themselves constitute the written proceedings for the Twelfth British National Conference on Databases, BNCOD-12, held at the University of Surrey, Guildford, UK.

Despite the maturity of database technology, and its widespread acceptance as being central to software and system development, a number of recurring themes have presented themselves again at this conference, as they do also at other database conferences. These range from the implementation challenges of parallel and distributed systems through the problems of exploiting object-orientation in databases and capturing temporal data to the formal models and techniques which underpin the abstractions inherent in databases. Whilst it is true that all of the refereed technical papers have been submitted from academia, the issues which they address are critical for system development and implementation; hence, we would hope that there will be as much in this volume to interest the commercial practitioner as the academic researcher.

The environment in which databases operate has evolved, and this has in itself brought a range of new challenges. Our first invited speaker, *Richard Barker*, addresses one such issue – the management of open systems, including multi-vendor databases – which is particularly pertinent to 'real' database implementations, just as it is to most other applications.

When first developed, databases represented, on the whole, snapshots of the world at particular instants. Much effort has been expended investigating the modelling and representation of temporal data. Our first group of technical papers addresses this area: *Schwiderski and Saake* explore the underlying temporal logic which pertains to active databases, whilst *Soukeras and King* discuss an event-based approach to modelling the temporal dimension of data.

Databases rely fundamentally on underlying formalisms. Often, these formalisms become most apparent as the basis for new query languages or manipulation algorithms. *Chan and Trinder* present a query notation for object-oriented databases founded on list comprehension techniques, and *Alagic and Sunderraman* discuss the expressivity of various logic paradigms in the context of strongly typed object databases. In a third paper in this group, *Bagai and Sunderraman* discuss an extension to the relational model of data, and an associated algebra, which can be applied to the manipulation of general deductive databases.

As the availability of suitable hardware permits the development of massively parallel databases, a number of issues arise which are addressed in the next group of papers. *Jelly, Kerridge and Bates* present an approach to benchmarking parallel database machines, which have, of course, performance characteristics which are fundamentally different from those of traditional mainframes. *Burger and Thanisch* discuss modifications to the standard concept of transactions which would promote the achievement of massive concurrency in parallel systems. *McCarroll and Kerridge* explore the issue of semantic integrity and the derivation of integrity tests appropriate to parallel database machines.

Object-oriented databases are proving to be far from the simple idea which was first espoused, and they offer a wealth of challenges which are being addressed by a number of researchers. Here, we have three papers which discuss three different areas of concern: the impedance mismatch at the interface, efficient access to stored objects, and an ad-hoc query language for objects. The papers by *Paton, al-Qaimari and Doan*, *Kemp, Iriarte and Gray* and *Barclay and Kennedy*, respectively, discuss these three topics.

The final pair of technical papers explore the area of federations of heterogeneous distributed database systems and the requirement for interoperability. *Murphy and Grimson* describe the Jupiter system, a multidatabase 'layer' which provides interoperability language, and *Jeffery et al.* propose a 5-layer model of information content to aid the reconciliation of the data models for autonomous heterogeneous information sources.

Our second invited speaker, *Peter Gray*, draws the conference to a close by discussing the challenge of releasing the knowledge that is now widely available on the so-called 'information highway'. He suggests that a combination of object databases, client-server architectures and 'knowledge brokers' will be necessary for the full potential of knowledge networks to be realised.

Acknowledgements

The task of selecting 13 papers for presentation from the 47 submitted fell to the programme committee of some 23 members, to whom I am deeply grateful. In addition to the papers included here, others were recommended for poster presentation during the conference. Bill Olle was a tower of strength as chair of the committee, in the initial preparation of the papers for refereeing, the collation of referees' comments for the programme committee meeting and the drafting of the outline programme, as well as guiding the committee itself through the material to hand. As always, the programme committee has attempted to maintain a balance of interest between academia and commerce, and I am especially grateful to Bill for his leadership in this area.

I am particularly indebted to the guidance and support of the BNCOD steering committee, especially Alex Gray, its chair, who has responded to countless phone-calls and email messages, as well as offering much useful practical advice. In addition, the organisers of previous conferences – especially Mike Worboys and Peter Gray – have offered invaluable advice at several stages. The conference itself could not have been organised at Surrey without the long-suffering assistance of Helen Slee and Caroline Leishman, who handled most of the administrative details, and postgraduate students in the Department have also been a major source of effort behind the scenes.

Guildford, May 1993   David S. Bowers

Conference Committees

Programme Committee
T. W. Olle (T. William Olle Associates) - Chair
T. J. Bourne (SIAM Ltd.)
D. S. Bowers (University of Surrey)
R. Cooper (University of Glasgow)
B. Eaglestone (University of Bradford)
D. J. L. Gradwell (Data Dictionary Systems Ltd.)
P. M. D. Gray (University of Aberdeen)
W. A. Gray (Univ College of Wales, Cardiff)
J. Hughes (University of Ulster)
M. Jackson (University of Wolverhampton)
K. G. Jeffery (Rutherford Appleton Laboratory)
J. Kennedy (Napier University)
R. Lucas (Keylink Computers Ltd.)
S. Malaika (IBM, Hursley)
J. K. M. Moody (University of Cambridge)
M. A. Newton (Open University)
A. Poulovassilis (Kings College, University of London)
N. Revell (City University)
C. Small (Birkbeck College, University of London)
P. M. Stocker (University of East Anglia)
R. Tagg (Independent Consultant)
M. Worboys (University of Keele)
M. H. Williams   (Heriot-Watt University)

Steering Committee
W. A. Gray (Univ College of Wales, Cardiff) - Chair
T. J. Bourne (SIAM Ltd.)
D. S. Bowers (University of Surrey)
P. M. D. Gray (University of Aberdeen)
M. Jackson (University of Wolverhampton)
M. Worboys (University of Keele)
M. H. Williams   (Heriot-Watt University)

Organising Committee
D. S. Bowers (University of Surrey)
C. Leishman (University of Surrey)
H. Slee (University of Surrey)

Contents

Invited Papers

Managing open systems now that the "glasshouse" has gone   1
R. Barker (OpenVision International, Camberley, UK)

Knowledge reuse through networks of large KBS   13
P.M.D. Gray (University of Aberdeen, UK)

Temporal Databases

Expressing temporal behaviour with extended ECA rules   23
S. Schwiderski and G. Saake (University of Cambridge, UK)

Temporal databases: an event-oriented approach   38
S. Soukeras and P. J. H. King
(Birkbeck College, University of London, UK)

Formal Approaches

Object comprehensions: a query notation for object-oriented databases   55
D. K. C. Chan and P. W. Trinder (University of Glasgow, UK)

Expressivity of typed logic paradigms for object-oriented databases   73
S. Alagic and R. Sunderraman (Wichita State University, USA)

Algebraic computation of the weak well-founded model for general   90
deductive databases
R. Bagai and R. Sunderraman (Wichita State University, USA)

Parallel Databases

Benchmarking parallel SQL database machines   105
I. Jelly (Sheffield Hallam University, UK),
J. Kerridge (University of Sheffield, UK) and
C. Bates (National Transputer Support Centre, Sheffield, UK)

Branching transactions: a transaction model for parallel databases   121
A. Burger and P. Thanisch (University of Edinburgh, UK)

A strategy for semantic integrity enforcement in a parallel database   137
machine
N. McCarroll and J. Kerridge (University of Sheffield, UK)

Object Oriented Databases

On interface objects in object-oriented databases   153
N. W. Paton, G. al-Qaimari and K. Doan
(Heriot-Watt University, UK)

Efficient access to FDM objects stored in a relational database   170
G. J. L. Kemp, J. J. Iriarte and P. M. D. Gray
(University of Aberdeen, UK)

A conceptual language for querying object-oriented data   187
P. J. Barclay and J. B. Kennedy (Napier University, UK)

Distributed Databases

The Jupiter system: a prototype for multi-database inter-operability   205
J. P. Murphy (Dublin City University, Republic of Ireland) and
J. B. Grimson (Trinity College, Dublin, Republic of Ireland)

A model for heterogeneous distributed database systems   221
K. G. Jeffery, L. Hutchinson, J. Kalmus, M. Wilson, W. Behrendt and
C. Macnee (Rutherford Appleton Laboratory, UK)

Managing Open Systems
Now that the Glass-house Has Gone

Richard Barker

OpenVision International, Camberley,
Surrey GU15 3HS

Abstract. Corporate mission-critical systems were once held in proprietary mainframe environments, the 'glass-house'. A single supplier and large team of systems experts enabled users and IT departments to see the system from a distance, using parts they were granted access to. When things went wrong, everything was restored, eventually, as if by magic. Modern systems are moving to vast networks of flexible distributed databases and open-systems technology where every user has a PC or workstation. Who manages geographically dispersed systems, comprising hardware and software from multiple suppliers, half of it bought by user departments themselves? The answer must include a computerized distributed system management facility. This paper covers systems management issues that must be addressed and some key initiatives that are emerging to tackle them. It focuses on open-systems operations, performance, storage and security. Without a good understanding of these issues, open-systems solutions may cause more damage than good to companies that implement them.

1 Introduction

The world is changing fast and many of our old certainties have been dashed, to be replaced by new uncertainties, which are sometimes stimulating and sometimes frightening. Not least of these in our computer technology industry is the replacement of one blue mug by thirty or forty widely coloured and exotic mugs. We are, of course, referring to the unstoppable move from the generic mainframe, or glass-house as it is sometimes known, to distributed open systems. The cost argument for this move is *apparently* undeniable, given that the price per million instructions executed on an INTEL or SPARC chip is around forty times cheaper than on the mainframe. And some companies claim that their replacement hardware is cheaper than the running costs of the air conditioning they used before. *So what is the problem, if any?*

2 Problem Definition

In some senses there is none. The hardware *is* much cheaper. We *can* chop and change between suppliers. The software costs are generally much higher, and new releases *do* occur at a frightening pace, but that is containable and often quite fun. In fact having the ease of use of object technology, windowing and all the great tools we get on Windows, NeXT, Mackintosh and even Motif has enabled us to deliver much more sophisticated applications for our users, with superb graphical user interfaces – no more the dumb terminals of the past. Both network and database technology have come on so well that they offer excellent point solutions to transferring and managing huge amounts of data across the network. CASE, fourth-generation languages, object-oriented tools have enabled us to rethink our methodology for development and slashed life-cycle timescales for delivery of business-process-oriented systems.

The problem is encountered not during development, nor even during the first year of application implementation. It comes later when the same system needs to be rolled out to the second tranche of a hundred users, or to the first one-thousand-user site and especially to a large global organization with perhaps ten or thirty thousand highly demanding and critical end users. *The root cause of the problem is that in systems management terms open systems are not scalable.*

Scalability with open global distributed heterogeneous systems has several challenges that must be met before it can be successful. Many of these are implied by the very terms used.

2.1 Openness

Open systems are generally seen as beneficial but some of the concepts may have a down side when considered on this scale. Open implies choice, freedom and ease of access and therefore raises the questions:

> "What about enforced business process?"
> "What about corporate policy and standardization?"
> "What about privacy, access control and authorization?"

Distributed, as opposed to centralized, systems enable the data and the process to be placed near the user, provide connectivity scalability by the inherent capability to add or modify extra nodes, and theoretically they also eliminate the risk of a single point of failure. This should also mean that any subsystem or part of the network can be separately tuned or secured to best meet the needs of that user population. On the other hand these same benefits generate further questions such as:

> "Who manages the data when it is on 2000 nodes? With what tools?"
>
> "Who loads backup tapes on remote sites or what happens to the network response time if we backup across the network?"
>
> "How much redundancy of hardware, networks and data must we build in to ensure reliability of service or performance?"
>
> "And who manages the security of sites that are hundreds or thousands of miles away?"

In many organizations this distribution opportunity is being handled by siting general-purpose systems experts at remote sites, or by asking users to take on the task without training or proper tools – the result can be huge cost escalation, loss of control and, of most importance, loss of business integrity.

And then there is the excellent concept of heterogeneous systems as opposed to the homogeneous, single-supplier, proprietary lock-in problem of the past. Personally I really like this concept because if I want a new PC, workstation, UNIX server or other component I can choose what I want from a variety of commodity suppliers and just plug in the extra capability. It is just like picking a can of baked beans from the store – we can choose from two or three well-known brands or get the same thing with an own brand label from any supermarket chain. Or can we? Does it taste the same? What about the little blackened beans you sometimes get in cheap tins? Why do the cheaper tins not open as easily and why will my children not eat them anyway? The concept of heterogeneous and open systems relies upon conformance to international or de facto standards and our expectation is that the quality and finishing from a second or third source will be as good as from the original. But the minor differences in connectivity, protocols, semantics or other characteristics on which we rely actually burn huge amounts of our resources to resolve – and I mean burn in the sense of wasting time and/or money – profits if you prefer.

2.2 New Applications

Coincidentally with these changes there is a new breed of application being aggressively pursued by leading-edge companies. On one hand there is the move within the telecommunications, entertainment and information providing sectors to bring the Information Highway into our homes, whether we want it or not. On the other hand large global companies are streamlining their business processes to integrate with their customers and suppliers, to provide 10:1 improvements in productivity, normally using *apparently* integrated distributed databases encompassing structured data, vast document repositories and an ever growing amount of business relevant multimedia information (such as corporate and competitive advertisements). The database technology from companies like Oracle, Sybase and Informix is converging with up and coming database capability from Microsoft, Lotus and other new vendors. All of these technology developments would have added huge new challenges to the proprietary single-site environment: in an open-systems environment the challenges are exponentially greater even if you only consider issues such as backup and security.

2.3 Business Perspective

Whilst all these technologies and changes are happening what do the executives of our organizations think? In many senses they do no want to be bothered by anything to do with system management. They simply want cheap, highly usable, easy to learn, trouble free, best of breed, completely integrated business applications with a common look and feel. They also implicitly want the system to be available *all of the time* (what the industry refers to as 365x24 availability). Totally secure. Completely open to them as an individual! Highly performant. And if we, the technologists, cannot provide it there are plenty of suppliers who can (apparently) supply exactly what is needed for $499 tomorrow. Our users have become intolerant of the IT department, having been educated by their children and the computer rags of what is possible at very low cost – admittedly only in a single-user, personal workstation environment.

This paper will now go on to examine the critical aspects of managing open systems and the types of solutions that need to be employed. The strong technical needs will be flavoured by their applicability to the survival or sound running of any company or large organization and the aspirations of its executives. The final part of the paper then poses a few challenges in the hope that the next few years will see a dramatic improvement in the management of open-systems so that they can be relied upon to provide a stable, reliable and cost-effective solution for the new breed of mission-critical systems being developed today.

3 System Management Needs

In some senses system management starts where a system development life-cycle leaves off. Hopefully, an organization has gone through the process of creating a business and IT strategy, defined the requirement, designed both the application system and system topography, bought or built the application, converted from the old to the new and gone live. Now that we have applications that are rolling out on hardware, network and operating systems from multiple vendors we have got to make it work properly all of the time. (In reality, open-systems management equally applies to the distributed and interrelated development environments that are prevalent in many organizations today.) Good IT shops have included the following aspects in their IT strategy and are at least in part prepared.

The management aspects that need to be considered carefully in an open system broadly fall into the major areas of *operations, performance, storage* and *security*. Operations cover topics such as knowledge of what is out there, what is happening, and control of anything that moves. Performance covers monitoring, trend analysis, prediction and tuning of files, databases, devices and the network. Storage covers the ability to backup, recover, archive, migrate and otherwise (automatically) manage an apparently infinite distributed file store. And security covers authentication, authorization, audit, repudiation and policy management.

3.1 Operations

Let us approach this topic from a business perspective. In our business scenario we will imagine a large corporation (or progressive academic organization) which is continuously changing the way it does business, contracting and expanding to meet different market pressures. It will therefore be bringing to bear new applications which are bought in or built by both the IT department and directly by the users, causing a continuous state of flux. Users may be wiring up their own buildings, acquiring PCs, workstations, printers and laptops and even servers. By acquiring other companies or merging, the corporation may inherit complete computer networks using different applications, hardware, network protocols, and so on. And the executives, if they even give it a moment's thought, will expect it to be integrated without any trouble. So the first question we might want to ask is very simple: *"What do we have in our system?"*

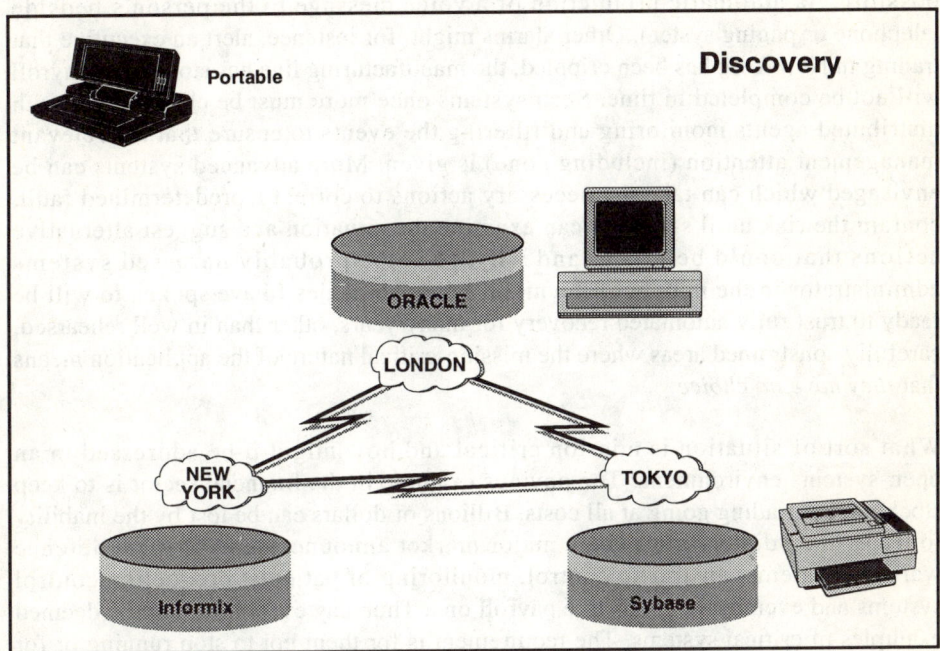

Fig. 1 What is out there on my network?

Discovery is the first major function that needs to be supported. We need to have a capability, or set of co-operating capabilities, to enable us to build up a logical and ideally physical picture of all our hardware, gateways, devices, operating systems, memory, protocols, database systems, applications, etc. This has several purposes from the mundane asset management through to the essential starting point for managing change. Ideally this sort of capability should be run in a client-server manner with agents on each node being able to collate the required information and provide it to one or more remote control consoles. This presents the first really difficult challenge, which is how do you distribute the agent software to all the nodes on the systems that exist in the newly acquired company? And later on how do you distribute new versions of software anyway to 2000 nodes? One way is to distribute the software in a manner analogous to the way a virus distributes itself across the network, but when we get round to considering security this may be perceived as 'not such a good thing!'.

Once we know what is out there, and how to get it, the next important question is: *"What happens when something goes wrong?"* Ideally we need an open-systems event management capability that can coexist with any proprietary capability and be easily configured to monitor automatically the wealth of possible events that could occur and at least notify some management console when an alarm is triggered. Some alarms should literally wake up a database administrator to correct a problem – possibly via automatic production of a voice message to the person's bedside telephone or paging system. Other alarms might, for instance, alert an executive that trading in New York has been crippled, the manufacturing line has stopped or payroll will not be completed in time. Such systems once more must be client-server with distributed agents monitoring and filtering the events to ensure that the relevant management attention (including none) is given. More advanced systems can be envisaged which can take the necessary actions to correct a predetermined fault, contain the risk until someone can examine the situation and suggest alternative actions that could be taken, and why, to some probably harassed systems administrator in the middle of the night. Few companies I have spoken to will be ready to trust fully automated recovery for many years, other than in well rehearsed, carefully constrained areas where the mission-critical nature of the application means that *they have no choice*.

What sort of situation is mission critical and how might it be addressed in an open-systems environment? The obvious example in the financial sector is to keep stock market trading going at all costs. Billions of dollars can be lost by the inability to trade immediately after some major market announcement. Critical defence warning systems, air traffic control, monitoring of patients, production control systems and even applications like payroll on a Thursday evening can all be deemed examples of critical systems. The requirement is for them not to stop running or for recovery that is so fast that it achieves the same effects. Proprietary systems from companies like Tandem have led the way, producing fault tolerant no-single-point-of-failure systems. Hewlett Packard and others have produced excellent shadow recovery systems. And the new massively parallel processing devices with shared-nothing architectures promise much in this area. But in an open-systems market we need the ability to exploit our diverse hardware and software, with minimal redundancy of equipment. The glass-house computer may be forty times more expensive than our new boxes but it is perhaps two hundred times more reliable. Given this *certainty* of regular failure on open systems we must have heterogeneous *fail-over* systems as illustrated below.

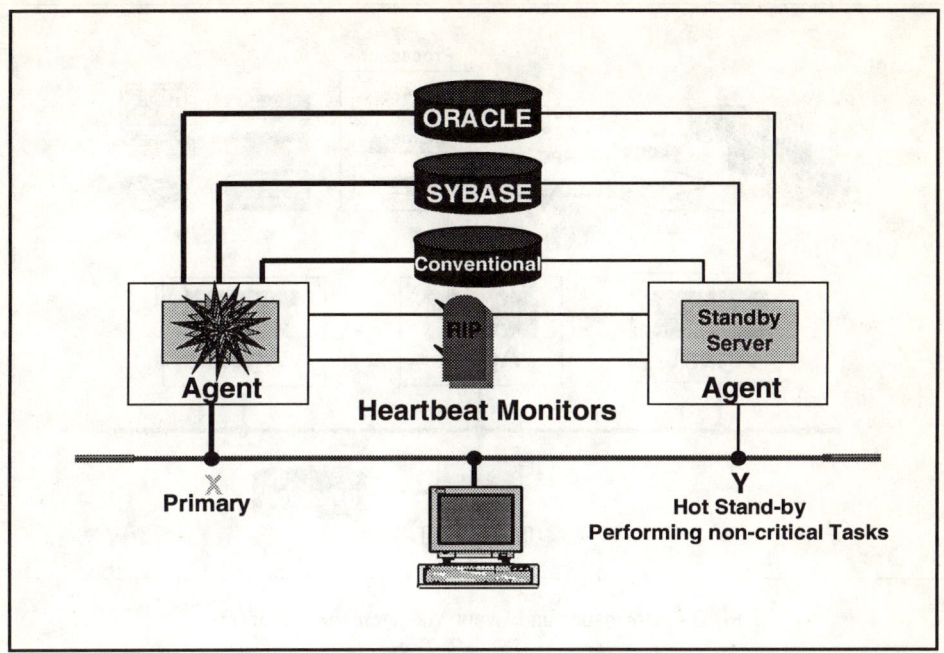

Fig. 2 Automatic Fail-over System

In these scenarios highly configured spare servers on the network could take on the role of *standby servers*, whilst performing non-critical tasks. They would deploy a variety of *heartbeat* monitoring capabilities to keep an eye on critical hardware and subsystems on one or more other servers. Should a failure occur on a subsystem, immediate normal recovery would be instigated (e.g. bringing up the ORACLE-based trading system again). If the failure were catastrophic the standby server would take over the original files, or shadows thereof, assume the network work identity of the original server, recover and restart all subsystems and help the users rapidly regain their service. Once recovered, the original server would become the standby machine – a bit like role reversal at home; but less emotionally stressful. The real challenge here is to enable a SUN UNIX machine, say, to act as hot standby for a variety of machines such as an IBM UNIX box, a SEQUENT NT server and an Alpha machine from Digital. And when do we believe that an Informix or ORACLE DBMS can act as hot standby for a Sybase system? Perhaps never. We may have to rely upon portable software and client-server monitoring agents to give the service that we require.

3.2 Performance

In an open-systems environment performance is a major problem in some senses when compared to the glass-house. With the older less capable systems we could predict throughput and response time to within 5% or so. Nowadays we rarely even attempt the task, for various reasons. The good news is that the rate of new capability

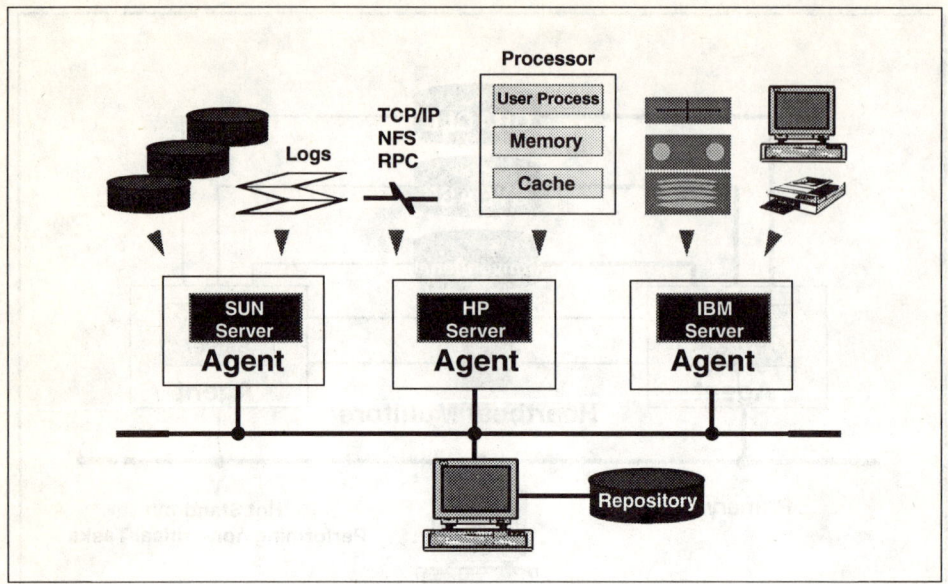

Fig.3 Performance and Event Management Station(s)

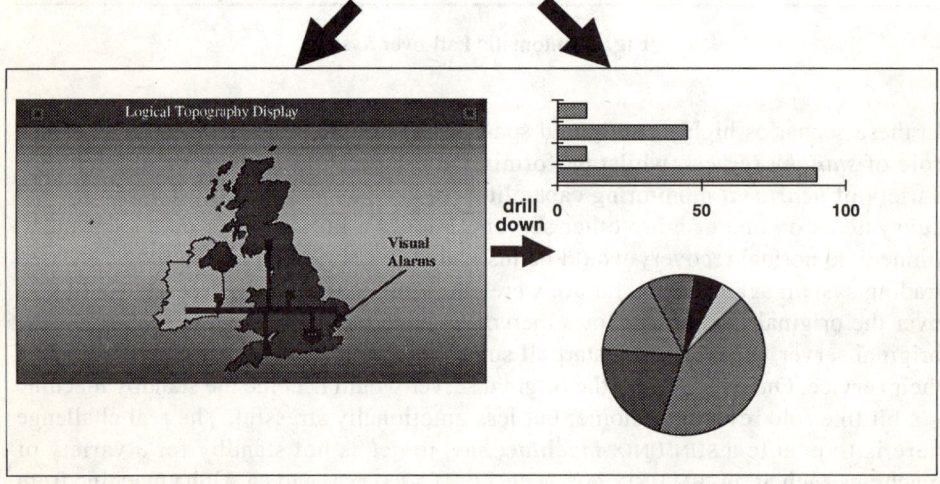

Fig.4 Management Monitors　　　　　　**Fig.5** Detailed Gauges

emerging on the market is outstanding. Every six to twelve months, processing speed, network capacity and nearly every other performance-related capability is doubling in power. In addition, by installing the latest version of a key component such as the database management system with say a new parallel server capability, we can dramatically change the characteristics of the system. On the down side we literally cannot accurately predict what will happen if we add a new application to the network or change some index – we have to try it and see. And where the systems consist of hardware and software from multiple suppliers their tools alone are insufficient.

What is required as a minimum therefore is performance management capability that can orchestrate performance monitoring agents on each host. These agents can work with vendor agents if available, or more likely they will actively collect the performance data required from every critical system component. The simple next step is to fire off alarms when preset simple or sophisticated thresholds are met, to provide online display gauges, trend analysis and other useful data to a systems management expert. More sophisticated capability would include integration with the event management capability mentioned earlier, to take remedial action to keep critical systems performing well, such as rescheduling jobs, reassigning user priority levels, rerouting network traffic and generally balancing the load. Such capability needs itself to be highly performant and capable of being educated rapidly in the field when new hardware, software or applications are added. And remember this may include nodes where no systems administrators can afford to be based across a wide geographical area.

So performance in an open-systems environment is a complex subject especially as our users naively expect non-stop instant response, and with many re-engineered business processes their businesses have come to rely upon it.

3.3 Storage

This relatively simple topic is now taking on a whole new life in the open-systems world. In the glass-house you might remember going into the rooms adjacent to the computers and seeing massive arrays of tapes and disks with lots of operators and perhaps robotic devices busily moving them around continuously. What was happening was the highly disciplined and essential task of taking backups, disaster recovery copies, archive and recovery of our critical data resource. More sophisticated systems allowed apparently infinite file stores, completely transparently to our users, except for a few moments delay while the data was brought back online automatically.

Today's requirement is slightly more complex. The data resides on perhaps 2000 nodes, few of which have any sort of permanent system staff to carry out even a simple backup process. In addition our database vendor friends have very kindly added capability for document management, multimedia, automatic data replication and will no doubt shortly give us dynamically relocating complex objects. The need is therefore to enable remote sites to have operatorless storage devices that remote storage agents can utilize to manage the normal backup situations. More sophisticated capabilities, perhaps driven automatically by an alarm from the event-management system, would carry out co-ordinated tasks such as network backup, defragmentation and selective archive of heterogeneous file subsystems across different nodes.

The laptop and other transiently connected devices need special attention as they may require automatic upload and download of mail and more complex local workgroup data. A typical example these days is a salesperson with a laptop containing prices, demonstrations, video-clip illustrations of products, order forms and up-to-date personal customer details. Every time they connect to the systems remotely, orders may be uploaded. When they connect for longer periods their entire portfolio may be updated, backups taken and reconciliation carried out between their recent local changes and the master distributed database. The system management capability might well need to *discover* what the salesperson has been doing and retrospectively create alarms and take corrective action. Which immediately brings up the most compelling concern – that of security.

3.4 Security

In an open-systems environment security is perhaps the hottest topic. This is the one where non-IT executives get seriously involved. One bank, for example, said: *"We don't really care about losing money – that is nothing compared to losing market confidence."* A legal company said: *"All out business is confidential... We sometimes need to stop our employees even knowing who our customers are, unless they really need to."*, and they were particularly concerned about the 'golden key' users in the IT department. These executives read the papers and hear about the uncontrolled millions of people who are joining the INTERNET each year. They also hear about competent INTERNET users being able to break into virtually any other system, and at the same time realize that they *must* communicate with the outside world to run their businesses properly.

So what do we need? The key words are authentication, authorization, audit, access control and repudiation. The starting point should be a business-level security risk assessment to ensure that the infinite number of things that *could* be done is reduced to a practical set. This will particularly highlight application-specific concerns and issues to do with user roles and third-party contacts.

Authentication Inevitably the first area to be addressed is some level of authentication – that is, to have electronic proof of identity. Another way of thinking about it is to ask the question: *"Are you **really** who or what you say you are?"* In an open-systems environment where users can have and may need multiple passwords to different systems, applications and databases this is not as easy as it sounds. The simplest requirement is to ensure that all users and groups of users are known and that their passwords are changed frequently. Privileged software agents across the network could identify potential problem areas, including identifying easily broken passwords.

The ideal situation, though, from a user perspective is to have a single logon that is authenticated and then used to give authorized access to all other systems. This sort of problem has been addressed very well by systems based upon the Kerberos™

capability which came from the Athena project at the Massachusetts Institute of Technology. A user would first log on to a highly secure node in the system which would authenticate the user and effectively issue tickets for authorized Kerberos-aware services that would enable the user to access the services transparently during the duration of the ticketed session. The key component of such capability is a sophisticated encryption algorithm to stop academics, UNIX hackers and others reading the passwords whilst it passes along the network. A new requirement here though is to enable different security systems around a global network to coexist, and of course to enable any such system to work on UNIX environments from multiple suppliers, and ideally on VAX VMS, NT, MAC, and so on. So now we are able to answer the question: *"What can you do, given who you are?"*

Access Control and Audit   What you can do must, however, be constrained by different levels of access control such as read, write, only the records for the people in your own department, internal mail only, perhaps to nominated groups. A serious issue though is security *across* these different subsystems to stop the expert *inferring* the data that they are after. This may need to be associated with sophisticated audit trails that identify who or what created, changed, accessed, removed data or other capabilities. Such audit trails need to bring together audit information from different subsystems, including those written by users and those produced by, say, stored procedures in database systems like Sybase and ORACLE.

In one company, a consultant told a trustworthy director from a different division that his management were fiddling the books. They managed to analyze the database audit trail of 'who had changed what and when' to identify the culprits, subsequently remove them and compensate the affected customers.

Repudiation   The final area is reasonably subtle. It is where someone has done something and then been able to change things so that it appears that it was not done at all or not done by that person. We need to stop people who have done something illegal, such as an insider trade, being able to say: *"I repudiate that I did that".*

The above theoretical needs must then be put in line with the hard realities of life such as:

"How do you protect the network against a PC user with PC-NFS?"
"How do you tie in smart-card security devices with a network security system?"
"How do you stop archive and backup files becoming security risks?"
"And how do you cater for all the non-computer security threats?"

Open-systems security, as in our personal lives, will always be a balance between the risk to the business and the cost of protection and therefore cannot be done without the direct involvement of executives.

4 Summary and Future

Open-systems management needs are way beyond those of the glass-house because of cost restrictions, distribution, multiple suppliers and a new breed of applications that will be used on them. All open-systems management tools need to be integrated within a client-server architecture. Agents on nodes must be able to coexist with proprietary capability and with management workstations, probably using a distributed common repository. Security has to be fundamental to the whole system, transparently allowing event management, performance tuning and network storage to occur in an ever changing system topography.

But there is a long way to go before the tools that we have today will provide the confidence levels in open systems that we have enjoyed with the glass-house. Research by open-systems vendors and academics must be done to answer questions such as:

"How do I predict the performance of a newly envisaged open-systems solution? And what will it cost? And which are the best suppliers?"

"How can I emulate a disaster and subsequent recovery?"

"How do I extend privacy and security to a laptop that is sometimes added to the network?"

These issues are important. They can break a company if not addressed properly. This means a careful blend of business acumen, intelligent application of technology, gentle but firm remote systems administration and a realistic attitude to the ratio of spend versus risk.

References

1. D. Geer: Lessons learnt from Project Athena. In: R. Khanna (ed.): Distributed Computing Implementation and Management Strategies. Prentice Hall 1993

2. W.R. Barker et al: CASE Method: Tasks and Deliverables. Addison and Wesley 1990

3. D.E. Geer, G.A. Champine: Distributed computing for the technical workplace. In: The Proceedings of the European UNIX Users Group. October 1990

Knowledge Reuse through Networks of Large KBS

Peter M.D. Gray

Department of Computing Science, University of Aberdeen
Aberdeen, Scotland, AB9 2UE

Abstract. The explosion of wide-band networks and the arrival of the information highway mean that large amounts of information are on-line, but where knowledge is in the form of procedures it is likely to be hard to re-use it or to adapt it to use knowledge in a variety of formats. Since database technology is about sharing information we need to rise to this challenge. Object database technology suggests a way forward by keeping procedures with class descriptors, but we need to combine this with client-server technology so that more computing takes place where the objects are, or where specialised knowledge servers are adapted to handle it. One consequence is that more knowledge will be stored declaratively (e.g. as constraints) and transformed before use instead of being frozen in a specific compiled form. Thus the technology will use more code-generation and compiling on-the-fly. A second consequence is the developing need for mediators and facilitators, acting as "knowledge brokers" and "knowledge transformers" at nodes on the network.

1 Introduction

The explosion of wide-band networks with the arrival of the InterNet and the long-expected Information Highway has finally arrived! But it doesn't just mean that there are more relational databases out there waiting to be joined together! Nor is it just about moving bitmaps and images and retrieving home videos from gigantic servers, which is what Oracle are concentrating on. Instead, I want to draw your attention to the coming together of knowledgebase technology and database technology! There is a great deal of knowledge available over the networks in the form of expert rules and procedures applicable to particular domains and to knowledge in a particular format. Now, since database technology is about sharing information, and making it available for a variety of applications (e.g. through subschemas), we need to think about how to put procedural knowledge from one server together with data from other servers. This is because, increasingly, data will be held on various servers and accessed on demand. We simply cannot have the alternatives of everyone keeping their own copies of large rapidly growing knowledge bases, or worse still, rediscovering the knowledge!

We need knowledge servers, some with problem-solving ability and some containing large nets of connected facts, probably structured as objects. But such sharing is not the only way of re-using knowledge. One theme running through this talk is that knowledge must be transformed in order to be re-used. Thus, instead of just shipping binary executable images around, we need to combine constraint declarations and procedures from various sources and use them to generate code that is tailored to the form of data on servers. Thus, *before knowledge can be re-used, it must be transformed*!

2 KSE and Ontologies

A persuasive vision of future Knowledge Networks comes from the Knowledge Sharing Effort (KSE) in USA. [Neches 91, Swartout 93] Their vision is one of Mediators, which are a kind of expert system acting as *Knowledge Brokers* on a network, which transform problems and requests so that they can be tackled by Knowledge Servers or specialist Problem Solvers on the net. One of the crucial ideas is that each Knowledge server has its own *ontology*, which is a rather abstract idea and not easy to grasp. [Neches 91] defines it as "the basic terms and relations comprising the vocabulary of a topic area, as well as the rules for combining terms and relations to define extensions to the vocabulary". However, it is something more than just a dictionary of terms together with grammar rules and semantic checks. There is the notion of an "ontological commitment", meaning that before one can even write down any assertion or theorem or other form of Knowledge then one must first take decisions committing one to a particular representational viewpoint. Thus if I start talking about the "salary of an employee" to another knowledge source, then we must first check that we use the same words for the same concepts (eg., is salary net of tax?) but more significantly we must share the same kind of entity-relationship model, and know about related things like "pay-day", "hiring" and "salary-cheque". This is all part of an ontology which is itself formally expressed in some meta-language or interlingua. The KSE is using Ontologinua developed by Gruber [93] at Stanford, and Gruber is currently collecting and comparing a variety of such ontologies, which provide a basis for the exchange of both problem-solving knowledge and domain specific knowledge.

The KSE was set up in 1991 with funding from ARPA and a coordinator paid for by NSF. Its aims were given in [Neches 91]. It has four working groups. One deals with collection of ontologies and is headed by Gruber and Tenebaum. Another deals with interchange of Knowledge expressed in different Knowledge Representation Languages. They are tackling this by developing a universal intermediate interchange format (KIF) into which each KRL can be translated, (much as is done with portable compilers). Another group is working on refining KRL's by specifying a layered structure (KRSS) for them. The main issue there is how much inference should be done by the KRL interpreter, and what inferential power it is assumed to possess, compared to the problem solver. The final group on External Interfaces headed by Finin and Wiederhold is developing a universal high level Knowledge Manipulation Language KQML. This is seen as a kind of Knowledge communications protocol for use by Mediators and Facilitators on a network. Each piece of Knowledge on the network will be encoded in KIF, but wrapped in a package with a KQML header, which will help the mediator to decide what to do with it. KQML is basically a command language with about 30 different commands. Parameters to commands describe what ontology to use and how to return the answers, independent of the implementation of the Knowledge server. It thus enables new servers to come on line and extend the capability of an existing network.

3 Re-Using Database Technology

This kind of architecture is very appealing. It makes use of the greatly increased communication bandwidth that is becoming available. Instead of concentrating on small grain parallelism it uses large grain division-of-labour parallelism, with mediators setting up tasks on a variety of servers. One big unknown, reported by the KQML group is how to return answers which point into a complex semantic network. This is very similar to the problem of returning objects from a remote object-oriented database. Indeed, one of the initial goals was to use an object-oriented DB as a "substrate under the Knowledge representation system to provide a persistent object store for Knowledge base objects". Thus we need to exploit the similarities between Frame-based KRL and OODB in order to make good use of database technology [Gray 92].

This same theme of re-using database technology has been taken up by John Mylopoulos (Toronto) [Mylop 93]. This ranges from basic storage management and object management, through concurrency control to query transformation and the storage of shared rules and constraints.

4 Knowledge Re-Use

A major reason for using object-oriented databases is the need for knowledge re-use. As applications get bigger and more complicated it becomes too hard for any one programmer to understand all the lines of code. In consequence more people are adopting the object oriented idea of encapsulating behavioural methods with the object class and hiding details of the implementation. Once a good class description has been built and tested it is encapsulated for re-use like an electronic component. This is the attraction of Smalltalk (and of C++ where it is well written).

The Smalltalk class library, which has evolved over almost a decade, has been a major success story in encouraging code re-use. It has been much more successful than a Fortran subroutine library for two reasons. Firstly, instead of having subroutines with a large number of parameters and some global variables we have methods with a small number of object identifiers or other parameters. In effect, the object becomes a natural bundle of parameters, whereas it is easy to make mistakes with long parameter lists and tedious to understand their description. Secondly, thanks to the use of inheritance, it is possible to specialise the description of an object by overriding some method definitions and adding others. Thus one can re-use inherited methods which saves rewriting. In fact, the first instinct of a Smalltalk programmer is to browse the class hierarchy for a suitable class definition, and then to specialise it where needed.

This theme of re-use extends naturally to object-oriented databases. Originally databases were about sharing large numbers of facts and maintaining them. With an OODB it becomes natural also to store the methods in the database, so that they too can be shared and re-used by a wide variety of users. This is important for maintaining the data in accordance with the principle of data independence. This principle was established in an early ANSI/SPARC report [1975] and it says that application programs must see data descriptions through a conceptual schema of abstract type declarations, which hides details of data storage. The reason for this is so that one could copy the data into a more suitable representation (for example with space for extra attributes or with extra indices or using a different kind of B-tree) without having to alter the application code. Clearly, this can only be done if the methods for accessing or updating the data items are simultaneously changed to correspond and thus they should be stored with the data. A description of our experience of the value of building an OODB (P/FDM) according to this principle, and of code-generating methods to suit the storage schema is given in [Kemp 94, Gray 94a]. Note that with an OODB we can extend this further to include methods that calculate with the data and derive new information, even though many of these will use more primitive methods to access the data, and so will not need to be changed following a change of storage.

There is another reason why it is valuable to store a wide variety of method definitions with an OODB, and this is to do with the growth of communications networks. With the availability of wideband networks we are less likely to bring the data to a monolithic program running on a single processor, and more likely to do parts of the computation on various remote processors. It thus makes more sense for this code to reside on remote machines. For many conventional programmers and scientists this involves quite a change of mindset. They are used to thinking of data as large Fortran arrays, and they start by sucking data from a database into these arrays. However, the client-server model is already beginning to change this. Here, part of the computation is done on the client and the part which is data intensive is done on the server. This saves time particularly when part of the computation is used to test and select data items. It thus makes sense to do these tests with stored methods on objects, where possible. With a distributed architecture of knowledge servers it makes sense to have them share an OODB, so that objects "carry their methods with them". In fact what are actually sent round the network are the object identifiers, whilst master copies of the objects and their methods are kept for update purposes on the OODB.

A consequence of this view is that people are concentrating on re-use of knowledge by sharing access to servers and expert problem solvers distributed over a network, but open to many users. The servers may have indexed collections of natural language sentences, like in an encyclopaedia, or they may be like large semantic nets in the object database form discussed earlier. The problem solvers incorporate compiled procedural knowledge which knows how to take the factual knowledge and solve certain classes of problem. Thus we take seriously the view that knowledge is compiled for a specific use, and move to a much more operational or encapsulated view of it. Each knowledge server or problem solver must present an external interface to users or other solvers on the network, whilst hiding details of knowledge storage and knowledge compilation. Instead, it offers various commands or operations on pieces of knowledge.

5 Constraints as Knowledge

There are various ways to store procedural knowledge in large knowledge bases. Many people have followed the simple idea of storing rules but, as argued in [Gray 94b], this has led to knowledge at too small a level of granularity which was too specialised to its application for it to be re-used. Hence there has been a reaction to use objects, with methods representing larger chunks of differently compiled knowledge. There is, however, another way to get slightly larger units of knowledge, which are indeed independent and can be held in a declarative form. These units are *constraints* referring to whole classes of objects or selected subsets of them. For example consider the following integrity constraint referring to an object model of patients:

> For each p in patient such that status (p) = "allergic"
> > not exists c in components (drugstaken(p))
> > > such that c isin allergies (p)

This constraint is what is known in database terminology as an integrity constraint. It prohibits certain kinds of updates, and describes a kind of invariant property of these object classes that must be maintained true by any update. It is more flexible than a rule in that it can be used in a variety of ways.

(i) It can be used to generate a number of data-driven rules which are triggered by a change to one of the attributes and which check whether the invariant is preserved, and if not carry out some abort or compensating repair action. [Embury 93]

(ii) It can be used as part of a backchaining system that is searching for suitable drugs for a patient. Effectively it adds an extra sub-goal to meet the constraint and restrict the solution set. [King 84]

(iii) The textual version of the constraint can be stored in the database and quoted by an explanation facility when a violation is detected.

Thus we see that constraints have to be transformed in some way before they can be used as part of a programming system. This is the price we pay for keeping them as independent units of knowledge. We are able to do this because some kinds of knowledge can conveniently be held in one form and transformed into several alternative forms on demand.

There are strong parallels here with query optimisation [Gray 84]. Indeed, a query on an object-oriented database can be thought of as a collection of constraints on the result and its components. The main technique of query optimisation is to transform the ordering of the constraints, usually so that some term in one of them can be used as a generator for a very restrictive set of values that is then used as the basis for generating the set of solutions. For example instead of generating all persons and testing for one whose age if 101 or name is Mxty, one can use an index to find such people directly. One can also do semantic query optimisation, where for example [King 84] if one is looking for a ship over 30,000 tons, one can use a constraint that only aircraft carriers displace over 25,000 tons and thus that one need only enumerate aircraft carriers in one's search. Thus, constraints can be used in an intelligent way to restrict a search space.

A further interesting development is in special purpose constraint satisfaction packages. We have been familiar with some of these, such as linear programming packages or equation solvers. The point about the newer class of solver is that they are not totally deterministic, and they can do an intelligent search through a combinatorially large search space, although they may not be guaranteed to find all solutions. In consequence they can improve on the performance of some of the techniques of backtrack search used in backward chaining. They can also do reasoning by elimination which is similar to setting up a number of possible worlds until all but one are eliminated. Thus it may in future be better to pass around knowledge in the form of constraints, which can then be transformed for internal use by a variety of packages and techniques, instead of passing knowledge as rules which can only be used by one kind of interpreter.

We can even consider constraints as a form of metadata, and ask queries about what constraints apply to what classes, or refer to which methods or attributes of those classes. This is necessary not just for an end-user browsing, but also for query optimisers.

There is an important connection between this view of constraints and the principle of Data Independence given earlier. That principle requires one to express queries in a set-theoretic form using only terms declared in the conceptual schema. The query then has to be evaluated against the storage schema. However, this is not just a simple macro-expansion or an interpretation. Instead, it involves re-thinking the query evaluation plan, making use of auxiliary data structures and indexes and choosing a good order of evaluation. The resultant form of the query may look very different depending on what kind of storage schema is used (relational tables, or a graph structure of objects, or Prolog clauses) [KJGF 94]. When we consider constraints instead of queries, the same principle applies. The final form of the constraint may look very different when expressed in a data-driven form as against a goal-driven form, but it is still the same knowledge being re-used.

This way of viewing re-use has some consequences for programming techniques. The dominant programming language is currently C++, and the dominant mode of re-use is by re-using procedures with strong static type checks. This encourages the programmer to think very precisely about the data representation often at the level of arrays, pointers and bitnaps, and to code it very tightly for fast execution. Once such code is encapsulated it cannot be taken apart or re-ordered. Whilst it is necessary to adopt this approach in real-time systems and in low level algorithms (eg., for B-trees or sorting) it is not good for higher levels of software which are knowledge-intensive or data-base applications. In fact, it may be that our approach to software engineering and formal methods is too conditioned by low-level software. Instead, at the higher levels, we need to keep our knowledge in a much more flexible form, using very high level languages and high level type declarations (conceptual schemas) that do not commit us to a precise storage representation. It means that we will get more compiling, code-generation and program transformation taking place at run-time. Programmers may spend more of their time writing code to transform code or generate pieces of C, or they make invoke tools to do it.

The argument for doing this is two-fold. Firstly it makes software evolution easier, and secondly it allows global optimisation. In the first case, we must take seriously the proposition that some data is so long-lived that it may well outlast the programming languages currently in fashion. Thus we must beware of the legacy problems caused by having fragments of code, compiled by elderly compilers for ageing languages, existing in large OODB or knowledge bases. There are already problems of legacy software, where people dare not replace procedures or change data formats, since they do not know what side-effects this may have. By hanging on to knowledge as high-level constraints and code-generating it for new forms of storage organisation we keep it fresh and active.

The second point concerns global optimisation. It is a well known phenomenon in operational research that one can optimise part of a system in a way that inhibits overall optimisation. Thus, we must stop programmers writing tight code committed to a particular storage representation which may tie the rest of the system to an unsuitable representation. Instead, as a positive example we can cite the optimisation of queries which include calls to Daplex method code stored in an object-oriented database. In this case the method code was not held in compiled form but as a list comprehension. Thus we could allow the optimiser as a privileged program to break the encapsulation of the code and combine it with the rest of the query so as to permit global query optimisation, with a new starting point and elimination of repeated computation of sub-expressions [Jiao 91], and hence very significant performance improvement. By analogy, we can see the possibility of collecting a variety of stored constraints from different sources concerned with a complex engineering design problem. We can then send them to an appropriate constraint solver which thus has all the information in a flexible form and can also retrieve measurements from a database, in order to solve the problem.

Another advantage of this architecture is that it reintroduces some of the more general non-deterministic problem solving techniques that were used in early rule-based systems and that were abandoned in the move to object-oriented systems. An important new development in this respect is constraint logic programming [van Hentenryck 91]. Prolog systems attempt to instantiate variables and then backtrack to a choice point in the program on encountering an unsatisfiable condition. The trouble is that this leads to a depth-first search in an order determined by the programmer. Instead of this, constraint logic systems use Prolog unification to set up constraints and then call to a special constraint solver which is able to re-order the constraints and choose more constraining ones first. The same search space is explored, but it is done more efficiently, with less chance of endless loops.[Embury 94] describes how to use this as part of a repair mechanism to find altered states of objects and new objects that fit constraints stored in the P/FDM object database.

6 Paying for Knowledge

Looking to the future, one can see that large Knowledge bases are expensive to build and maintain. They require careful cross-checking and continuous expansion and schema evolution. Experience teaches us that organising and indexing information so that it can be re-used in a variety of applications requires a lot of time and effort. The Smalltalk class library cited earlier, which is probably one of the most successful examples of code re-use, took many years to evolve, being rewritten several times, and this continues to be the case with developing in-house class libraries.

This raises the question of how to pay for Knowledge. Many people feel that Knowledge produced as a result of basic research, funded by governments, should be made available free of charge, over networks. There is a precedent for this in Molecular Biology, where the three-dimensional structures of proteins, discovered by crystallographers after painstaking experiment with government funding are made available from Brookhaven over networks at nominal charge. The US government also funds a lab of over 25 people working on data validation and maintaining network software and answering queries, etc. The argument for this is that the Knowledge was expensive to discover, and it is far better to pay a little extra to have it widely distributed for people to use and take advantage of the investment than to have the data sit there unused.

However, it is not so clear what will happen with genome data [Frenkel 91], which is produced from a much wider variety of sources and at a much greater rate. A network called EMBNET has been established, with the major existing European centres for genome and structural data acting as Knowledge Servers. In some ways this is an interesting fore-runner of networks of very large KBS. The genetic code is written with a twenty letter alphabet, and has a much more restricted semantics than the whole of natural language. Thus it has been possible to develop a common data model and set of descriptive terms for information interchange, acting as an ontology. There are also a variety of commercial products available which can extract data from network databases and present them in various ways. The 'Entrez' package is very interesting. It is available in executable form by ftp from NIH (Washington) and can be used in interactive gopher style to browse selected Brookhaven and NIH databases, particularly looking for textual descriptions accompanying the data. This sort of package makes the data available to a very wide variety of users at very low cost. Similar packages are available from EMBL (Heidelberg) [Rost 93] which will search for data across a range of different databases on the network without the user specifying or knowing which to search, and effectively acts as a Facilitator (kind of mediator). However, users also process the data with expensive commercial packages with full facilities for molecular modelling and interactive 3-D graphics. Likewise some commercial vendors sell added-value data derived for each protein, or for carefully selected groups of proteins with some biological function. Thus it appears that people will pay for a variety of software licenses to use data on the network. Also, they will pay for some specialist providers of data, but what establishes the "base load" for the network is the large amounts of structure and genome data provided free, together with various utility browsing programs and early forms of Facilitator and Mediator.

I have introduced this material on protein data networks, which concerns my own research area [KJGF 94], because it illustrates many of the principles of the Knowledge Sharing Effort (KSE) and also because it points to an alternative funding model. The crucial observation is that once one can get a very large number of people on a network then one can charge them each a small sum for the convenience of using up-to-date data and well-maintained packages. Thus it is not worth their while to obtain data "off the back of a lorry" or by other routes. Furthermore, the small sums accumulate into something worthwhile, which encourages other data providers and graphic interface providers to come on to the network. Effectively the network becomes a marketplace with a large number of consumers easily reached, and known to be interested in a specific area. Here, in the database community, we need to develop the techniques of program transformation and data sharing that will allow this new information marketplace to expand and develop!

Acknowledgements

I am grateful to the UK SERC for funding work by Graham Kemp and ZhuoAn Jiao and Suzanne Embury, and to the EC for funding under the BRIDGE Biotechnology Program together with co-workers at EMBL, where I have had stimulating discussions.

References

[ANSI-SPARC 75] "Interim Report of ANSI/X3/SPARC Study Group on Data Base Management Systems", ACM SIGFIDET, 7, pp 3-139.

[Embury 93] Embury, S.M., Gray, P.M.D. and Bassiliades, N. (1993), "Constraint Maintenance using Generated Methods in the P/FDM OODB", in Proc. 1st Workshop on Rules in Database Systems, N.W. Paton and M.H. Williams (eds), Springer-Verlag (in press).

[Embury 94] Embury, S.M. and Gray, P.M.D. (1994) "Non-deterministic updates in Daplex" technical report TR9401, Department of Computing Science, University of Aberdeen.

[Frenkel 91] Frenkel, K.A. (1991) "The Human Genome Project and Informatics", CACM 34(11), pp 41-51.

[Gray 84] Gray, P.M.D. (1984), "Logic, Algebra and Databases", Ellis-Horwood/Wiley.

[Gray 92] Gray, P.M.D., Kulkarni, K.G. and Paton, N.W. (1992) "Object-Oriented Databases: A Semantic Data Model Approach", Prentice-Hall.

[Gray 94a] Gray, P.M.D. and Kemp, G.J.L. (1994) "In praise of Daplex", technical report, Department of Computing Science, University of Aberdeen.

[Gray 94b] Gray, P.M.D. (1994) "Large Scientific Databases and Knowledge Reuse" in "Research Directions in Computer Science", R. Milner and I. Wand (eds.), Cambridge Univ. Press, (to appear).

[Gruber 93] Gruber, T.R. (1993) "A translation approach to portable ontology specifications", Knowledge Acquisition 5(2), pp 199-220.

[Kemp 94]   Kemp, G.J.L., Iriarte, J.J. and Gray, P.M.D. (1994) "Efficient Access to FDM Objects stored in a Relational Database", Proc. Twelfth British National Confeence on Databases (BNCOD-12), ed. D. Bowers, Springer-Verlag.

[KJGF 94]   Kemp, G.J.L., Jiao, Z., Gray, P.M.D. and Fothergill, J.E. (1994) "Combining Computation with Database Access in Biomolecular Computing", Proc. ADB-94 International Confce (Sweden), W. Litwin and T. Risch (eds.), Springer-Verlag.

[King 84]   King, J.J. (1984), "Query Optimisation by Semantic Reasoning", UMI Research Press.

[Mylop 93]   Mylopoulos, J., et al (1993) "Adapting Database Implementation Techniques to Manage Very Large Knowledge Bases", Proc. International Conference on Building and Sharing of Very Large-Scale Knowledge Bases '93, JIDDEC (Tokyo), pp 215-224.

[Neches 91]   Neches, R., Fikes, R., Finin, T., Gruber, T., Patil, R., Senator, T. and Swartout, W.R. (1991) "Enabling Technology for Knowledge Sharing", AI Magazine 12(3), pp 36-56.

[Rost 93]   Rost, B., Sander, C. and Schneider, R. (1993), "PHD - an automatic mail server for protein secondary structure prediction", CABIOS (in press), also research report EMBL (Heidelberg).

[Swartout 93]   Swartout, W.R., Neches, R. and Patil, R.S. (1993) "Knowledge Sharing: Prospects and Challenges" in Proc. International Conference on Building and Sharing of Very Large-Scale Knowledge Bases (KB & KS '93 Tokyo, JIPDEC, pp 95-102).

[van Hentenryck 91]   van Hentenryck, P. "Constraint Logic Programming", Knowledge Engineering Review 6, 151-194.

Expressing Temporal Behaviour with Extended ECA Rules

Scarlet Schwiderski[1] and Gunter Saake[2]

[1] Computer Laboratory, University of Cambridge, Cambridge, CB2 3QG, UK
[2] Informatik, Abt. Datenbanken, Technische Universität Braunschweig,
38023 Braunschweig, FRG

Abstract. The ECA (EventConditionAction) model constitutes the underlying theoretical model for active databases. The action of an ECA rule is triggered, when the event is detected and the condition is satisfied. Currently, only predicate logic expressions are allowed as conditions in ECA rules. We want to consider the use of temporal logic expressions instead. This allows the specification of situations involving the temporal database development. Temporal conditions are necessary for, among other things, the maintenance of dynamic integrity constraints. We introduce initialized temporal ECA rules which allow the explicit specification of the evaluation-periods of temporal conditions. Moreover we discuss the construction and evaluation of an IT-ECA automaton for the evaluation of intialized temporal ECA rules.

1 Introduction

The promising prospects of using *active database mechanisms* in various application areas (for example CIM, office automation systems, banking systems, air traffic control systems) have encouraged substantial research, on the theoretical as well as on the practical side. The ever increasing interest finds expression in the existence of a considerable number of prototype systems (Starburst [WiFi90], POSTGRES [SHP88, SJGP90], HiPAC [DBB88, DBM88], Ariel [Han89], Adam [DPG91], AIS [BeJa93], Samos [GaDi93], Ode [GJS92b]). The theoretical background of active database systems is constituted on the *ECA (EventCondition-Action) model* [McDa89, GJS92a, GJS92b]. *Events* are specified "happenings of interest" [GJS92a, GJS92b] in the active database, such as data manipulation events (creation, method execution and deletion events in the case of an object-oriented database system; insert, update and delete events in the case of a relational database system), time events, transaction events or abstract events. These *basic events* can be composed to *complex events* using specific operators (for example ";" for the successive occurrence of two events). If the event, denoted in the event-part of an ECA rule, is detected, the *condition* in the condition-part is checked and if it is valid, the *action* is triggered (that is, the action-part is evaluated). The action-part of an ECA rule contains an executable program, written in the DML of the underlying database system.

In most recent approaches to the ECA model, conditions are simple predicate logic expressions [McDa89, GJS92a, GJS92b, DBB88, DBM88], although

[DBB88, DBM88] mention the necessity to define conditions on "trends and historical data". "Ariel" introduces an operator **previous** which allows the specification of transition constraints [Han89]. "HiPAC" supports an operator `Changes` which allows "to express conditions involving changes to stored as well as derived objects" [Cha89]. Neither **previous** nor `Changes` offer general theoretical concepts. On the whole, temporal expressions as conditions do not coincide with current ECA approaches.

Several papers mention *integrity constraint maintenance* to be one application area of the ECA model (e.g. [DBM88]). Dynamic integrity constraints are conditions on the temporal development of the database and are formulated in *temporal logic* [ELG84, Ser80, LiSa87, SaLi88, Ara91]. Therefore, there is a need to incorporate temporal expressions as conditions into ECA rules.

We want to investigate the use of temporal logic for the condition-part of ECA rules. We show, how *temporal ECA rules* can be used for monitoring dynamic integrity constraints. Then we consider temporal ECA rules in general and introduce an enhanced version of *initialized temporal ECA rules* which allow the explicit specification of an activation-event. This is necessary, because temporal logic formulae are evaluated in state sequences, and with the help of an activation-event, we can specify the corresponding evaluation-state-sequence. Initialized temporal ECA rules provide a number of advantageous features for modelling complex temporal situations, namely

- The points in time, when temporal conditions are to be checked, can be specified explicitly.
- The evaluation-periods of temporal conditions can be specified explicitly.
- Temporal situations can be specified which involve absolute points in time.

Then we discuss an evaluation-method for initialized temporal ECA rules. This evaluation-method is based on existing methods for detecting complex events [GJS92a, GJS92b] and for monitoring temporal logic expressions [Schw92, ScSa92, SHS93].

The paper is organized as follows. We motivate our work in Sect. 2 with the help of a simple example. Section 3 contains an introduction into the temporal logic PTL and evaluation schemata for PTL formulae (so-called transition graphs). In Sect. 4 we describe ECA rules. We confine ourselves to the event-part of rules and give only a short overview over the condition- and action-part. In Sect. 5 we consider ECA rules extended with temporal conditions. We introduce temporal and initialized temporal ECA rules. We also discuss an evaluation-method which enables monitoring initialized temporal ECA rules during database runtime. A summary follows in Sect. 6.

2 Motivation

In this section we present our ideas with the help of a simple example: A bank account is to be checked once a day at 8pm. If the balance of this bank account differed by more than 2000 units downward within the last working day (that is, since 8am that morning), the bank is to be informed. We first show, how this situation can be modelled as a formula of PTL, and then as initialized temporal ECA rule.

$x = bank\_account.balance \Rightarrow$
$closing\_hour \land$ **sometime** $bank\_account.balance - 2000 > x$ **since_last previous** $opening\_hour$

The variable x contains the balance of the bank account at the time the temporal formula is checked. Since we cannot use absolute time in PTL, we cannot model "once a day at 8am" and "once a day at 8pm" directly. Instead, we introduce an event *opening_hour* and assume that it is signalled once a day at 8am. Also, we introduce an event *closing_hour* and assume that it is signalled once a day at 8pm. We realize that there are no means to specify the evaluation-period of a temporal formula directly. We have to encode this information inside the formula.

I **EVERY DAY 8:00**
E **EVERY DAY 20:00** [$x = bank\_account.balance$]
C **sometime_past** $bank\_account.balance - 2000 > x$
A $inform\_bank(bank\_account)$

Here we can model "once a day at 8am" and "once a day at 8pm" directly, since the evaluation-time and -period can be encoded in the initialization(I)- and event(E)-part of the initialized temporal ECA rule and time events are allowed as events therein. "Once a day at 8am" is expressed as **EVERY DAY 8:00** and "once a day at 8pm" as **EVERY DAY 20:00**. The parameters necessary to evaluate the condition are defined inside the square brackets in the event(E)-part of the rule, which indicates that the parameters are bound when the corresponding event (namely **EVERY DAY 20:00**) is detected. In this case we bind the current value of *bank_account.balance* to the variable x. The condition is evaluated in the evaluation-period of the initialized temporal ECA rule, that is, from 8am to 8pm the same day. We check, whether there was an old bank account balance some time in the past, but after 8am, which was by more than 2000 units higher than the current bank account balance stored in x. In the action(A)-part of the rule we specify the action to be taken, if the condition is valid (that is, if there was an old bank account balance more than 2000 units higher than the current one). In this case we inform the bank about the bank account in question.

3 Temporal Logic

Temporal logic is an extension of predicate logic. Here, we present a past-directed first-order temporal logic (PTL), which goes back to the work of Manna and Pnueli [MaPn83, MaPn91]. The underlying notion of time is linear and discrete. We assume that there is an initial point in time. Syntax and semantics of PTL correspond to known linear temporal logics [Ara91, SaLi88, MaPn91, Ser80, ELG84].

3.1 Syntax and Semantics of PTL Formulae

Syntax. The syntax of a mathematical logic is given in terms of formulae. Formulae are built from symbols, which are defined as follows.

Definition 1. The *symbols of PTL* are

- a signature $\Sigma = (S, \Omega, \Pi)$ with
  - $S = \{s_1, s_2, \ldots\}$, a set of *sorts*
  - $\Omega = \{f_1 \colon s_{1_1} \times \ldots \times s_{1_{n1}} \to s_{1_0}, f_2 \colon s_{2_1} \times \ldots \times s_{2_{n2}} \to s_{2_0}, \ldots\}$, a set of *function symbols*
  - $\Pi = \{p_1 \colon s_{1_1} \times \ldots \times s_{1_{m1}}, p_2 \colon s_{2_1} \times \ldots \times s_{2_{m2}}, \ldots\}$, a set of *predicate symbols*
- a set of *variables* $X = \{x_1 \colon s_1, x_2 \colon s_2, \ldots\}$
- *special symbols* like $\neg, \wedge, \vee, \exists, \forall$, **previous, existsprevious, always_past, sometime_past, always...since_last, sometime...since_last**

Example 1. *real* is a sort, *abs* represents a 1-ary and $*$ a 2-ary function. $<, >$, and $=$ depict 2-ary predicates. The special symbols are used to construct formulae.

Definition 2. The *formulae of PTL* are built as follows

- Each predicate logic formula φ is a formula.
- If φ and ψ are formulae, then $\neg \varphi$ and $\varphi \vee \psi$ are formulae.
- If φ is a formula, then **previous** φ and **existsprevious** φ are formulae.
- If φ and ψ are formulae, then **always_past** φ, **sometime_past** φ, **always** φ **since_last** ψ and **sometime** φ **since_last** ψ are formulae.

Example 2. $abs(x) > 0$ and $x * y = 100$, where x and y denote variables of sort *real*, form predicate logic formulae, whereas **always_past**$(x > 0)$ represents a formula of PTL (because it contains the temporal operator **always_past**).

Semantics. The semantics of a mathematical logic is given by the definition of an interpretation structure, in which the symbols of the language are interpreted. In the case of PTL we need state sequences as interpretation structures, because PTL formulae are evaluated in a sequence of database states; as opposed to predicate logic (PL hereafter) formulae, which are evaluated in a single database state.

Definition 3. An *interpretation of a signature* $\Sigma = (S, \Omega, \Pi)$ is a Σ-structure $A(\Sigma) = (A(S), A(\Omega), A(\Pi))$ where

- $A(S)$ a set containing $A(s)$ for each sort $s \in S$
- $A(\Omega)$ functions $A(f) \colon A(s_1) \times \ldots \times A(s_n) \to A(s_0)$ for each $f \colon s_1 \times \ldots \times s_n \to s_0 \in \Omega$
- $A(\Pi)$ predicates $A(p) \subseteq A(s_1) \times \ldots \times A(s_m)$ for each $p \colon s_1 \times \ldots \times s_m \in \Pi$

Example 3. In the example presented above (example 1), the interpretation of the sort, the functions and the predicates is given intuitively: *real* denotes the set of real numbers, *abs* gives the absolute value of a real, $*$ multiplies two reals, and $<$ is true, if the left-hand real is smaller than the right-hand one.

Definition 4. A *state sequence* $\hat{\sigma} = \langle \sigma_0, \sigma_1, \ldots, \sigma_i \rangle$ is a non-empty sequence of Σ-structures $\sigma_j = A_j(\Sigma)$, where $0 \leq j \leq i$. $\hat{\sigma}_{i-j}$, where $0 \leq j \leq i$, denotes the partial sequence $\langle \sigma_0, \sigma_1, \ldots, \sigma_{i-j} \rangle$ of $\hat{\sigma}$.

In PL we are looking at single database states, that is, at single Σ-structures $\sigma = A(\Sigma)$. Here, however we are looking at sequences of database states and therefore at sequences of Σ-structures $\hat{\sigma} = \langle \sigma_0, \sigma_1, \ldots, \sigma_i \rangle = \langle A_0(\Sigma), A_1(\Sigma), \ldots, A_i(\Sigma) \rangle$. In this way we can evaluate formulae containing the temporal operators **previous, existsprevious, always_past, sometime_past, always ...since_last, sometime...since_last**.

Definition 5. A *local substitution* β_j of variables X is an assignment $\beta_j(x:s) \in A_j(s)$ for each variable $(x:s) \in X$. A *global substitution* $\hat{\beta}$ of variables X is a sequence $\langle \beta_0, \beta_1, \ldots, \beta_i \rangle$ of local substitutions, which satisfies the following condition for each $(x:s) \in X$ with $0 \leq m, n \leq i$.

$$\beta_m(x) \in (\sigma_m(s) \cap \sigma_n(s)) \Rightarrow (\beta_m(x) = \beta_n(x))$$

Most PL and PTL formulae contain free variables, whose values must be determined before the formulae themselves can be evaluated. In case of PL we need one variable-value-mapping for one database state (local substitution). In case of PTL we need a sequence of these mappings, one for each state of the state sequence. We demand that each of these local substitutions maps variables to the same elements as long as possible (global substitution) [Saa91].

Lemma 6. For a given state sequence $\hat{\sigma} = \langle \sigma_0, \sigma_1, \ldots, \sigma_i \rangle$ and a given global substitution $\hat{\beta} = \langle \beta_0, \beta_1, \ldots, \beta_i \rangle$, the validity of a PTL formula is derived by

$(\hat{\sigma}, \hat{\beta}) \models \varphi$ iff $(\sigma_i, \beta_i) \models \varphi$ for PL formulae φ
$(\hat{\sigma}, \hat{\beta}) \models \neg\varphi$ iff not $(\hat{\sigma}, \hat{\beta}) \models \varphi$
$(\hat{\sigma}, \hat{\beta}) \models \varphi \vee \psi$ iff $(\hat{\sigma}, \hat{\beta}) \models \varphi$ or $(\hat{\sigma}, \hat{\beta}) \models \psi$
$(\hat{\sigma}, \hat{\beta}) \models$ **existsprevious** φ iff $|\hat{\sigma}| > 1$ and $(\hat{\sigma}_{i-1}, \hat{\beta}_{i-1}) \models \varphi$
$(\hat{\sigma}, \hat{\beta}) \models$ **previous** φ iff $|\hat{\sigma}| > 1$ and $(\hat{\sigma}_{i-1}, \hat{\beta}_{i-1}) \models \varphi$ or $|\hat{\sigma}| = 1$
$(\hat{\sigma}, \hat{\beta}) \models$ **always_past** φ iff $(\hat{\sigma}_{i-j}, \hat{\beta}_{i-j}) \models \varphi$ for all $0 \leq j \leq i$
$(\hat{\sigma}, \hat{\beta}) \models$ **sometime_past** φ iff there exists j, where $0 \leq j \leq i$,
                                                         such that $(\hat{\sigma}_{i-j}, \hat{\beta}_{i-j}) \models \varphi$
$(\hat{\sigma}, \hat{\beta}) \models$ **always** φ **since_last** ψ iff $(\hat{\sigma}_{i-j}, \hat{\beta}_{i-j}) \models \varphi$ for all $0 \leq j < k$,
                                                         such that $k =$
                                                         $min \; \{\{m | (\hat{\sigma}_{i-m}, \hat{\beta}_{i-m}) \models \psi\} \cup \{i+1\}\}$
$(\hat{\sigma}, \hat{\beta}) \models$ **sometime** φ **since_last** ψ iff there exists j, where $0 \leq j < k$,
                                                         such that $(\hat{\sigma}_{i-j}, \hat{\beta}_{i-j}) \models \varphi$, where $k =$
                                                         $min \; \{\{m | (\hat{\sigma}_{i-m}, \hat{\beta}_{i-m}) \models \psi\} \cup \{i+1\}\}$

Example 4. $(\hat{\sigma}, \hat{\beta}) \models abs(x) > 0$ states that the absolute value of x (given by β_i in $\hat{\beta}$) in the current state (given by σ_i in $\hat{\sigma}$) is greater than 0.

$(\hat{\sigma}, \hat{\beta}) \models$ **always_past** $(x > 0)$ is valid, if the value of x has always been greater than 0 throughout the whole state sequence $\hat{\sigma}$.

It should be noted that the state sequence $\hat{\sigma} = \langle \sigma_0, \ldots, \sigma_i \rangle$ is evaluated backwards starting at the last state σ_i which corresponds to the current state.

3.2 Evaluation Schemata for PTL Formulae

The semantics of PTL gives no hint on how PTL formulae can be evaluated systematically. An evaluation method allowing a stepwise formulae evaluation is therefore needed. Transition graphs, whose construction and evaluation is briefly introduced in this section, represent such an evaluation method.

Definition 7. A *transition graph* $T = (G, \nu, \eta, m_0, F)$ consists of

1. a directed graph $G = (N, E)$ with nodes N and edges E,
2. a *node labelling* $\nu: N \to PTL$,
3. an *edge labelling* $\eta: E \to PL$,
4. a non-empty *initial marking* $m_0 \subseteq N$ and
5. a set of *final nodes* $F \subseteq N$.

A transition graph T_φ can be constructed from every PTL formula φ [LiSa87, Saa88, SaLi88]. The transition graph T_φ of a PTL formula φ is the basis for the stepwise evaluation of φ in a state sequence $\hat{\sigma} = \langle \sigma_0, \sigma_1, \ldots, \sigma_i \rangle$, starting in state σ_i and going backwards to state σ_0.

Example 5. Figure 1 shows the transition graph of the PTL formula **sometime_past** *(A)*.

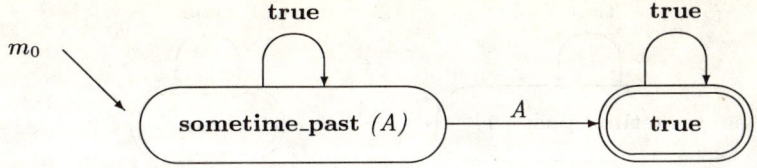

Fig. 1. Transition graph of **sometime_past** *(A)*

The evaluation of a transition graph starts with the nodes of the initial marking. We say the node is marked, or the node belongs to the current marking. Then we evaluate the given state sequence $\hat{\sigma} = \langle \sigma_0, \ldots, \sigma_i \rangle$, starting with state σ_i which corresponds to the current database state and decreasing the index stepwise from i to 0. In each state, we evaluate the edge-labels of the outgoing edges of the currently marked nodes. If the edge-label is valid, we unmark the start-node of the edge and mark the end-node. If all edge-labels of the outgoing edges of a certain node are invalid, we unmark the start-node only. Finally, φ is valid, if there is a marked final node[3] in state σ_0.

Although the described method evaluates any PTL formula stepwise in a state sequence $\hat{\sigma}$, it is not appropriate for the practical use, because it assumes that the whole state sequence $\hat{\sigma} = \langle \sigma_0, \ldots, \sigma_i \rangle$ is known in state σ_i. That, however, implies that the whole state sequence (that is the whole database history) is stored. The fact that the database history is continuously growing thwarts this easy solution. In [Schw92, ScSa92, SHS93] we present an efficient method for evaluating PTL formulae. There the transition graph T_φ of a PTL formula φ is evaluated in the reverse direction. We use the so-called *reversed transition graph* T_φ^{-1}. The latter is the transition graph T_φ with reversed edges. We start the evaluation in state σ_0 with the final nodes of T_φ^{-1} and increase the index stepwise from 0 to i. The problem is that the values of the free variables in φ are not known until state σ_i and the reversed transition graph can therefore only be partially evaluated. Certain information, must be kept for later evaluation. We store this information with the nodes of the reversed transition graph and call it *state information*. The state information of a node contains conditions on the possible values of the free variables under which the corresponding node is currently marked. Finally, φ is valid, if the node of the initial marking is marked in state σ_i and the corresponding state information is evaluated to **true**.

Example 6. Figure 2 shows the reversed transition graph of the PTL formula **sometime_past** *(A)*.

4 ECA Rules

The ECA approach originates with the work of Dayal and McCarthy [DBM88, McDa89]. At present, research in this field captures a lot of attention [DBB88,

---
[3] Final nodes are indicated by a double line.

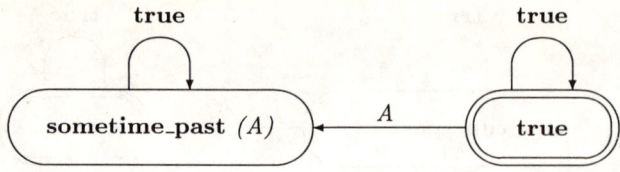

Fig. 2. Reversed transition graph of **sometime_past** *(A)*

SHP88, SJGP90, Han89, Cha89, WiFi90, GeJa91, GJS92a, GJS92b, DPG91, BeJa93, GaDi93]. Presented ECA models differ mostly in the expressiveness of their event language. Here we present an event language that goes back to [DBM88, GaDi93].

[DBM88] states that "conditions to be monitored may be complex, and may be defined not only on single data values or individual database states, but also on sets of data objects, transitions between states, trends and historical data". At present, however, conditions are either simple predicate logic expressions, or collections of queries. In the latter case, the condition is satisfied, if all queries return non-empty answers.

An action is an executable program, written in the DML of the underlying database system. This program can contain database operations as well as messages to an external program or process [DBM88].

In this section we confine ourselves to a detailed description of the event-part of ECA rules. For a detailed description of the condition- and action-part of current approaches, we refer to the given literature.

Event expressions are either *basic events* or *complex events*, which are built from basic events by applying certain event-operators. We distinguish the following classes of basic events [DBM88, GJS92b, GaDi93]:

- *Data manipulation events* are signalled (before or after) an object is created, deleted, updated and so on.
- *Time events* are signalled at absolute points in time (e.g. 1 April 1993, 9.00 a.m.), relative points in time (e.g. 30 min after event E is signalled), or periodic points in time (e.g. every day at 8.00 a.m.).
- *Transaction events* are signalled (before or after) a transaction begins, commits, or aborts.
- *Abstract events* are signalled by users or application programs.

Basic events can be composed to complex events by using the following operators:

$(E_1; E_2)$ denotes the *sequence* of two events E_1 and E_2. $(E_1; E_2)$ is signalled when E_2 is signalled, provided that E_1 has been signalled at some earlier time.

(E_1, E_2) denotes the *conjunction* of two events E_1 and E_2. (E_1, E_2) is signalled when both events are signalled in an arbitrary order.

$(E_1 \mid E_2)$ denotes the *disjunction* of two events E_1 and E_2. $(E_1 \mid E_2)$ is signalled when either E_1 or E_2 is signalled.

(E^*) denotes the *closure* of event E. (E^*) is signalled everytime E is signalled.

(**not** $E\ [E_1 - E_2]$) denotes the *absence* of event E in the intervall $[E_1 - E_2]$. (**not** $E\ [E_1 - E_2]$) is signalled when event E is not signalled in the interval starting with event E_1 and ending with event E_2.

Events can have attributes. An attribute of a basic event can hold information about the current database state or about the activity that caused the event to occur (the occurrence-time of the event, the occurrence-transaction of the event, the user-id that initiated the occurrence-transaction). Attributes of complex events are derived from the attributes of the constituent basic events. The attributes are passed on to the condition-part and to the action-part of a rule, when the event in the event-part is detected.

Complex events can be detected using finite automata [GJS92a, GJS92b]. The evaluation of an automaton starts in a start-state and each occurrence of a basic event causes a state transition into a new successor state. The accepting states of an automaton indicate the detection of the complex event.

5 Extended ECA Rules

5.1 Specifying Extended ECA Rules

In this section we want to consider the implications of using PTL formulae as conditions in ECA rules.

Definition 8. An ECA rule with a PTL formula as condition is called *temporal ECA rule*. The PTL formula itself is then called *temporal condition*.

Integrity constraint maintenance is one major application area of ECA rules [DBM88, GeJa91]. Dynamic integrity constraints, which are used to monitor the dynamic (that is temporal) behaviour of a database, are formulae of temporal logic. Temporal ECA rules are therefore an appropriate means for their maintenance. In the following, we consider integrity constraints before we discuss temporal conditions in general.

Dynamic integrity constraints ensure that the temporal development of a database obeys certain rules. The set of integrity constraints must not be violated in any state of the database lifecycle.

Example 7. The following dynamic integrity constraint states that a person is always a member of the college in which he/she matriculated sometime in the past.

$\forall p : Person\ \forall c : College$ **always_past**($\neg\ matriculation(p, c)$) $\vee$
    always $member(p, c)$ **since_last** $matriculation(p, c)$

In the classical approach such a constraint must be evaluated after each state transition. In case of a violation, the DBMS must react in a certain way to enforce the constraint. The DBMS can either forbid the database operation that causes the violation, roll back the transactions that result in an inconsistent database state, or evaluate system-generated compensating database operations that lead to a consistent database state [FPT92]. Therefore, temporal ECA rules can be used in the following way for integrity constraint maintenance:

E $\textbf{any}_{dme}$
C $\neg \varphi$ $\quad\quad\quad\quad\quad\quad\quad \Diamond\Diamond$ where φ is an integrity constraint $\Diamond\Diamond$
A • rolling back of transactions
    • forbidding of database operation
    • evaluating system-generated compensating transactions

The event expression $\textbf{any}_{dme}$ denotes the disjunction of all data manipulation events in the event algebra.

Using temporal ECA rules for integrity constraint maintenance in the classical sense, as shown above, makes only very limited use of the potential of the ECA model. Now we want to point out the prospects of using temporal ECA rules in general.

The first step in increasing the expressive power, in comparison to temporal ECA rules used for integrity constraint maintenance, is to allow arbitrary event expressions in the event-part of a rule. This way, we make it possible to specify precisely when a constraint is to be checked, as it is often not necessary to check a constraint after each state transition (that means after the $\textbf{any}_{dme}$ event is signalled), but only in certain situations. We can specify these situations in the event-part of a rule. This increases the efficiency of constraint maintenance.

Dynamic integrity constraints are evaluated in the whole former lifecycle of the database, starting with the initial state and ending with the current state. Often it would be desirable to state constraints which consider only sub-state-sequences, starting with an arbitrary state in the lifecycle and ending with the current state. With temporal ECA rules, we can achieve that by restricting the evaluation-period of a temporal condition to the activation-period of the corresponding rule.

In the following we define initialized temporal ECA rules, which allow the explicit specification of an activation-event, in addition to the event-, condition- and action-part of a temporal ECA rule. With the help of an activation-event, we can specify the evaluation-period of a temporal condition explicitly.

Definition 9. A temporal ECA rule with an additional activation-event is called *initialized temporal ECA rule (IT-ECA rule)* and is written in the form IECA, where I and E denote event expressions, C a PTL formula and A a procedure call indicating the action to be taken.

Besides clarity and ease of specification, there is another important advantage in encoding complex temporal situations in temporal ECA rules, and initialized temporal ECA rules respectively, rather than in PTL formulae. Time events are allowed as basic events in event expressions. Time events are, however, not allowed in our temporal logic PTL. It is therefore not possible to formulate the situation shown in the motivating example (Sect. 2) in PTL directly.

5.2 Monitoring Extended ECA Rules

In the last section we showed that (initialized) temporal ECA rules provide a powerful tool for modelling complex temporal situations in a database. In this section we want to introduce a method for evaluating initialized temporal ECA rules during database runtime. We refer to evaluation methods for temporal formulae (see Sect. 3.2 and [Schw92, ScSa92, SHS93, Saa88, LiSa87, Saa91]) and for event expressions (see Sect. 4 and [GJS92a, GJS92b]).

The idea for evaluating initialized temporal ECA rules is to combine the finite automata of event expressions and the reversed transition graphs of temporal conditions into a combined evaluation schema. That is possible, because transition graphs are similar to finite automata [Saa88] and can be easily transformed. We describe the construction and evaluation of an IT-ECA automaton for an initialized temporal ECA rule.

Algorithm 10 Construction of an IT-ECA automaton. Given is an initialized temporal ECA rule IECA. The IT-ECA automaton of IECA is constructed as follows:

1. Construct the finite automata for I and E and call them A_I, A_E.
2. Construct the reversed transition graph of C and call it T_C^{-1}.
3. Connect each accepting state of A_I with ε (empty event) transitions to the start state of A_E
4. Connect each accepting state of A_I with ε (empty event) transitions to each final node of T_C^{-1}.

Algorithm 10 simply consists of joining together finite automata and reversed transitions graphs into a combined evaluation schema. The finite automaton for I builds the first part of the schema; then follow the finite automaton for E and, in parallel, the reversed transition graph of C.

The evaluation of an IT-ECA automaton in a given state sequence $\hat{\sigma} = \langle \sigma_0, \sigma_1, \ldots \rangle$ starts with the start state of A_I in state σ_0. A_I is evaluated until the activation-event I is detected (A_I enters an accepting state). The start state of A_E and the final nodes of T_C^{-1} are activated via empty event transitions. Both, automaton A_E and the reversed transition graph T_C^{-1} are evaluated in parallel until event E is detected. The reversed transition graph can then be evaluated under the given variable-binding. We find that the corresponding temporal condition is **true** or **false** (depending on whether the state information of the start node of the reversed transition graph is evaluated to **true** or **false**).

Example 8. Figure 3 shows the IT-ECA automaton for the initialized temporal ECA rule

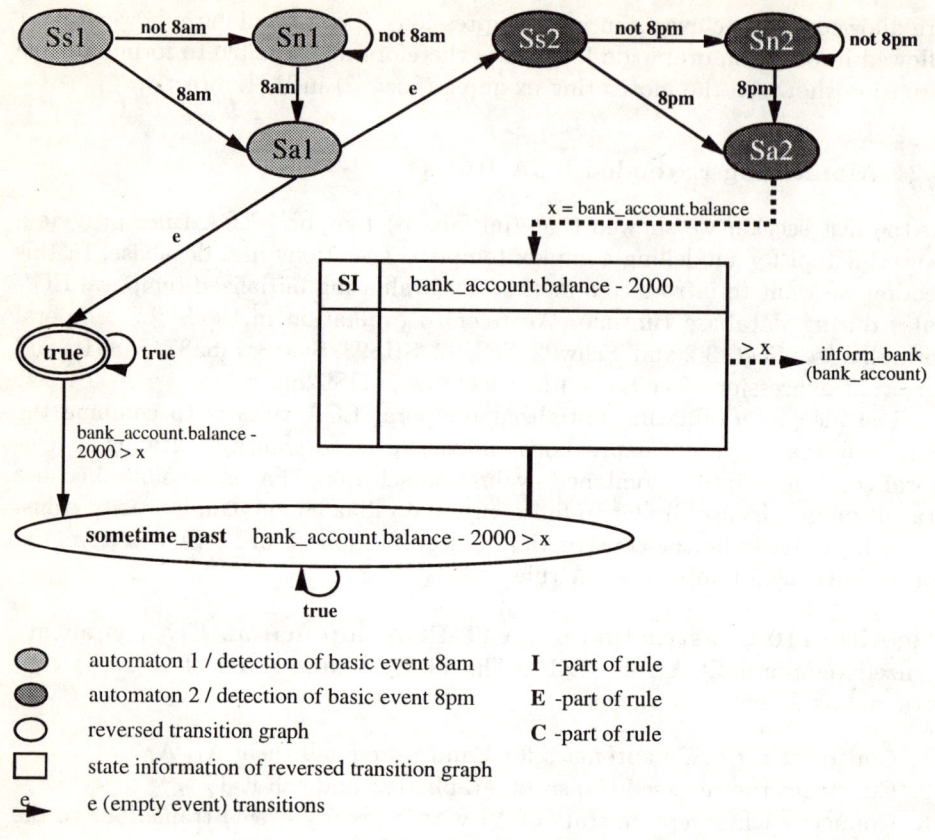

Fig. 3. IT-ECA automaton

I **EVERY DAY 8:00**
E **EVERY DAY 20:00** [$x = bank\_account.balance$]
C **sometime_past** $bank\_account.balance - 2000 > x$
A *inform_bank(bank_account)*

The automaton is evaluated as follows: The evaluation starts in state σ_0 with the start state **Ss1** of automaton 1. On the occurrence of event **8am** the automaton moves into the accepting state **Sa1**. On the occurrence of all other basic events the automaton moves into the non-accepting state **Sn1**. Once the automaton is in state **Sa1** both, the start state **Ss2** of automaton 2 and the final node of the reversed transition graph are activated via empty event transitions (see [GJS92a]). Automaton 2 detects the occurrence of event **8pm** (that is, it enters its accepting state **Sa2**). The reversed transition graph is evaluated until automaton 2 enters its accepting state **Sa2**. After each state transition the edge label $bank\_account.balance - 2000 > x$ is checked. The edge label depends on the value of the variable x, which is unknown before a certain state σ_i in which the event corresponding to the event-part of the rule is detected (that is, automaton 2 enters its accepting state **Sa2**). Therefore, we store all occurring values of *bank_account.balance*-2000 in an auxiliary relation **SI** (that is the state information of the start node) until the value of x is determined and we can check, whether there is a value greater than x. In that case, the temporal condition is valid in state σ_i and the trigger can fire. The dotted lines illustrate the flow of control. On the occurrence of event E (automaton 2 is in state **Sa2**), the free variable x of the temporal condition **sometime_past** *bank_account.balance*$-2000 > x$ is bound to the current value of *bank_account.balance*. x is then compared with the values stored in **SI**. If *bank_account.balance*$-2000 > x$ is evaluated to **true** for at least one entry in **SI**, the action is triggered (that is, *inform_bank(bank_account)* is executed).

The example above is straightforward in that both I and E are basic events and C is a simple PTL formula. In general the finite automata for I and E can be much more complex, e.g. there may exist several accepting states. Also the automata in our example are deterministic. That is not the case, if complex event expressions include the sequence- and closure-operator. The evaluation of a non-deterministic IT-ECA automaton must be further investigated. The evaluation depends on the chosen parameter context [ChMi93]: *recent*, *chronicle*, *continuous* or *cumulative*. The parameter context determines which event occurrence of a specific event is considered in the evaluation of a corresponding complex event. Moreover, more complex PTL formulae lead to more complex reversed transition graphs and therefore to a more complex evaluation (for more details see [SHS93]).

6 Conclusions

In this paper we have applied temporal logic to the condition-part of ECA rules. Temporal ECA rules are, among other things, needed for the maintenance of dynamic integrity constraints. But we have shown that we achieve much more: Initialized temporal ECA rules are a powerful means for modelling and monitoring complex temporal situations and enhance the expressiveness of pure dynamic integrity constraints by far. One main advantage is that we can include time events into constraint specification in a natural way. Moreover, we can specify the evaluation-time and the evaluation-period of temporal conditions in the initialization- and event-part of an initialized temporal ECA rules. Finally, we have introduced a method for evaluating initialized temporal ECA rules during database runtime.

References

[Ara91]   Arapis, C., *Temporal Specification of Object Behaviour*, in: Thalheim, B.; Demetrovics, J.; Gerhardt, H.-D. (Eds.): Proc. 3rd Symp. Mathematical Fundamentals of Database and Knowledge Base Systems MFDBS '91, Rostock, 1991, LNCS 495, pp. 308–324.

[BeJa93]   Behrends, H., Jasper, H., et.al., *Endbericht der Projektgruppe "Aktive Informationssysteme"*, Interne Berichte IS 15, Abteilung Informationssysteme, Universität Oldenburg, October 1993, in german.

[Cha89]   Chakravarthy, S., *Rule Management and Evaluation: An Active DBMS Perspective*, SIGMOD RECORD, Vol. 18., No. 3, September 1989, pp. 20–28.

[ChMi93]   Chakravarthy, S., Mishra, D., *Snoop: An Expressive Event Specification Language for Active Databases*, Technical Report UF-CIS-TR-93-007, University of Florida, 1993.

[DBB88]   Dayal, U., Blaustein, B., Buchmann. A., et. al., *The HiPAC Project: Combining Active Databases and Timing Constraints*, SIGMOD RECORD, Vol. 17, No. 1, March 1988, pp. 51–70.

[DBM88]   Dayal, U., Buchmann, A.P., McCarthy, D.R., *Rules are Objects Too: A Knowledge Model for an Active, Object-Oriented Database System*, in: Dittrich, K.R. (Ed.), Advances in Object-Oriented Database Systems, 2nd International Workshop on Object-Oriented Database Systems, Bad Münster am Stein-Ebernburg, FRG, September 1988, pp. 129–143.

[DPG91]   Diaz, O., Paton, N., Gray, P., *Rule Management in Object-Oriented Databases: A Uniform Approach*, Proceedings of the 17th International Conference on Very Large Databases, Barcelona, Spain, 1991, pp. 317–326.

[ELG84]   Ehrich, H.-D., Lipeck, U.W., Gogolla, M., *Specification, Semantics, and Enforcement of Dynamic Database Constraints*, in: Proceedings of the 5th International Conference on Very Large Databases, Singapore, 1984, pp. 301–308.

[FPT92]   Fraternali, P., Paraboschi, S., Tanca, L., *Automatic Rule Generation for the Correction of Constraint Violations in Active Databases*, in: Lipeck, U., Thalheim, B. (Eds.), Modelling Database Dynamics, Volkse, 1992, Germany, Springer-Verlag, pp. 153–173.

[GaDi93]   Gatziu, S., Dittrich, K.R., *Eine Ereignissprache für das aktive, objektorientierte Datenbanksystem SAMOS*, in: Stucky, W., Oberweis, A. (Eds.), Datenbanksysteme in Büro, Technik und Wissenschaft, GI-Fachtagung, Braunschweig, March 1993, pp. 94–103, in german.

[GeJa91]   Gehani, N.H., Jagadish, H.V., *Ode as an Active Database: Constraints and Triggers*, Proceedings of the 17th International Conference on Very Large Databases, Barcelona, Spain, 1991, pp. 327–336.

[GJS92a]   Gehani, N.H., Jagadish, H.V., Shmueli, O., *Composite Event Specification in Active Databases: Model & Implementation*, Proceedings of the 18th International Conference on Very Large Databases, Vancouver, British Columbia, Canada, 1992, pp. 327–338.

[GJS92b]   Gehani, N.H., Jagadish, H.V., Shmueli, O., *Event Specification in an Active Object-Oriented Database*, Proc. ACM SIGMOD, June 1992, pp. 81–90.

[Han89]   Hansen, E.N., *An Initial Report on the Design of Ariel: A DBMS with an Integrated Production Rule System*, SIGMOD RECORD, Vol. 18., No. 3, September 1989, pp. 12–19.

[HüSa91]   Hülsmann, K., Saake, G., *Theoretical Foundations of Handling Large Substitution Sets in Temporal Integrity Monitoring*, Acta Informatica, Vol. 28, 1991, Springer-Verlag, pp. 365–407.

[Lip90]   Lipeck, U.W., *Transformation of Dynamic Integrity Constraints into Transaction Specification*, Theoretical Computer Science, Vol. 76, 1990, pp. 115–142.

[LiSa87] Lipeck, U.W., Saake, G., *Monitoring Dynamic Integrity Constraints Based on Temporal Logic*, Information Systems, Vol. 12, No. 3, 1987, pp. 255–269.

[MaPn83] Manna, Z., Pnueli, A., *How to Cook a Temporal Proof System for your Pet Language*, 10th ACM Symposium on Principles of Programming Languages, January 1983, pp. 141–154.

[MaPn91] Manna, Z., Pnueli, A., *The Temporal Logic of Reactive and Concurrent Systems, Vol. 1 : Specification*, Springer-Verlag, New York, 1991.

[McDa89] McCarthy, D.R., Dayal, U., *The Architecture of an Active Database Management System*, Proc. ACM SIGMOD 1989 International Conference on the Management of Data, Portland, Oregon, May-June 1989, pp. 215–224.

[Saa88] Saake, G., *Spezifikation, Semantik und Überwachung von Objektlebensläufen in Datenbanken*, Informatik-Skripten 20, TU Braunschweig, 1988, in german.

[Saa91] Saake, G., *Descriptive Specification of Database Object Behaviour*, Data & Knowledge Engineering, Vol. 6 (1991), pp. 47–73.

[SaLi88] Saake, G., Lipeck, U.W., *Using Finite-Linear Temporal Logic for Specifying Database Dynamics*, in: Börger, E.; Kleine Büning, H.; Richter, M.M. (Eds.), Proc. CSL '88, 2nd Workshop Computer Science Logic, Duisburg, 1988, LNCS 385, 1989, pp. 288–300.

[Schw92] Schwiderski, S., *Realisation von Objekten in einem Relationalen Datenbanksystem*, Diplomarbeit, TU Braunschweig, 1992, in german.

[ScSa92] Schwiderski, S., Saake, G., *Monitoring Temporal Permissions using Partially Evaluated Transition Graphs*, in: Lipeck, U., Thalheim, B. (Eds.), Modelling Database Dynamics, Volkse, 1992, Germany, Springer-Verlag, pp. 196–217.

[SHS93] Schwiderski, S., Hartmann, T., Saake, G., *Monitoring Temporal Preconditions in a Behaviour Oriented Object Model*, Informatik-Berichte 93-07, TU Braunschweig, 1993.

[Ser80] Sernadas, A., *Temporal Aspects of Logical Procedure Definition*, Information Systems, Vol. 5, 1980, pp. 167–187.

[SHP88] Stonebraker, M., Hanson, E.N., Potamianos, S., *The POSTGRES Rule Manager*, IEEE Transactions on Software Engineering, Vol. 14, No. 7, July 1988, pp. 897–907.

[SJGP90] Stonebraker, M., Jhingran, A., Goh, J., Potamianos, S., *On Rules, Procedures, Caching and Views in Data Base Systems*, SIGMOD RECORD, Vol. 19, Issue 2, June 1990, pp. 281–290.

[WiFi90] Widom, J., Finkelstein, S.J., *Set-Oriented Production Rules in Relational Database Systems*, SIGMOD RECORD, Vol. 19., Issue 2, June 1990, pp. 259–270.

Temporal Databases: an Event Oriented Approach

S. Soukeras and P.J.H. King

Department of Computer Science, Birkbeck College,
University of London, Malet Street, London WC1E 7HX
E-mail : ubacr17@uk.ac.bbk.dcs

Abstract. This paper introduces a new approach to incorporating the temporal dimension in database systems. Instead of introducing time as an attribute in a conventional state database the paper proposes that state databases are derivatives from event databases which are regarded as fundamental. A data modelling approach is introduced together with a realization in terms of a Temporal Functional Database Language (TFDL).

1. Introduction

Conventional database systems, i.e. those that offer no explicit facilities for temporal support, provide for the maintenance of a view of the current state of a real world system. We term this view the *current database state*. As changes in the real world system occur, this current database state is updated to reflect the new situation. Previous states could be recovered by use of the log tape to back out transactions.

Most previous research into the explicit representation of the temporal dimension within database systems has concentrated on extending the relational model. Typically, temporal information is included by providing for the timestamping of tuples [1, 4, 11, 16, 18], or for incorporating the temporal dimension in the attribute domain [6, 21], or both [5]. Effectively, such systems provide for the representation of a series of states of the database, each timestamped with the period during which it was valid.

In our view, a database state, whether the current or a previous one, though vitally important from the point of view of database querying and transaction processing, is essentially secondary information in the sense that it is derivative from a series of *events* or change transactions, which constitute the primary information. In a conventional database system the lack of explicit temporal facilities implies that the database itself cannot include knowledge of how an event affects a state. Therefore, the interpretation and calculation of the consequences of event occurrences on the current database state is done outside the database system, with the resulting modifications being applied to the current state to produce the new current state.

It is our view that a temporal database system should offer facilities for capturing the events that occur in the real world, and for describing how they affect a database state. Using these descriptions, it should then compute the database states and the periods of their validity, as required for query and transaction processing. The approach is different from previous approaches to the explicit incorporation of temporal information.

Our view is that a record of the events which occur, which we term the *event database*, is the fundamental information which should persist. From this information the conventional database view, the *state database*, can always in principle be derived (figure 1). We believe that the approach to temporal databases of maintaining a history of timestamped database states is restrictive and troublesome. Whilst for convenience it may be on occasions expedient to compute the database state at a particular point in time from an earlier state and the intervening events, this is a matter of efficiency only and should not be allowed to confuse the basic semantic theory. It is the event database that is fundamental. We believe that our approach is better in offering the capability and flexibility necessary for modelling a world evolving in time.

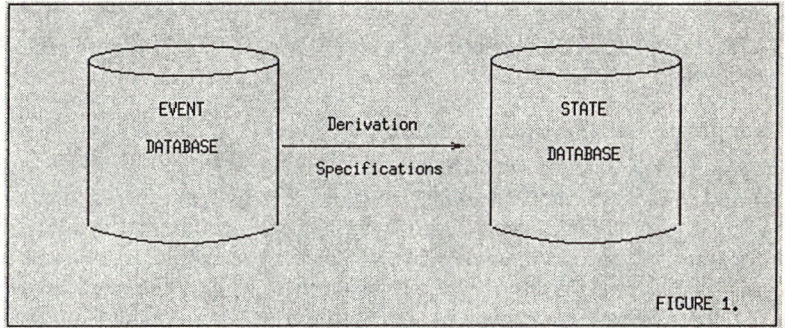

FIGURE 1.

2. Functional databases and Functional programming languages

A functional database supports the Entity Function data model, which sees the world as consisting of entities, or primitive objects, and functions between them. The entities model the things of the real world, and the functions the relationships between them. Advantages of the Entity Function model have been discussed by Shipman [17], Kulkarni and Atkinson [9] and summarized by King and Poulovassilis [8] :

1) it is conceptually natural,
2) it is entity-based so that referential integrity is implicitly maintained,
3) functions are semantically irreducible units of information, hence there is ease of schema specification and update, and
4) an inference mechanism is available in the form of derived functions.

An early example of a functional database system is DAPLEX [16].

Functional programming languages are based on the lambda calculus and allow the user to define a set of functions and perform computations by application of the functions to arguments. The computational power of functional languages is that of the lambda calculus. All recursive functions, that is all Turing-computable ones, may be expressed in this calculus [7]. An important feature claimed for functional programming languages is *referential transparency*, *i.e.* an expression evaluated any number of times gives the same result (as long as the definitions of the functions involved remain the same). Examples of functional programming languages include HOPE [3] and Miranda [23]. Theoretical foundations of functional programming may be found in Hindley and Seldin [7].

In most database systems, the data manipulation language is not powerful enough to support the computations that are required by the applications; it is not computationally complete. To gain the required computational power the data manipulation language is usually embedded into a programming language such as C or COBOL, termed the *host language*. The disadvantage of this approach is the mismatch of the paradigms between the embedded and the embedding language, particularly in relation to types, the so called impedance mismatch problem.

Some functional database languages, such as FQL[2] and FDL[13, 15], exploit the natural correspondence between the functional data model and functional programming to achieve a computationally complete database language. The database itself consists of a set of function definitions, which model either data or computation, and expression evaluation serves as the querying mechanism. Thus, application programs can persist in the database in the same way as data [13].

3. The Temporal Entity Function database model

Database design involves the creation of a model of that part of the real world which is of interest, an analysis of the activities that the database is required to support against the model, and finally a mapping from that model to the persistent constructs which the database management software to be used supports. Thus, for example, much current practical database design involves the use of one of the various semantic data models based upon the concepts of entity, attribute and relationship, with a mapping from these to the n-ary relations supported by such systems as Oracle, Ingres, etc. Clearly, the closer the correspondence between the data modelling constructs of the modelling technique and the persistent structures of the database software, the more straightforward the second stage of the process will be, a particular advantage with the functional approach.

The semantic data models currently used in this way aim at providing a means of modelling the current database state. They do not provide a means of capturing what we call the event database, which we regard as fundamental. To achieve this, new database models or radically extended versions of the present state oriented ones are required. In this section we describe an extension of the entity function model, the *Temporal Entity Function Model* (TEFM) which achieves the above in the functional context.

The basic constructs of TEFM are Entity Types, Event Types, History Types and Functions.

Entity types are distinguished into abstract entity types, (those without printable value), *e.g.* a person, and printable entity types, *e.g.* a person's name, referred to as lexical entity types. The distinction between abstract entities and lexical entities is the same as that between non-lexical and lexical entities in NIAM [23].

Time itself is modeled by a printable (lexical) entity type. It is a discrete, point-based, and totally ordered set. It models the time when events take place in the real world, so called *valid time* [19]. In this paper we consider time as having only one granularity which our system supports. Further developments will support multiple granularities, with time viewed as a partially ordered set of points.

Functions represent time invariant relationships between, and time invariant attributes of, entity, and event types. Functions may be wholly extensionally defined ones modelling facts, intensionally defined modelling computation, or of mixed definition modelling facts with an intentional equation serving as a default rule for missing information, or computation with the extensional equations serving as exceptions to the rule expressed.

Event types model instantaneous happenings and are the means for capturing the dynamic properties of the system being modelled. The function *tof* returns for each instance of an event type the time of its occurrence. Further information about events is modelled in the form of functions representing attributes and relationships.

The event database consists of the entities, events, the lexicals and functions between them, and its purpose is to capture the fundamental information of a system.

History types model historical information *i.e.* time variant relationships in the system. If we use the set of natural numbers as our model of time, $t = \{0,1,2,3,...\}$, and τ is some type, then any total function from t to τ is called a *history of τ*, or τ *history*. A history could be visualized as a sequence of the successive values an object takes across time, or as a set of pairs $\{(0,\tau_0), (1,\tau_1),...\}$, or as a time series. If (n,τ_n) belongs to a history, then τ_n is the value of this history at time point n. The set of all histories of τ is called the *history type of τ* and is written as *history(τ)*. Thus, if temp is a type representing temperature then history(temp) is the set of all possible temperature time series. A particular history might be the time series representing the body temperature of a particular person taken at the points in our time model.

In TEFM, histories are derived from the information in the event database via history specification functions that describe i) when and how events influence histories; and ii) how histories persist when they are not influenced by events. These functions are described in detail in section 4.5

In a simple example, we have lamps in a room. Each lamp has its own switch. The only events that take place in the system are the switchings of the lamps, and the event that marks the time of the beginning of the system.

The event database schema of this example follows. Its graphical representation is shown in figure 2.

```
Entity   : lamp.
Event    : switch, start.
Function :
    switched : switch  -> lamp
```

The function switched specifies which of the lamps a switch event applies to.

A lamp can be in one of two operational states, on or off. We model this lamp attribute with a type called state = {ON, OFF}. The histories of the operational states of the lamps can be modelled by the type history(state). The specification functions of such a history should describe how its value (the lamp's operational state) is affected by the occurrencies of start and switch events and how it persists in between. We should note that the type history(state) can be used to model the state history of any object with two operational modes *e.g.* a television set, a car engine, or a central heating system.

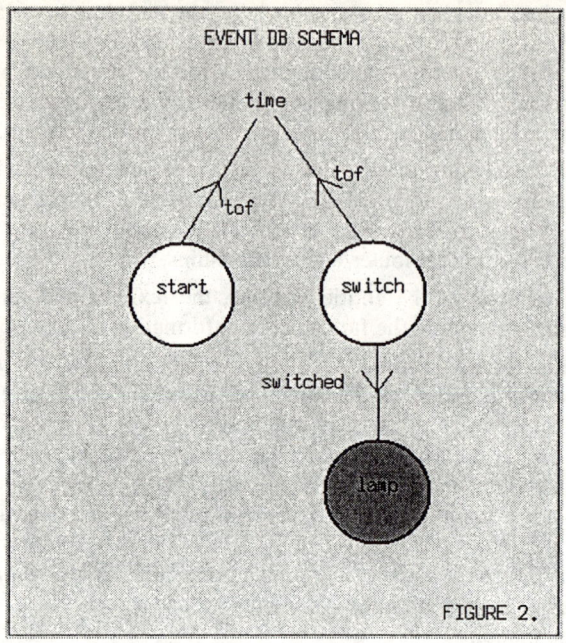

FIGURE 2.

A set of temporal operators is provided for querying histories, offering the means for constructing the database states in time. Their semantics follow the history specification functions. The history querying operators will be discussed in detail in the next section where we introduce the temporal database language TFDL.

TEFM offers the means for capturing events that occur in a system and describing their effect on a database state and thus realizes a new database modelling approach whose principle is, that in an evolving system the events are the significant information which should be recorded.

4. Temporal Functional Database Language (TFDL)

TFDL is a true superset of FDL extended to include events, times and histories, and features for their manipulation.

Our description of TFDL will be brief for those aspects of the language that are common with FDL, sections 4.1 and 4.2, and go into more detail for its new features, sections 4.3, 4.4 and 4.5.

4.1. Data Types

The primitive data types of TFDL are string, integer, bool and time. In addition, the user can declare extensible data types corresponding to abstract entities - called entity types, and to events - called event types. Another category of types corresponding to histories is available, and the types belonging to it are called history types.

Also inherited from FDL are arbitrarily nested lists, sums and products. *e.g.* [1,4,5,10] belongs to the type list(integer). Sum types represent union of types and their components are tagged by upper-case identifiers termed constructor functions, which can be thought as functions without reduction rules:

```
tree :: sum;
LEAF : integer -> tree;
NODE : integer tree tree -> tree;
```

The tree sum type contains binary trees of integers which are constructed from the union of their leaves and nodes. Sum types can also be used to define types which are equivalent to enumerated types in programming languages such as C. *e.g.*

```
state :: sum;
ON : -> state;  OFF : -> state;
```

Product types represent the Cartesian product of types. Values of product types can be thought as records. The product constructor '**' is used to declare product types. For example, the product of integer type and string type called tup may be declared thus :

```
tup :: integer ** string;
```

The value {3, "Paul"} is a value of tup.

Elements are added and removed from the extent of an entity type via creation and deletion commands. The values of instances of entity types are hidden by displaying a transient global variable of the form $x, where x is an alphanumeric identifier. For any entity type τ, a zero-argument generator function All_τ returns the current extent of τ in the form of a list. *e.g.*

```
person :: entity;
create person $p;   /* Create an instant of entity type person*/
All_person;
 [$p]  /* The function All_person returns the extension of the
        person type */
```

4.2. Functions

The type of a function must be declared before it is defined. The following declarations,

```
name : person -> string;
factorial : integer -> integer;
```

declare name to be a function whose argument is a person and whose result is a string, and factorial to be a function which takes an integer argument and returns an integer result. The definition of functions is incremental with the insertion and deletion of equations. The left hand side (LHS) of each equation consists of the function name followed by a number of patterns which may contain variables, constants, or constructors. Thus,

```
name $p   <=   "Jim";

factorial 0   <=   1;
factorial x   <=   x * factorial (x-1);
```

In the above definitions $p, 0 and x are all patterns. x is a variable, $p and 0 are constants.

Functions are evaluated by pattern matching. When the function is applied to an argument, or arguments, the evaluator determines which equations have patterns that match those arguments. A pattern consisting of a constant will only match an argument which is equal to that constant, whilst a variable matches any argument. Thus,

```
name $p;
 "Jim"
factorial 1;
 1
```

If more than one equations match the arguments of a function then the evaluator will use a Left to Right Best Fit (LRBF) algorithm [14] to choose one. Thus;

```
factorial 0; /* best match by the first equation of the definition */
 1
```

The LHS of equations must be unique, so if an equation is specified with the same LHS as an existing one, the existing right hand side (RHS) of the equation is replaced with the new RHS. Thus,

```
name $p   <=   "Paul";
name $p;
 "Paul"
```

For any function *f*, which has only entities or events for arguments, its inverse function is a list valued function and defined by the system with the name inv_*f*. Thus,

```
inv_name "Paul";
 [$p]
```

Finally, lambda calculus anonymous functions can be directly expressed in TFDL. For example the identity function :

```
lambda x. (x);
```

4.3. Time Type

Time is modelled as a totally ordered set of time points isomorphic to the integers. Values of time type have the form Tx, where x is an integer.

The built-in functions *timeoforder* and its inverse *orderoftime* define the isomorphism of the times with the integers.

```
timeoforder : integer -> time;
orderoftime : time -> integer;
```

The functions *before*, *after* and *at* define redundantly the total order in the set.

```
before : time time -> bool;
before Tx Ty   <=   (orderoftime x < orderoftime y);
```

```
after : time time -> bool;
after T x Ty   <=   (orderoftime x > orderoftime y);

at    : time time -> bool;
at Tx Ty   <=   (orderoftime x = orderoftime y);
```

The constants Tmin and Tmax represent the earliest and latest times in the system. Other useful functions for the manipulation of time are given in the appendix.

It has to be pointed out, that the above model of time is adequate for demonstrating our ideas for representing and manipulating historical information, but is perhaps too simple for most practical purposes, its restriction to one granularity of time being unrealistic. Our future target is a time model, flexible enough to satisfy most of the users view of how time requires to be represented and, additionally, one that offers enough support for easily constructing such user views. It should include the ability to refer to different time granularities and operate between them, and to define calendar systems. An approach to DBMS support for time can be found in [10].

4.4. Event Types

Events represent instantaneous happenings, *i.e.* those occurring at a specific time point and having no duration. They model the dynamic part of a system. They are the only objects of the system that have a time reference associated with them, and therefore they represent the means of entering information in the database, which is explicitly qualified by time. Events are central to our manipulation of the historical dimension, which is presented in section 4.5 below.

Event types are very similar to entity types. As with entity types, elements are added and removed from the extent of an event type via creation and deletion commands. The values of events are also hidden by assigning them transient global variables of the form $x, where x is an alphanumeric identifier. Finally, for any event type τ, a zero-argument generator function All_τ returns the current extent of τ in the form of a list. Additionally, for each instance of an event type the user defined function *tof* returns the time of its occurrence. Other information about an event is modeled with functions.

In our lamps example,

```
lamp :: entity;
switch :: event;
switched : switch -> lamp;
```

the switching of a lamp at time T10 would be recorded as :

```
create lamp $lamp;
create switch $sw;
tof $sw1   <=   T10;
switched $sw1   <=   $lamp;
```

4.5 History Types

The type constructor *history* when applied to any type τ, constructs the history type of τ, written history(τ). τ is the *value* type of history(τ). As mentioned earlier in section 3, the instances of history(τ) model functions from time to τ.

A history type is realized in TFDL as a sum type, and thus consists of a number of constructor functions applied to zero or more arguments. The argument type of such a constructor function is called the *owner* type of the histories it constructs. Thus, these history constructing constructor functions define disjoint partitions within a history type.

For example, to model the histories of operational states of lamps, we could construct histories of type history(state) by using a constructor function LSTATE that takes a lamp as argument and returns a history(state).

```
LSTATE : lamp -> history(state);
```

Thus, LSTATE $lamp is an instance of history(state).

Additionally, another constructor function could be used to define a partition of the type history(state) for modelling the states of a television set (tv) in time :

```
TVSTATE : tv -> history(state);
```

The above mechanism of history representation provides for the treatment of temporal values as first class objects in the language. Therefore, TFDL has *temporal value integrity* as defined in [22].

TFDL provides three families of specification functions for the description of the semantics of histories,

i) *events_ε*, takes a history as argument and returns the list of ε type events that might modify it. Thus, the following equations in the definition of events_switch and events_start specification functions describe which switch and start events might affect a lamp's operational state history:

```
events_switch (LSTATE x) <= inv_switched x;
/* A lamp's operational state history is affected by the
   switchings of this lamp */


events_start (LSTATE x) <= All_start;
/* A lamp's operational state history is affected by all
   the start events (expected to be only one).*/
```

ii) *impact_ε*, takes a history of type history(τ) and a type ε event as arguments, and returns a list of tuples, whose first element is the time that the event affects the history and the second is its impact. The event's impact on the history is defined as a function (τ -> τ), that is a function from the value that the history would have at the time of the event's impact if the event had not taken place to its value due to the occurrence of the event. The following equations of the specification functions impact_switch and impact_start describe the time and nature of the impact that switch and start events have on the histories of operational states of lamps :

```
impact_switch (LSTATE l) s <= [{tof s, reverse}];
```

```
        /* A switch event affects a lamps' operational state history
           at the time of its occurrence and it reverses its state.
           reverse is a function (state -> state) defined in the
           appendix. */

        impact_start (LSTATE x) st  <=  [{Tmin, undef}, {tof st, off}];
        /* A start event affects a lamp's operational state history
           at the beginning of time and at the time of its
           occurrence. undef is a constant function (state -> state)
           that returns (@), an TFDL null value meaning undefined;
           off is a constant function (state -> state) that returns
           OFF (see appendix). */
```

Note, that it is possible for an event to affect a history at more than one times in a different way at each of them.

The above specification functions provide a way of describing how events modify a history (how they change its values) and characterizes our approach as event oriented. The next specification function defines the semantics of a history's persistence, that is what is its value at a time point, when no event occurs that modifies it.

iii) *persists*, takes a history as an argument and returns its persistency. The persistency of a history describes how the value of a history persists when it is not affected by events, and it is modelled in TFDL with a sum type called *persistency*. All elements of persistency are constructed by applying the constructor function PERSIST to a function from time to the value type of the history, whose persistency is defined. In the case of a lamp's operational state history, its persistency should specify that its value remains constant until it is changed by the impact of an event:

```
        persists (LSTATE x) <=
            PERSIST lambda t. (value (LSTATE x) last t);
```

Value, is one of the temporal operators offered by the system for the manipulation of histories and it returns the value of a history at a time point. Histories with the same type of persistency as LSTATE histories are called stepwise constant histories. Due to their overwhelming majority in real life, the 0-argument constructor function STEPWISE_CONST is added to the persistency sum type, abstracting the stepwise constant persistency semantics.

```
        STEPWISE_CONST :-> persistency;
        persists (LSTATE x) <= STEPWISE_CONST;
```

Nevertheless, any type of persistency can be defined via the PERSIST constructor function.

TFDL provides a set of temporal operators for extracting historical information from histories in accordance to their semantics as defined via the specification functions. In the core of this set are two operators, *value* and *timelist*, which are not TFDL expressible and therefore their definition is built in the system.

i)   `value : history (alpha) time -> alpha;`
     Value, is a polymorphic function (alpha is a type variable), which takes a history

and a time for arguments and returns the value of the history at this time. *e.g.* value (LSTATE $lamp) T10. The value of a history at a time point is computed by collecting the events that are affecting the history at this time point, and then applying the composition of their impacts to the value that the history would have had in the absence of any event, as it is defined by the persists function. Note, that in the case of more than one event affecting the history at the same time, their impacts are composed in an undeterministic order.

ii) `timelist : history (alpha) -> (list time);`
Timelist is a polymorphic function that takes a history as arguments and returns a list of times, at which events modify the history. *e.g.* timelist (LSTATE $lamp);

This small optimized core of temporal operators combined with the computational power of our functional language it would appear to be at least as powerful as any other historical query language. Nevertheless, we believe that despite the computational completeness of the language, built-in efficient historical operators are important for the success of a historical database system due to the massiveness of the expected data. Therefore, finding useful operators to be included in the language is a matter of great interest. Two extra operators, *when* and *extent*, are provided by the language although they are TFDL expressible. Their declaration and description follows :

iii) `when : history(alpha) (alpha -> bool) -> list(time ** time);`
when, takes as arguments a history of type history(τ) and a function from τ to bool (a condition on the value of the history) and returns a list of tuples. The first element of each tuple is a time point from the timelist of the history, such that the history's value at that point satisfies the condition but the value at the previous time in the timelist does not. The second, is the next time in the timelist that the history's value does not satisfy the condition. Therefore, if the persistency semantics of the history is stepwise constant, the function returns the maximal time intervals during which the condition is satisfied. For other persistency semantics further interpolation will be needed. *e.g.* when (LSTATE $lamp) (is_on);
is_on is a function (state -> bool), that returns true if its argument is ON and false if it is OFF (see appendix).

iv) `extent : history(alpha) -> list(alpha ** (time ** time));`
extent, takes a history as argument and returns its whole extent, that is all its values accompanied with their time interval, assuming that the history's persistency is stepwise constant. *e.g.* extent (LSTATE $lamp);

Additionally, the identification of useful operators for comparisons between histories is still a matter of on going research.

In the lamps example, let us assume that the following scenario took place:

```
create lamp $l1, $l2; /* Lamps $l1 and $l2 are created*/

create start $st1;
tof $st1   <=   T3;   /* The start of the system event takes place at T3*/

create switch $s1;
tof_switch $s1   <=   T6;
switch_of $s1   <=   $l1; /* Lamp $l1 is switched at time T6 */
```

```
create switch $s2;
tof_switch $s2   <=   T16;
switch_of $s2    <=   $12; /* Lamp $12 is switched at time T16 */

create switch $s3;
tof_switch $s3   <=   T26;
switch_of $s3    <=   $11; /* Lamp $11 is switched at time T26 */
```

Then, the following queries would result:

```
value LSTATE $11 T3;
 OFF
value LSTATE $12 T18;
 ON
timelist LSTATE $11;
 [Tmin, T3, T6, T26];
when LSTATE $11 (is_on);
 [{T6, T26}]
extent LSTATE $11;
 [{@, {Tmin, T3}}, {OFF, {T3, T6}}, {ON, {T6, T26}}, {OFF, {T26, Tmax}}]
```

4.6 Lamps and Sockets Example

We will slightly extend our lamps example to make it more realistic and demonstrate the power of the event-oriented approach. The room now contains lamps and sockets. Lamps are plugged to and unplugged from sockets, and they are switched (figure 3).

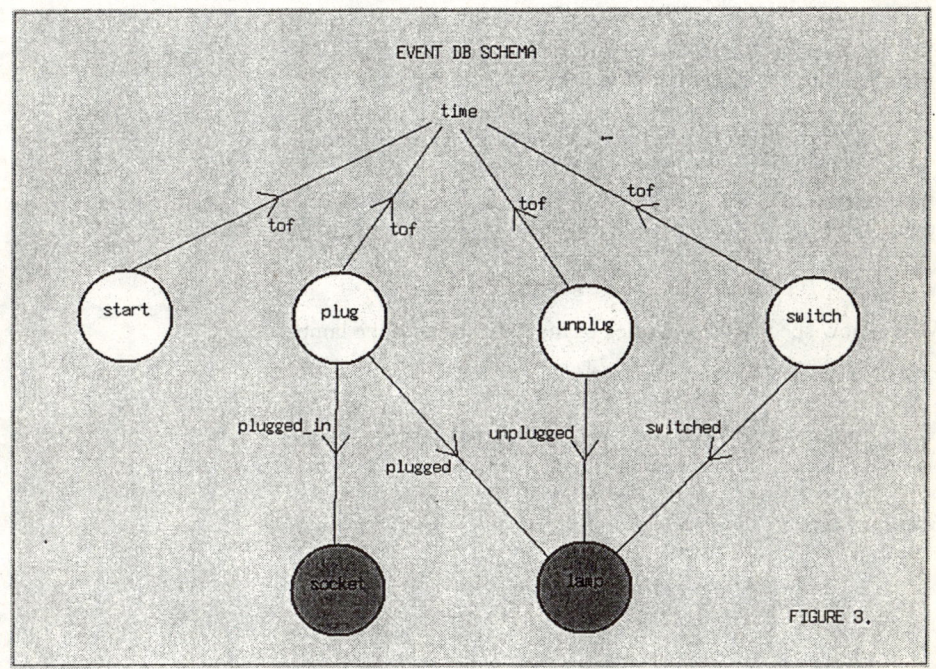

FIGURE 3.

```
lamp :: entity;          socket :: entity;
start :: event;  plug :: event;  unplug :: event;  switch ::event;

plugged     : plug -> lamp;  /*returns the lamp a plug event refers to*/
plugged_in  : plug -> socket; /*returns the socket a plug event refers to*/
unplugged   : unplug -> lamp; /*returns the lamp an unplug event refers to*/
switched    : switch -> lamp;
```

Let us derive from these events the histories of the operational states of the lamps (whether a lamp's switch is in the on or off position).

```
OP_STATE : lamp -> history(state);

events_start   (OP_STATE x)    <=  All_start;
impact_start   (OP_STATE x) y  <=  [{Tmin, undef}, {tof y, off}];

events_switch  (OP_STATE) x    <=  inv_switched x;
impact_switch  (OP_STATE x) y  <=  [{tof s, reverse}];

persists       (OP_STATE x)    <=  STEPWISE_CONST;
```

Let us now specify the histories of plugging states of the lamps (whether a lamp is plugged in or not) :

```
PL_STATE : lamp -> history(state);

events_start   (PL_STATE x)    <=  All_start;
impact_start   (PL_STATE x) y  <=  [{Tmin, undef}, {tof y, off}];

events_plug    (PL_STATE x)    <=  inv_plugged x;
impact_plug    (PL_STATE x) y  <=  [{tof y, on}];

/* on is a constant function (state -> state) that returns ON (see appendix) */

events_unplug  (PL_STATE) x    <=  inv_unplugged x;
impact_unplug  (PL_STATE x) y  <=  [{tof y, off}];

persists       (PL_STATE x)    <=  STEPWISE_CONST;
```

We can now specify the histories of the light states of the lamps:

```
LSTATE : lamp -> history(state);

events_start   (LSTATE x)      <=  ALL_start;
impact_start   (LSTATE x) y    <=  [{Tmin, undef}, {tof y, off}];

events_switch  (LSTATE x)      <=  inv_switched x;
impact_switch  (LSTATE x) y    <=  [{tof y,
                   if (value (PL_STATE x) (tof y) = OFF)   off   reverse}];
```

```
/* A plug event modifies the history of the light state of a lamp
   at the time of its occurrence and it makes its value OFF if
   its plugging state is OFF otherwise it reverses its
   light state; function if is defined in the appendix */

events_plug    (LSTATE x)    <=   inv_plugged x;
impact_plug    (LSTATE x) y  <=   [{tof y,
           if (value  (OP_STATE x) (tof y) = ON)   on  off}];

/* A switch event modifies the history of light state of a lamp
   at the time of its occurrence, and its value is modified to be
   the same with the value of the history of the lamp's switch state*/

events_unplug   (LSTATE x)    <=   inv_unplug x;
impact_unplug   (LSTATE x) y  <=   [{tof y, off}];

persists       (LSTATE x)    <=   STEPWISE_CONST;
```

Other histories that could be specified if needed, include the history of the sockets a lamp was plugged in, a history of lamps that a socket had plugged in, and so on.

5. Event-oriented against state-oriented databases

An important advantage that the event-oriented approach offers is the flexibility to expand the view it provides at any time. That is, if the events that occur in a real world system are recorded in the database, the system can in principle offer any valid history at any time required. In a state-oriented database the histories that will be recorded must be decided in advance. If at a later date other histories are required it is possible that its construction cannot be realized due to lack of data.

Another important feature of the event-oriented database is that they evolve by simply recording information about the events that occur in the real world system. No derivation of any historical information is needed, because the knowledge about them is either already stored in the database, or will be stored when the particular historical information becomes important. The system will deduce this information when it is queried. On the other hand, state-oriented databases require an interpretation of the consequence of the events occurrences on the current database state and a computation of the modifications required to apply to it, in order to produce the new current state. As a result, besides providing less automation than the event-oriented ones, they also run into trouble when a retroactive event takes place, requiring recomputation of all the subsequent states.

Thus, deriving states from events rather than *vice versa* greatly raises the semantic level of the database making it more flexible to manipulate.

In particular, our approach to specifying the semantics of the histories by the provision of specification functions for each event type, offers great flexibility in updating history semantics, either in the way events affect histories or by adding new event types that contribute to the histories. Thus, if we wanted to add to the lamps and sockets example the event of lamp destruction and update the lamp light state history accordingly:

```
destr::   event;
destr_of  :  destr  ->  lamp;

events_destr    (LSTATE x)   <=   inv_destr_of x;
impact_destr    (LSTATE x) y <=   [{tof y, undef}];
```

6. Conclusions and Future Work

A new approach to incorporating the temporal dimension in database systems was introduced and realized by the data model TEFM, and its data language TFDL. The approach is event oriented and is shown to offer greater flexibility, more automation and better handling of retroactive events than the state oriented one adopted until now.

An assumption made in this paper is that temporal information is precise. We realize that in real life it is very common for time related information to be imprecise. Nevertheless, we decided to establish our basic theory under this assumption for clarity reasons. The incorporation of the features of Fudal [20], a functional database language which uses modal logic for handling incomplete information, will be investigated.

The temporal dimension we referred to in this paper corresponds to the time when events take place in reality, what used to be known as the historical dimension [19]. We believe that our approach could be used to incorporate transaction time as well, that is the time when events are recorded in the database. Thus, making our database model bi-temporal is included in our future work.

TFDL runs as a simulation on top of FDL and thus is inherently slow. Our immediate plan is its full implementation, and optimization of its temporal operators.

REFERENCES

[1] J. Ben-Zvi. *The Time Relational Model.* PhD. thesis, computer Science department, UCLA, 1982.

[2] P. Buneman, R.E. Frankel and R. Nikhil. *An implementation technique for database query languages.* ACM Trans. on Database Systems, 7(2):164-186, June 1982.

[3] R.M. Burstall, D. B. McQueen and D. T. Sannella. *HOPE : An experimental applicative language,* Edinburgh University Research Report CSR-62-80.

[4] J. Clifford and D.S. Warren. *Formal semantics for time in databases.* ACM Transactions on Database Systems, 8(2):214-254, June 1983.

[5] J. Clifford and A. Croker. *The historical relational model (HRDM) and algebra based on lifespans.* In Proceedings of the Third International Conference on data Engineering, 528-537, Los Angeles, CA, February 1987.

[6] S.K. Gadia. *A homogeneous relational model and query languages for temporal databases.* ACM Transactions on Database Systems, 13(4):418-448, December 1988.

[7] J.R. Hindley and J.P. Seldin. *Introduction to combinators and the lambda calculus.* Cambridge University Press 1986.

[8] P.J.H. King and A. Poulovassilis. *FDL: A language which integrates database and functional programming.* Actes du Congres INFORSID 88, pp. 167-181, La Rochelle (1988).

[9] K.G. Kulkani and M.P. Atkinson. *EFDM: Extended Functional Data Model*, Computer Journal, 29:38-46, Jan 1986.

[10] Lorentzos N.A. *DBMS support for time and totally ordered compound data types.* Information systems Vol 17, No 5, pp. 347-358

[11] N.A. Lorentzos and R.G. Johnson. *Extending relational algebra to manipulate temporal data.* Information Systems ,13(3):289-296, 1988.

[12] S.B. Navathe and R. Ahmed. *A temporal relational model and a query language.* Information Sciences, 49(2):147-175, 1989.

[13] A. Poulovassilis. *The Implementation of FDL, a Functional Database Language.* The Computer Journal, 35(2):119-128, 1992. C.U.P.

[14] A. Poulovassilis. *A pattern-matching algorithm for functional databases.* The Computer Journal, 36(2):195-199, 1993.

[15] A. Poulovassilis and P.J.H. King. *Extending the functional data model to computational completeness.* Advances in Database Technology (EDBT 90), Lecture Notes in Computer science, No 416, Springer-Verlag, 1990.

[16] N.L Sarda. *Extensions to SQL for historical databases.* IEEE Transactions on knowledge and data Engineering, 2(2):220-230, July 1990.

[17] D.W. Shipman. *The functional data model and the data language DAPLEX.* ACM Trans. on Database Systems, 6:140-173, March 1981.

[18] R. Snodgrass. *The temporal query language TQuel.* ACM Transactions on database systems, 12(2):247-298, July 1987.

[19] R. Snodgrass and I. Ahn. *A taxonomy of time in databases.* SIGMOD 1985, pp 236-246

[20] D.R. Sutton and P.J.H. King. *Integration of modal logic and the functional model.* BNCOD 10, Lectures Notes in Computer Science, 156-174, Springer-Verlag 1992.

[21] A.U. Tansel. *A historical query language.* Information Sciences, 53:101-133, 1991.

[22] A.U. Tansel, J. Clifford, S. Gadia, S. Jajodia, A. Segev and R. Snodgrass. *Temporal Databases theory, design, and implementation.* Chapter 20: 496-533, Benjamin/Cummings 1993.

[23] D.A Turner. *Miranda: A non-strict functional language with polymorphic types.* Lecture Notes in Computer Sciense, Vol 201, Springer-Verlag 1985.

[24] J.J.V.R. Wintraecken. *The NIAM Information Analysis Method: Theory and Practice.* Kluwer, Deventer, The Netherlands, 1990.

APPENDIX

Auxiliary functions:

```
if : bool alpha alpha -> alpha;
if true x y <= x;
if false x y <= y;
```

```
ago : integer time-> time;
ago x y  <=   timeoforder ((orderoftime y) - x);

ahead : integer time -> time;
ahead x y  <=   timeoforder ((orderoftime y) + x);

last : time -> time;
last x  <=  ago 1 x;

next : time -> time;
next x  <=   ahead 1 x;

which_times : (time -> bool) (list time) -> (list time);
which_times f []  <= [];
which_times f [h|t] <= if (f h)  [h| which_times f t]  which_times f t;

/*which_times takes a boolean condition on time and a list of times and
  returns the times in this list that satisfy the condition */

off : state -> state;
off x  <=   OFF;

on : state -> state;
on x  <=   ON;

is_on : state -> bool;
is_on x <=  (x = ON);

undef : state -> state;
undef x  <=   @;

reverse : state -> state;
reverse ON   <=   OFF;
reverse OFF   <=   ON;
```

Object Comprehensions:
A Query Notation for Object-Oriented Databases

Daniel K.C. Chan * and Philip W. Trinder

Computing Science Department, Glasgow University
Glasgow G12 8QQ, United Kingdom

Abstract. Existing object-oriented query notations have been criticised for being unclear, verbose, restrictive, and computationally weak. This paper introduces a new query notation, *object comprehensions*, that allows queries to be expressed clearly, concisely, and processed efficiently. Object comprehensions are designed for object-oriented databases and include features that are missing from or inadequate in existing object-oriented query languages. Novel features include: a predicate-based optimisable sub-language providing support for the class hierarchy; numerical quantifiers for dealing with occurrences of collection elements; operations addressing collection elements by position and order; a high-level support for interaction between different collection kinds; and recursive queries with computation.

1 Introduction

Many object-oriented query languages [Ser87, CDV88, Bee88, BM89, Kim90, BTA90, Ont91b, BDK92, DGJ92, KKS92] have been implemented and proposed. Some of these query languages are designed particularly for object-oriented databases, e.g. LIFOO [BM89] and ORION [Kim90]. Many are, however, adapted from other areas: the relational data model and its extensions, e.g. ONTOS SQL [Ont91b]; semantic data models, e.g. OSQL [Bee88]; and object-oriented programming languages, e.g. OPAL [Ser87]. All of them, however, are inadequate in one way or another [CHT93]. Their inadequacies can be categorised into four groups: support of object-orientation, structuring power, computational power, and support of collection.

A few object-oriented query languages do not capture all the fundamental properties of object-oriented data models, e.g. the class hierarchy. The class hierarchy is defined by the *ISA* relationship between classes defined in a database schema. An object can be used wherever an object of its superclass is expected. A collection can therefore contains elements of different but related classes. A query selecting elements of a particular class from such a collection is therefore not

---

* Supported by the Overseas Research Award Scheme of the Committee of Chancellors and Vice-Principals of the Universities of the United Kingdom (ORS/8817021), the Glasgow University Postgraduate Scholarship, and ESPRIT Project 2071 Comandos. Electronic mail: daniel@dcs.glasgow.ac.uk.

unnatural - note that the class hierarchy is a form of classification. Nevertheless, support given to the class hierarchy by existing query languages is incoherent. ORION, for example, provides four constructs to support the class hierarchy: (1) class extents and the membership test *is-in*; (2) the operators * (meaning including instances of all subclasses), *union*, and *difference* over class extents to form class extent expressions; (3) specifying the class of the object returned by a method call using *class*, this specification can be sandwiched between method calls that are composed in a sequence; and (4) specifying the class of objects used and returned in a recursive query using *is-a*. It is worth noticing that many query languages support the class hierarchy by assuming the existence of class extents and rely on the membership test operator. Such an assumption is invalid in some cases, for example, class extents are optional in the data models of LIFOO and ONTOS SQL. Our proposal provides a predicate-based sub-language allowing selection on classes without assuming the existence of class extents. Actually it supports a more general form of selection that may involve calling methods conditionally [BNPS92] which is especially useful in manipulating lists.

Structuring power refers to the ability to explore and synthesise complex objects which are the components of an object-oriented database. For instance, the creation of a new object may require a collection of objects as a parameter. To do that, a query language must go beyond, for example, what is provided by ONTOS SQL. What is needed is something like nested queries. The proposed notation allows orthogonal composition of constructs and hence does not suffer the same problem.

Recursion and quantification are two examples that characterise the computational power of a query language. Traversal recursive queries are supported only by ORION among the query languages mentioned earlier. None of them, however, supports recursive queries with computation. The support of quantification is generally poor. OSQL does not support any quantifier. However, it is claimed that such support can be obtained using foreign functions (i.e. user-defined functions written in a programming language that are imported to Iris [FAC$^+$89] using an OSQL command). Without a root class, a class which is a superclass of all other classes, it is difficult to see how polymorphic functions can be defined to enable quantification over all possible element classes. Our proposal include powerful quantifiers that can be used to express sophisticated queries succinctly. Among them the numerical quantifiers are particularly interesting. Furthermore recursive queries with computation can be expressed.

Multiple collection classes are supported in several object-oriented data models [Ser87, Ont91a, ZM91, BDK92]. *Set* is widely supported and its operations are well understood. Unfortunately it is not the case for other collection classes. Interaction between different collection classes is even most puzzling. By and large, support in this area is far from satisfactory. For instance, the support provided by O_2Query [BDK92] is rather low-level. A case in point is that to return a list from a query involving both sets and lists O_2Query requires all the sets to be turned into lists explicitly. A high-level support for interaction between different collection classes using a concise notation is included in our proposal.

It allows order and duplicate elements to be preserved when it is required and in other cases it provides more opportunities for optimisation. Also included are operations that manipulate lists based on positions and the order of elements.

The aim of this research is to provide a good query notation that takes into consideration the fundamental properties of object-oriented data models. This paper introduces a new query notation called *object comprehensions*. It is based on *list comprehensions* [PJ87], which has been argued to be a good query notation for being clear, concise, powerful, and optimisable [Tri91]. Object comprehensions extend list comprehensions by consolidating and improving constructs found in existing query languages. Furthermore they incorporate new constructs that are missing from existing query languages. Optimisation opportunities have been identified for some of the novel constructs. Some of the optimisations allow syntax-level transformations at compile-time while others suggest optimisations at run-time. These optimisation rules reported in [CT94b] not only subsume previous work of the same kind but also include many new optimisations.

The organisation of this paper is as follows. Section 2 reveals the origin, development, and benefits of comprehensions. Section 3 describes a reference object-oriented data model and a running example defined in terms of this reference model. Section 4 presents object comprehensions using queries posed to the example database. Section 5 concludes.

2 Comprehensions: Past and Present

2.1 Set, List and Collection Comprehensions

In mathematics the set of square of all the odd numbers in a set s is conventionally written:

$$\{\, square\ x \mid x \in s \wedge odd\ x\,\}$$

This standard mathematical notation for sets was the inspiration for *comprehensions*. Comprehensions first appeared as *set comprehensions* in an early version of the programming language NPL. This language later evolved into Hope [BMS80] but without comprehensions. Later *list comprehensions* were included in KRC [Tur81], which was also the first to utilise the now familiar set-based syntax. List comprehensions have since been incorporated into several popular functional languages, e.g. Miranda [Tur85] and Haskell [HW90]. A full description of list comprehensions can be found in [PJ87].

Using list comprehensions the above mathematical expression can be written:

$$[\, square\ x \mid x \leftarrow s;\ odd\ x\,]$$

where s stands for a list instead of a set.

The syntax of list comprehensions is as follows, where E stands for an expression, Q stands for a qualifier, P stands for a pattern, and Λ stands for an empty qualifier:

$$
\begin{array}{rcl}
E & ::= & \ldots \\
  & | & [\,E \mid Q\,] \\
Q & ::= & E \\
  & | & P \leftarrow E \\
  & | & \Lambda \\
  & | & Q\,;\,Q
\end{array}
$$

The result of evaluating the comprehension $[\,E \mid Q\,]$ is a new list, computed from one or more existing lists. The elements of the new list are determined by repeatedly evaluating E, as controlled by the qualifier Q.

A qualifier is either a *filter*, E, or a *generator*, $P \leftarrow E$, or a sequence of these. A filter is just a boolean-valued expression, expressing a condition that must be satisfied for an element to be included in the result. An example of a filter was *odd x* above, ensuring that only odd values of x are used in computing the result. A generator of the form $V \leftarrow E$, where E is a list-valued expression, makes the variable V range over the elements of the list. An example of a generator was $x \leftarrow s$ above, making x range over the elements of the list s. More generally, a generator of the form $P \leftarrow E$ contains a pattern P that binds one or more new variables to components of each element of the list.

Recently, list comprehensions have been generalised to *collection comprehensions*, which provides a uniform and extensible notation for expressing and optimising queries over many collection classes including sets, bags, lists, trees, and ordered sets [WT91]. The most significant benefit is that, although each primitive operation will require a separate definition for each collection class, only one query notation is needed for all these collection classes; besides, a single definition is all that is required for higher-level operations defined in terms of collection comprehensions. In other words, it significantly reduces the syntactic complexity of the query notation.

2.2 Other Extensions and Implementations

An extension to support local definitions in list comprehensions was suggested in [Ham90]. Side-effecting qualifiers were proposed in [GOPT92]. They permit data to be manipulated by side-effects in addition to being queried. The strong point is that such queries can still be optimised.

The advantage of comprehensions over SQL, on which many object-oriented query languages are based, becomes clear when side-effecting qualifiers are taken into consideration. It is difficult to see how SQL-based languages can be extended in a similar way to cope with side-effects.

List comprehensions have also been applied to imperative languages such as an experimental version of PS-algol [TCH90]. The new version of Napier [MBCD89] about to be released supports collection comprehensions. List comprehensions are also included in a new functional database language called PFL

[SP91]. In P/FDM [PG90], DAPLEX queries are translated to an abstract form of list comprehensions with which optimisation is carried out. The authors also commented that list comprehensions allow queries to expressed declaratively while DAPLEX has a navigational style of querying. It is interesting that the optimisation rules are defined at the abstract comprehension level and many of them are already reported earlier in [Tri89].

2.3 Simplicity, Power and Optimisation

It was argued convincingly in [Tri91] that comprehensions are a good query notation for being concise, clear, expressive, and easily optimised. The essence of the argument is as follows. Comprehensions are concise because they are a declarative specification of the query. Comprehensions are clear because they are composed of consistent and general constructs. For each of the well-known optimisation strategies on relational queries, there exists an equivalent list comprehension transformation [TW89] and two of the transformations were demonstrated [TCH90].

3 The Running Example

3.1 The Reference Data Model

A reference data model is used to define the example database, which will be used in the next section to illustrate object comprehensions. The model fulfills the requirements as stated in [ABD+89, Ban89, Dit91] for object-oriented data models and therefore is similar to many existing data models[ZM90]. It supports the following features:

- base values
- encapsulation
- classes
- static type checking
- complex objects
- method calling
- class hierarchy
- dynamic binding
- object identity
- method overloading
- multiple inheritance
- sets, bags, and lists

Note that tuples (or records) are not supported by the reference model and a collection, e.g. a set, is an object with its own object identifier. Class extents are not supported - no class is automatically associated with a set containing all instances of that class. A formal specification of the reference data model is given in [CHT92, CT94a]. A comparison of object-oriented data models including the reference data model can be found in [CHT93].

3.2 The Example Database

The example database is a simplified university administration system that records information about students and staff members of a university, its academic departments and courses. The relationships between classes defined in the schema are shown in Fig. 1.

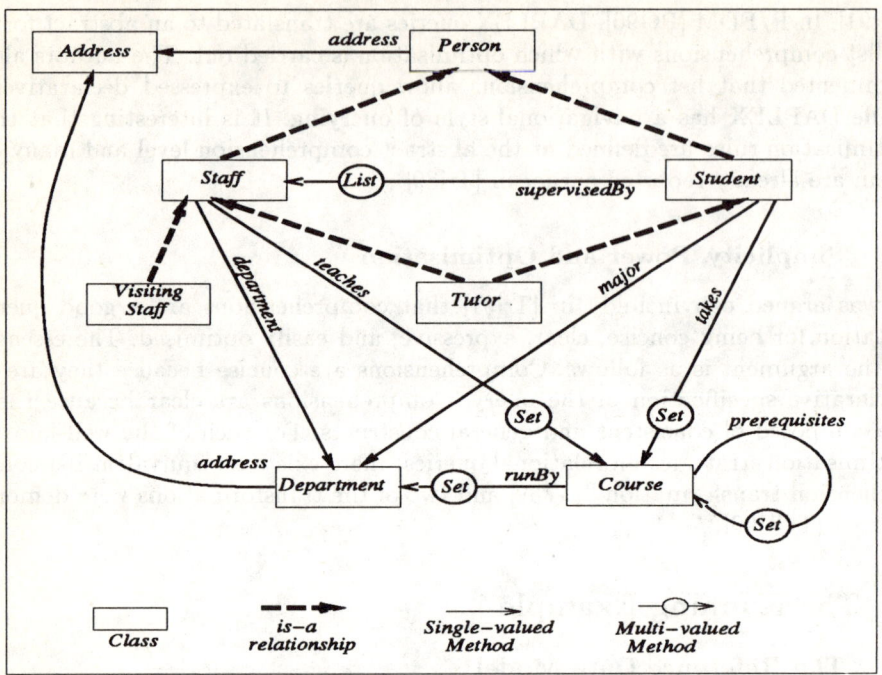

Fig. 1. Simplified Schema Diagram

The class *Person* has two subclasses: *Student* and *Staff*. *VisitingStaff* is a subclass of *Staff*. *Tutor* inherits from both *Student* and *Staff* to represent students doing part-time teaching. The calculation of the salary of a tutor is different from that of a staff member. This variation is captured by giving an overloaded method *salary* to *Tutor*. Every person is given an address which is an object of class *Address*. A student can have a principal supervisor, a second supervisor, and so forth. This relationship is modelled by the method *supervisedBy* as a list of staff members. Every staff member and student are associated to an academic department of class *Department* via *department* and *major* respectively. Courses given by each staff member and taken by each student are also recorded. They are represented by set-valued methods, *teaches* and *takes*. A course may have a set of prerequisite courses (*prerequisites*) and is administered by one or more academic departments (*runBy*). Also recorded is the percentage weights of assessments (*credits*) given in each course. A course is an instance of the class *Course*.

The schema definition is given in Fig. 2. In order to keep it simple, only the relevant method signatures are given, attributes and method implementations are omitted. It is assumed that the database contains six set collections: *Persons*, *Departments*, and *Courses*, containing all instances of their corresponding classes; and *StaffMembers*, *Students*, and *Tutors*, containing instances of the corresponding classes that are members in the Science Faculty.

```
Class Person isa Entity              Class Department isa Entity
methods                              methods
    name :→ String,                      name :→ String,
    address :→ Address.                  address :→ Address.

Class Staff isa Person               Class Course isa Entity
methods                              methods
    department :→ Department,            code :→ String,
    teaches :→ Set of Course,            runBy :→ Set of Department,
    salary :→ Integer.                   prerequisites :→ Set of Course,
                                         assessments :→ Bag of Integer,
Class Student isa Person                 credits :→ Integer.
methods
    major :→ Department,             Class Address isa Entity
    supervisedBy :→ List of Staff,   methods
    takes :→ Set of Course.              street :→ String,
                                         city :→ String.
Class Tutor isa Staff, Student
methods                              Database is
    salary :→ Integer.                   Persons : Set of Person,
                                         Departments : Set of Department,
Class VistingStaff isa Staff.            Courses : Set of Course,
                                         StaffMembers : Set of Staff,
                                         Students : Set of Student,
                                         Tutors : Set of Tutor.
```

Fig. 2. Simplified Schema Definition

4 Object Comprehensions

The following subsections demonstrate object comprehensions using queries posed to the example database described in the previous section. Methods used in the examples are assumed to be without side-effects. Side-effecting methods can be dealt with as proposed in [GOPT92]. The focus of each query is underlined. A discussion is given after each query. Queries involving staff members, students, and tutors should be read as staff members, students, and tutors of the Science Faculty, unless stated otherwise.

4.1 Support of Object-Orientation

Method Calling and Dynamic Binding

Q1. Return staff members earning more than £1000 a month.

$Set[\, s \leftarrow StaffMembers;\ \underline{s.salary} > 1000 \mid s\,]$

Encapsulation protects attributes of an object from being accessed directly. Such an access must be made via a method. In Q1, *s.salary* represents the calling of method *salary* on a staff member object *s* drawn from *StaffMembers*. Recall that a tutor is a staff member whose salary is calculated differently using an overloaded method. Since *StaffMembers* may contain tutor objects, the method to be used will be dynamically determined depending on the class of *s* (details of the resolution scheme can be found in [CT94a]).

Complex Objects and Path Expressions

Q2. Return tutors living in Glasgow.

$Set[\,t \leftarrow Tutors;\ \underline{t.address.city} = \text{``Glasgow''} \mid t\,]$

Support of complex objects implies that a method call may return an object. The returned object can, in turn, receive another method call. This can go on for several method calls until, for example, a base value is returned. In Q2, *t.address.city* represents the calling of method *city* on the result returned by calling *address* on a tutor object *t*. Such a sequence of method calls is usually referred to as a *path expression*.

Object Identity

Q3. Return tutors working and studying in the same department.

$Set[\,t \leftarrow Tutors;\ t.department \equiv t.major \mid t\,]$

In object-oriented data models, objects are represented by object identifiers which are essential for object sharing and representing cyclic relationships. Equality between objects is defined by the equality between their object identifiers. In Q3, the equality operator, "≡", compares two department objects using their object identifiers.

Class Hierarchy

Q4. Return all visiting staff members in the university.

$Set[\,p \leftarrow Persons;\ p\ \underline{hastype}\ VisitingStaff \mid p\,]$

Recall that *StaffMembers* contains only members in the Science Faculty. The only collection in the database that contains all visiting staff members is *Persons*. It is the reason why *Persons* is used in Q4. The elements of *Persons* can be of class *Person* or its subclasses. One way of selecting elements from such a collection is to specify the class of interest. In Q4, *hastype* returns true if person object *p* is an instance of class *VisitingStaff*.

To fully support the class hierarchy using *hastype*, it is necessary to support three boolean operators, namely *and*, *or*, and *not*. Together they form a sublanguage, which is powerful enough to express any class-based selection.

> Q5. Return all staff members in the university. For a visiting staff member, only return him if he earns more than £1000 a month.
>
> $Set[\,p \leftarrow Persons;\ p\ \underline{hastype}\ VisitingStaff\ \underline{implies}\ p.salary > 1000\mid p\,]$

The method *salary* is defined for visiting staff members but not for persons in general. Therefore calling *salary* on a person object may result in an error. To allow selection that is applicable only to objects of a particular class, the *hasclass & implies* construct can be used. The filter after *implies*, e.g. *p.salary > 1000* above, is applied only if the object is of the class specified after *hastype*, e.g. *VisitingStaff* above. This construct is crucial for manipulating lists as other ways of expressing the same query may destroy the order of the elements.

Local Definitions

> Q6. Return students whose major departments are in either Hillhead Street or University Avenue.
>
> $Set[\,s \leftarrow Students;\ a\ \underline{as}\ s.major.address.street;$
> $\quad a =$ "Hillhead Street" or $a =$ "University Avenue" $\mid s\,]$

Local definitions simplify queries by providing symbolic names to expressions. They are particularly useful when a path expression is used in more than one place. In Q6, *s.major.address.street* would have been written twice if local definitions were not supported. The use of the symbolic name *a* for the expression saves repeating the long expression twice.

4.2 The Result Expression

Returning New Objects

> Q7. Return students and the courses taken by them. The result is obtained by creating new objects using the student objects and the sets of courses.
>
> $Set[\,s \leftarrow Students \mid AClass.new(s, s.takes)\,]$

Operations that create new objects should be allowed in the result expression. In Q7, the method *new* takes two parameters: *s* and *s.takes* and creates a new object of class *AClass* for each object in *Students*. *AClass* is not automatically generated by the query but should be defined before the query is executed (its definition would be similar to those in Fig. 2). So it is really a requirement for orthogonal support of object-creating methods.

Many systems, e.g. IRIS, would use *tuples* to return the result of Q7. The drawbacks with this approach are (1) tuples are values and duplicates are always eliminated and (2) new objects have to be generated using perhaps a programmatic interface. This is unsatisfactory in terms of semantics and functionality. Another approach that solves a subset of the general problem involves creating new classes and factorising existing classes [MS89, HS91a, AD94]. Detailed discussion on this issue can be found in [HS91b, US92, CK94].

Nested Queries

> Q8. Return students and the courses taken by them with a credit rating greater than one. The result is obtained by creating new objects using the student objects and the sets of courses.
>
> $Set[\,s \leftarrow Students \mid AClass.new(\,s,\, \underline{Set[\,c \leftarrow s.takes;\ c.credits > 1 \mid c\,]})\,]$

Nested queries enable richer data structures to be returned as well as complex selection conditions to be expressed. In Q8, the inner query returns a set of courses and is used as a parameter to the method call in the result expression of the outer query.

4.3 Generators

Multiple Generators

> Q9. Return students studying in the same department as Steve Johnson.
>
> $Set[\,\underline{x \leftarrow Students};\ \underline{y \leftarrow Students};\ x.name = \text{``Steve Johnson''};$
> $x.major = y.major \mid y\,]$

Multiple generators allow relationships that are not explicitly defined in the database schema to be "re-constructed". In Q9, x is ranged over *Students* and y is ranged over the same set but independently. The missing relationship is established using the major departments of x and y. Multiple generators are particularly useful in processing nested collections as shown in the next example.

Dependent Generators

> Q10. Return courses taken by the students.
>
> $Set[\,\underline{s} \leftarrow Students;\ c \leftarrow \underline{s.takes} \mid c\,]$

The result of a method call can be a collection containing many elements. To facilitate querying over the elements in such a "nested" collection, a dependent generator can be used. In Q10, c is ranged over the collection returned by calling *takes* on the current student object s (i.e. the element in *Students* that is currently bound to s). The range of c changes whenever s is given a new object.

Literal Generators

> Q11. Return those courses among DB4, AI4, HCI4, OS4, and PL4 which have a credit rating over 1.
>
> $Set[\,c \leftarrow Courses;\ x \leftarrow \underline{Set\{\text{``DB4''},\text{``AI4''},\text{``HCI4''},\text{``OS4''},\text{``PL4''}\}};$
> $c.code = x;\ c.credits > 1 \mid c\,]$

Collection literals can simplify queries by making them more concise and arguably clearer. In Q11, a set literal of strings is specified by listing the elements within curly brackets. They are, however, more often used in specifying filters as in the next example.

4.4 Quantifiers

The quantifiers introduced in this subsection concerns the occurrences of collection elements and they have the same semantics for sets, bags, and lists. Yet the different constraints of these collection classes on their elements can be exploited for semantic query optimisation.

Existential Quantifiers

Q12. Return those courses among DB4, AI4, HCI4, OS4, and PL4 which have a credit rating over 1.

$Set[\,c \leftarrow Courses;\ c.credits > 1;$
$\quad c.code = \underline{some}\ Set\{\text{"}DB4\text{"}, \text{"}AI4\text{"}, \text{"}HCI4\text{"}, \text{"}OS4\text{"}, \text{"}PL4\text{"}\} \mid c\,]$

Q13. Return students taking a course given by Steve Johnson.

$Set[\,l \leftarrow StaffMembers;\ l.name = \text{"}Steve\ Johnson\text{"};\ s \leftarrow Students;$
$\quad \underline{some}\ s.takes = \underline{some}\ l.teaches \mid s\,]$

A restricted form of existential quantification is provided by *some*, which can appear on either side of an operator. In Q12, the first filter succeeds if a course code is one of the members listed in the set literal. That is,

$$\exists x : Set\{\text{"}DB4\text{"}, \text{"}AI4\text{"}, \text{"}HCI4\text{"}, \text{"}OS4\text{"}, \text{"}PL4\text{"}\} \bullet x = c.code$$

In Q13, the filter returns true if there is a common element between the two sets: *s.takes* and *l.teaches* (i.e. an non-empty intersection). That is

$$\exists x : s.takes\ \exists y : l.teaches \bullet x = y$$

Universal Quantifiers

Q14. Return students taking only courses given by Steve Johnson.

$Set[\,l \leftarrow StaffMembers;\ l.name = \text{"}Steve\ Johnson\text{"};\ s \leftarrow Students;$
$\quad \underline{every}\ s.takes = some\ l.teaches \mid s\,]$

In Q14, the last filter succeeds if all the course elements in *s.takes* are also in the set *l.teaches*. That is,

$$\forall x : s.takes\ \exists y : l.teaches \bullet x = y$$

Numerical Quantifiers Numerical quantifiers are based on numerical quantifiers used in logic [BB89], and are constructs that have not appeared before in other languages. They are very useful in dealing with duplicate elements in collections and the number of elements that are common between two collections (i.e. the size of the intersection).

Q15. Return students taking two or more courses given by Steve Johnson.

$Set[\,l \leftarrow StaffMembers;\ l.name = \text{``Steve Johnson''};\ s \leftarrow Students;$
$some\ s.takes = \underline{atleast\ 2\ l.teaches}\ |\ s\,]$

Q16. Return students taking exactly two courses given by Steve Johnson.

$Set[\,l \leftarrow StaffMembers;\ l.name = \text{``Steve Johnson''};\ s \leftarrow Students;$
$some\ s.takes = \underline{just\ 2\ l.teaches}\ |\ s\,]$

Q17. Return students taking no more than two courses given by Steve Johnson.

$Set[\,l \leftarrow StaffMembers;\ l.name = \text{``Steve Johnson''};\ s \leftarrow Students;$
$some\ s.takes = \underline{atmost\ 2\ l.teaches}\ |\ s\,]$

In Q15, the last filter becomes true if there are at least two elements that are common between $s.takes$ and $l.teaches$. That is

$$\exists_{\geqslant 2}\ x : l.teaches\ \exists\, y : s.takes \bullet x = y$$

where

$$\exists_{\geqslant n}\ x : C \bullet P(x) \equiv \exists_{\geqslant n-1}\ x : C \bullet (P(x) \wedge (\exists\, y : C \bullet P(y) \wedge y \neq x))$$
$$\exists_{\geqslant 1}\ x : C \bullet P(x) \equiv \exists\, x : C \bullet P(x).$$

In Q16, the last filter succeeds if there are exactly two elements that are common between the operand sets. That is,

$$\exists_{=n}\ x : C \bullet P(x) \equiv (\exists_{\geqslant n}\ x : C \bullet P(x)) \wedge \neg\, (\exists_{\geqslant n+1}\ x : C \bullet P(x))$$

While in Q17, the number of common elements must be less than or equal to two. That is,

$$\exists_{\leqslant n}\ x : C \bullet P(x) \equiv \neg\, (\exists_{\geqslant n+1}\ x : C \bullet P(x))$$

Quantifiers are bound in the following order: universal quantifier then numerical quantifier and followed by existential quantifier. When two numerical quantifiers are used together the following semantics is given,

$$q_1\ e_1\ cs_1\ \theta\ q_2\ e_2\ cs_2 \equiv q_1\ e_1\ cs_1\ \theta\ some\ cs_2\ \wedge\ some\ cs_1\ \theta\ q_2\ e_2\ cs_2$$

4.5 Support of Collection

Aggregate Functions

> Q18. Return courses with less than two assessments.
>
> $Set[\,c \leftarrow Courses;\ c.assessments.\underline{size} < 2 \mid c\,]$

The aggregate function *size* returns the number of elements in a collection. It is defined for all collection classes. For bags and lists duplicate elements are included in the counting. Some aggregate functions are, however, defined only for certain collection classes.

Equality

> Q19. Return courses requiring no prerequisite courses.
>
> $Set[\,c \leftarrow Courses;\ c.prerequisites \underline{==} Set\{\} \mid c\,]$

In many occasions it is necessary to compare two collections based on the elements, their occurrences, and their order. Two bags are equal if for each element drawn from either collection there is equal number of occurrences in both bags. For lists, the number of occurrences and the positions must be the same. In Q19, the filter becomes true if *c.prerequisites* is an empty set. Note that object comprehensions do not support equality on objects that are not collections.

Occurrences and Counting

> Q20. Return courses with 4 25% assessments.
>
> $Set[\,c \leftarrow Courses;\ just\ \underline{4}\ c.assessments = 25 \mid c\,]$
>
> Q21. Return the number of assessments counted 25% in DB4 assuming that the course object is represented by an identifier *db4*.
>
> $Set[\,i \leftarrow List\{0..db4.assessments.size\};\ just\ \underline{i}\ db4.assessments = 25 \mid i\,]$

Bags and lists allow duplicate elements. Q20 and Q21 show how the occurrences of elements can be used and retrieved using object comprehensions. In Q21, the possible number of occurrences is generated from a literal generator ranging from zero to *db4.assessments.size*.

Positioning and Ordering

> Q22. Return the first and second supervisors of Steve Johnson.
>
> $Set[\,s \leftarrow Students;\ s.name\ =\ \text{``Steve Johnson''};$
> $\quad sup \leftarrow s.supervisedBy.[1..2] \mid sup\,]$
>
> Q23. Return students having Steve Johnson before Bob Campbell in their supervisor lists.
>
> $Set[\,s \leftarrow Students;\ s.supervisedBy.[Steve : Bob] \sim==\ List\{\} \mid s\,]$

A list allows duplicate elements and keeps track of the order of the elements. Naturally queries involving lists may question on the order or positions of elements. In Q22, the first two elements of the list are returned and used in a generator. In Q23, a sublist whose first element is Steve (assuming that Steve is an identifier holding the person object corresponding to Steve Johnson) and whose last element is Bob (similarly an identifier) is returned. It returns an empty list if Steve Johnson does not come before Bob Campbell in a supervisor list. Otherwise it returns the first match.

Union and Differ

> Q24. Return students in the Computing Science and Electrical Engineering Departments.
>
> $Set[\,s \leftarrow Students;\ s.major.name\ =\ \text{``Computing Science''} \mid s\,]$
> $\underline{union}$
> $Set[\,s \leftarrow Students;\ s.major.name\ =\ \text{``Electrical Engineering''} \mid s\,]$

The *union* operator combines two collections to form a new collection of the same class but having all the elements. If the two operand collections have different element classes, the element class of the result collection is the unique least general superclass of the original element classes. The union of two bags contains all the elements including all duplicates. The union of a list to another list appends the latter one to the former one.

> Q25. Return cities where students, but no staff, live.
>
> $Set[\,s \leftarrow Students \mid s.address.city\,]$
> $\underline{differ}$
> $Set[\,s \leftarrow StaffMembers \mid s.address.city\,]$

For *differ*, the class of the result elements is determined in the same way as in *union*. The number of occurrences for an element in the result collection is the difference of that in the operand collections. For lists, *differ* will remove the last match.

Converting Collections

> Q26. Return the salary of tutors and keep the possible duplicate values.
>
> $\underline{Bag}[\, t \leftarrow Tutors \mid t.salary\,]$

This query is based on a set of tutor objects and naturally the result will be a set of integers. However that will result in duplicates being eliminated. If duplicates are to be kept the result can be specified to be a bag. This provides a high-level mechanism to control the management of duplicates. Converting into a set will eliminate duplicates while converting into a list will have the additional effect of assigning an arbitrary order over the result elements. The latter is therefore non-deterministic.

Mixing Collections

> Q27. Return courses taught by the supervisors of Steve Johnson.
>
> $Set[\, s \leftarrow Students;\; s.name = \text{``Steve Johnson''};$
> $\quad\; \underline{sup \leftarrow s.supervisedBy};\; c \leftarrow sup.teaches \mid c\,]$

If an object-oriented data model supports more than one kind of collection, the corresponding query notation should support not only different collection classes but also the mixing of them in the same query. In Q27, *s.supervisedBy* returns a list and is mixed with two generators drawing from sets. If the result collection is to be a list, the generators must be handled with care. For example, swapping of generators will no longer be possible. If all the generators are drawn from lists, the result elements must be computed in the order specified by the generators. If only some of the generators are drawn from lists, the order of the result elements can only be partially determined. In all other cases, an arbitrary order is given.

4.6 Query Functions and Recursion

> Q28. Return all direct and indirect prerequisite courses for the "DB4" course.
>
> let $\underline{f}(\, cs\, :\, Set\; of\; Course\,)$ be
> $\quad \overline{Set}[\, x \leftarrow cs\; union\; \underline{f}(\, x.prerequisites\,) \mid x\,]$
> in $Set[\, c \leftarrow Courses;\; c.code = \text{``DB4''};\; p \leftarrow \underline{f}(c.prerequisites) \mid p\,]$

In object-oriented data models, it is possible to find cyclic relationships involving one or more classes. This suggests that recursive queries should be supported. With object comprehensions, recursive queries can be expressed using query functions. In Q28, the result of the query is generated by retrieving elements, p, from a collection returned by a recursive function, $f(\,c.prerequisites\,)$. Function f takes a set of courses and returns a set of courses. For each element x drawn from the input collection cs, f is applied recursively on the prerequisite courses of x, $x.prerequisites$, and the result is then used as part of the input. The recursion stops when f is passed an empty set.

5 Concluding Remarks

The salient features of a new query notation for object-oriented databases were presented. The notation, object comprehensions, is capable of expressing sophisticated queries in a clear and concise fashion. This is achieved via the support of a number of powerful predicates, orthogonal composition of constructs, query functions, local definitions, manipulation of different collection classes, and recursion. Despite of being a powerful notation, object comprehensions can be optimised using existing optimisation techniques. Some optimisations for class testing and quantification were identified and presented in [CT94b]. Even though only side-effect free expressions were considered in this paper, the notation can be easily extended to cope with expressions with side-effects and still be optimisable.

References

[ABD+89] M. Atkinson, F. Bancilhon, D. DeWitt, K. Dittrich, D. Maier, and S. Zdonik. The Object-Oriented Database System Manifesto. In *Proceedings of the International Conference on Deductive and Object-Oriented Databases*, pages 40–57. Elsevier, 1989.

[AD94] R. Agrawal and L.G. DeMichiel. Type Derivation Using the Projection Operation. In *Proceedings of the International Conference on Extending Database Technology*. Springer-Verlag, 1994.

[Ban89] F. Bancilhon. Query Languages for Object-Oriented Database Systems: Analysis and a Proposal. In *Proceedings of the GI Conference on Database Systems for Office, Engineering, and Scientific Applications*, pages 1–18. Springer-Verlag, 1989.

[BB89] E.J. Borowski and J.M. Borwein. *Dictionary of Mathematics*. Collins, 1989.

[BDK92] F. Bancilhon, C. Delobel, and P. Kanellakis, editors. *Building An Object-Oriented Database System - The Story of O_2*. Morgan Kaufmann, 1992.

[Bee88] D. Beech. A Foundation for Evolution from Relational to Object Databases. In *Proceedings of the International Conference on Extending Database Technology*, volume 303 of *Lecture Notes in Computer Science*, pages 251–270. Springer-Verlag, 1988.

[BM89] O. Boucelma and J.L. Maitre. Querying Complex-Object Databases: the LIFOO Functional Language. Technical report, Université de Provence, France, 1989.

[BMS80] R.M. Burstall, D.B. MacQueen, and D.T. Sanella. Hope: an Experimental Applicative Language. In *Proceedings of the 1st ACM Lisp Conference*, pages 136–143. ACM Press, 1980.

[BNPS92] E. Bertino, M. Nagri, G. Pelagatti, and L. Sbattella. Object-Oriented Query Languages: The Notion and the Issues. *IEEE Transactions on Knowledge and Data Engineering*, 4(3):223–237, June 1992.

[BTA90] J.A. Blakeley, C.W. Thompson, and A.M. Alashqur. OQL[X]: Extending a Programming Language X with a Query Capability. Technical Report 90-07-01, Texas Instruments Incorporated, U.S.A., November 1990.

[CDV88]   M.J. Carey, D.J. DeWitt, and S.L. Vandenberg. A Data Model and Query Language for EXODUS. In *Proceedings of the ACM SIGMOD International Conference on Management of Data*, pages 413–422. ACM Press, 1988.
[CHT92]   D.K.C. Chan, D.J. Harper, and P.W. Trinder. A Reference Object-Oriented Data Model Specification. Technical Report DB-92-2, University of Glasgow, U.K., November 1992.
[CHT93]   D.K.C. Chan, D.J. Harper, and P.W. Trinder. A Case Study of Object-Oriented Query Languages. In *Proceedings of the International Conference on Information Systems and Management of Data*, pages 63–86. Indian National Scientific Documentation Centre (INSDOC), 1993.
[CK94]   D.K.C. Chan and D.A. Kerr. Improving One's Views of Object-Oriented Databases. In *Proceedings of the Colloquium on Object-Orientation in Databases and Software Engineering*, 1994.
[CT94a]   D.K.C. Chan and P.W. Trinder. An Object-Oriented Data Model Supporting Multi-methods, Multiple Inheritance, and Static Type Checking: A Specification in Z. In *Proceedings of the 8th Z User Meeting*, Workshops in Computing Series. Springer-Verlag, 1994.
[CT94b]   D.K.C. Chan and P.W. Trinder. Optimising Object Comprehensions. In *Prcoeedings of the 6th International Conference on Computing and Information*. IEEE Press, 1994.
[DGJ92]   S. Dar, N.H. Gehani, and H.V. Jagadish. CQL++: A SQL for the ODE Object-Oriented DBMS. In *Proceedings of the International Conference on Extending Database Technology*, volume 580 of *Lecture Notes in Computer Science*, pages 201–216. Springer-Verlag, 1992.
[Dit91]   K.R. Dittrich. Object-Oriented Database Systems: The Notion and the Issues. In *On Object-Oriented Database Systems*, pages 3–10. Springer-Verlag, 1991.
[FAC+89] D.H. Fishman, J. Annevelink, E. Chow, T. Connors, J.W. Davis, W. Hasan, C.G. Hoch, W.Kent, S. Leichner, P. Lyngbaek, B. Mahbod, M.A. Neimat, T. risch, M.C. Shan, and W.K. Wilkinson. Overview of the Iris DBMS. In W. Kim and F.H. Lochovsky, editors, *Object-Oriented Concepts, Databases, and Applications*, pages 219–250. ACM Press, 1989.
[GOPT92] G. Ghelli, R. Orsini, A. Pereira Paz, and P.W. Trinder. Design of an Integrated Query and Manipulation Notation for Database Languages. Technical Report FIDE/92/41, University of Glasgow, U.K., 1992.
[Ham90]   K. Hammond. Definitional List Comprehensions. Technical Report 90/R3, University of Glasgow, U.K., January 1990.
[HS91a]   A. Heuer and P. Sander. Classifying Object-Oriented Query Results in a Class/Type Lattice. In *Proceedings of the 3rd Symposium on Mathematical Fundamentals of Database and Knowledge Base Systems*, volume 495 of *Lecture Notes in Computer Science*, pages 14–28. Springer-Verlag, 1991.
[HS91b]   A. Heuer and M.N. Scholl. Principles of Object-Oriented Query Languages. In *Proceedings of the GI Conference on Database Systems for Office, Engineering, and Scientific Applications*, pages 178–197. Springer-Verlag, 1991.
[HW90]   P. Hudak and P. Wadler. Report on the Functional Programming Language Haskell. Technical Report 89/R5, University of Glasgow, U.K., February 1990.
[Kim90]   W. Kim. *Introduction to Object-Oriented Databases*. MIT Press, 1990.
[KKS92]   M. Kifer, W. Kim, and Y. Sagiv. Querying Object-Oriented Databases. In *Proceedings of the ACM SIGMOD International Conference on Management of Data*, pages 393–402. ACM Press, 1992.

[MBCD89] R. Morrison, A.L. Brown, R.C.H. Connor, and A. Dearle. The Napier88 Reference Manual. Technical Report PPRR-77-89, University of Glasgow & University of St. Andrews, U.K., 1989.

[MS89] M. Missikoff and M. Scholl. An Algorithm for Insertion into a Lattice: Application to Type Classification. In *Proceedings of the 3rd International Conference on Foundations of Data Organisation and Algorithms*, volume 367 of *Lecture Notes in Computer Science*, pages 64–82. Springer-Verlag, 1989.

[Ont91a] Ontologic Inc., U.S.A. *ONTOS Developer's Guide*, 1991.

[Ont91b] Ontologic Inc., U.S.A. *ONTOS SQL Guide*, 1991.

[PG90] N.W. Paton and P.M.D. Gray. Optimising and Executing DAPLEX Queries using Prolog. *The Computer Journal*, 33(6):547–555, 1990.

[PJ87] S. Peyton-Jones. *The Implementation of Functional Programming Languages*, chapter 7, pages 127–138. Prentice-Hall, 1987.

[Ser87] Servio Logic Development Corporation, U.S.A. *Programming in OPAL, Version 1.3*, 1987.

[SP91] C. Small and A. Poulovassilis. An Overview of PFL. In *Proceedings of the International Workshop on Database Programming Languages*, pages 89–103. Morgan Kaufmann, 1991.

[TCH90] P.W. Trinder, D.K.C. Chan, and D.J. Harper. Improving Comprehension Queries in PS-algol. In *Proceedings of the 1990 Glasgow Database Workshop*, pages 103–119, U.K., 1990. University of Glasgow.

[Tri89] P.W. Trinder. *A Functional Database*. D.Phil thesis, Oxford University, December 1989.

[Tri91] P.W. Trinder. Comprehensions: a Query Notation for DBPLs. In *Proceedings of the 3rd International Workshop on Database Programming Languages*, pages 55–70. Morgan Kaufmann, 1991.

[Tur81] D.A. Turner. Recursion Equations as a Programming Language. In Darlington, Henderson, and Turner, editors, *Functional Programming and its Application*. Cambridge University Press, 1981.

[Tur85] D.A. Turner. Miranda: a Non-strict Functional Language with Polymorphic Types. In *Proceedings of the 2nd Conference on Functional Programming Languages and Computer Architectures*, volume 201 of *Lecture Notes in Computer Science*, pages 1–16. Springer-Verlag, 1985.

[TW89] P.W. Trinder and P.L. Wadler. Improving List Comprehensions Database Queries. In *Proceedings of the TENCON'89*, pages 186–192. IEEE Press, 1989.

[US92] R. Unland and G. Schlageter. Object-Oriented Database Systems: State of the Art and Research Problems. In K. Jeffery, editor, *Expert Database Systems*, chapter 5, pages 117–222. Academic Press, 1992.

[WT91] D. Watt and P.W. Trinder. Towards a Theory of Bulk Types. Technical Report FIDE/91/26, University of Glasgow, U.K., July 1991.

[ZM90] S.B. Zdonik and D. Maier, editors. *Readings in Object-Oriented Database Systems*. Morgan Kaufmann, 1990.

[ZM91] S.B. Zdonik and G. Mitchell. ENCORE: An Object-Oriented Database Systems. *IEEE Data Engineering Bulletin*, 14(2):53–57, June 1991.

Expressivity of Typed Logic Paradigms for Object-Oriented Databases

Suad Alagić and Rajshekhar Sunderraman

Department of Computer Science
The Wichita State University
Wichita, KS 67260-0083, U.S.A.
E-mail: {alagic,raj}@cs.twsu.edu

Abstract. We investigate three logic paradigms of increasing level of expressivity in modeling strongly typed, polymorphic, object-oriented database systems and their applications. The first paradigm is based on Horn clauses with equality, the second on normal logic programs (with negation in the body) and the third on logic programs that may have an arbitrary first order formula in the clause body. Our contribution is that we make these paradigms object-oriented and strongly-typed with advanced polymorphic facilities. We demonstrate how features of these paradigms are used for high-level semantic specification of a variety of standard database abstractions, both system and application-oriented. The presented strongly typed object-oriented database language departs significantly from either strongly typed programming or database programming languages, as it allows specification of methods associated with an object type (class) in a high-level, logic programming style. It accomplishes the simplicity of non-procedural data languages and the richness of the object-oriented paradigm in modeling complex systems and applications. The associated prototyping tool, based on the paradigm developed in the paper, is a powerful assistant in designing complex database applications in a strongly typed manner, allowing complex design decisions to be tested structurally and behaviorally prior to the major database implementation efforts.

1 Introduction

The logic programming paradigm [8, 25] is based on mathematical logic and is therefore very versatile in its applications. It has been used as a declarative programming language [17]. The same framework is also used in deductive databases to represent knowledge [19]. Due to its roots in mathematical logic, the paradigm can potentially be used in any situation that requires logic. In this paper, we propose to use the logic programming paradigm as a semantic specification language for object-oriented databases. The object-oriented database paradigm used in this paper is strongly-typed and comes equipped with advanced polymorphic features. By integrating the logic programming features into a strongly typed object-oriented paradigm, we achieve the advantages of declarative data languages, in addition to the richness of the object-oriented paradigm in modeling complex applications.

The semantic specification language proposed in this paper provides a framework under which the semantics of methods can be specified[1]. We distinguish between two types of methods: observer methods and constructor/mutator methods. The observer methods allow the programmer to make observations about the state of an object. The second type of methods are mutators and constructors. Mutators change the state of an object and constructors create new objects. The semantics of the methods is essentially a complete specification of the effect of mutators and constructors on observers. The effect must be specified for each type correct mutator/constructor–observer combination. If a mutator or constructor does not have any effect on any of the observers, such a fact must be stated in the specification. Alternatively, these invariance rules could be automatically introduced by the system.

The most general form of a constraint in the specification of an abstraction is of the form A :- W, where A is an atom and W is a first-order formula. In our paradigm, an atom is specified in the object-oriented style as a sequence of method applications to an object, the last of which must be an observer method. This way, we ensure that a truth value could be assigned to the atom. Formulas are constructed in the usual way as in logic programs.

The simplest form of the constraint would be when W is a conjunction of atoms. This is the same as Horn clauses and its semantics are well understood. Any set of Horn clauses has a unique minimal model [10] and although it is quite sufficient for most applications, it has its limitations in its expressivity, as we will demonstrate in the paper.

The first logic paradigm that we consider is based on typed Horn clause logic with equality. Such a paradigm has been used for EQLOG [20] and its extension called the rewriting logic in MaudeLog [28]. Its advantages are that the initial algebra semantics is available, as is a modified E-unification algorithm [20]. Our approach is somewhat different as we have a separate equality theory expressed in purely equational form. This equality theory is meant to be an extension of the standard equality theory [25]. In this, as well as in the more expressive paradigms, a model must satisfy the equality theory in the first place.

The expressivity of the language can be extended by including negation in the bodies of the clauses. A restricted form of negation, called stratified negation, in which recursion via negated goals in the body is prohibited, is introduced and we present some examples of specifications where this is needed. A set of stratified clauses also has a unique intended minimal model [9]. However, there are some situations which require non-stratified negation. We present some examples where this is the case. The semantics of a set of non-stratified clauses is given in terms of a partial model, referred to as the well-founded model [35].

There are other situations where it would be convenient to allow a general first-order formula in the body of a clause. We demonstrate that in order to provide high-level, strongly typed but polymorphic, object-oriented specifications of a variety of standard database abstractions, this level of generality is indeed required. The relationship with the previous paradigm has been elaborated in [25, 26], which presents a straightforward transformation procedure to convert such clauses into clauses which have a conjunction of literals in their bodies.

The rest of the paper is organized as follows: In Section 2, we describe the speci-

---

[1] We refer to this part of the specification as the Constraint section.

fication block, as the unit of encapsulation, information hiding and inheritance. These fundamental properties of the object-oriented database paradigm are described in [11]. Parametric polymorphism, as supported by the specification block, is discussed in Section 3, and higher-order (F-bounded) polymorphism [14] in Section 7. The distinction between inheritance and subtyping, as well as a recently proposed notion of behavioral subtyping [23], are discussed in Section 4. Usage of multiple inheritance is illustrated in Section 5. In all the sections quoted above, Horn clause logic with separate equality theory is used. In Section 6, we consider a more powerful paradigm allowing constraints with negation in the body. Sections 8 and 9 explore constraints with arbitrary first order formulae in their bodies. In these two last sections we consider generic database abstractions such as sorting and indexing, and present their object-oriented, strongly typed polymorphic specifications based on the most powerful logic paradigm explored in the paper. In Section 10, we present comparisons with the related research and discuss a prototyping tool based on the paradigm developed in the paper.

2 Specification Block

The specification language is strongly typed, polymorphic and declarative. Its main construct is the specification block as a unit of encapsulation, information hiding, inheritance, parametric and higher-order polymorphism. A specification block defines an object type (class) and includes the following components:

- Optional type parameters.
- A collection of observers. Observers are predicates whose result type is thus omitted from the specifications.
- A collection of mutators that affect the underlying object (while preserving the object identity). The result type is thus omitted.
- A collection of constructors. The result of a constructor application is an object with a new identity.
- Constraints expressed as logic programs.
- Equality theory, expressed in the equational form.

In addition, a specification block (class) has creators associated with it, which when invoked, return newly created objects of that class. A creator can be viewed as a method on the class itself, rather than on its objects.

Throughout this paper, we shall illustrate the proposed paradigm by strongly-typed, parametric, object-oriented specifications of widely used database abstractions with logic-based constraints and equations.

Example 1. Our first example, shown below, is a specification for Account abstraction which uses the specification Money, assumed to be previously defined.

```
Specification Account;
Imports Money;
Creators:
    open(Money);
Predicates:
    balance(Money);
Mutators:
    deposit(Money);
    withdraw(Money);
Constraints:
    open(M).balance(M);
    A.deposit(M).balance(N.add(M)) :- A.balance(N);
    A.withdraw(M).balance(N.sub(M)) :- A.balance(N), M.less_than(N);
Equality
    A.deposit(M).deposit(N)=A.deposit(N).deposit(M);
    A.deposit(M).withdraw(M)=A;
End Account.
```

The specification of the class Account uses the type Money, hence the Imports declaration. The result of the application of a creator is always of this type, so it is omitted. It defines a predicate (balance), and two mutators (deposit and withdraw). The Constraint section contains axioms that define the effect of mutators on the only observer, balance.

The equational theory in the above Account specification states that withdrawing an amount after depositing the same amount into an account returns the account object to its original state, as far as what can be observed about it using the observer balance, and that the order of deposit is not important. An equality axiom contains two sequences of mutators that are equivalent with respect to what can be observed in terms of their effect on the state of the underlying object by invoking observers. □

The language for the constraints is the same as used in logic programs. Horn clauses have the following general form:

$$A :- B1, B2, ..., Bn$$

where A, B1, B2, ..., and Bn are atomic predicates. The meaning of the above clause is the following: In order for A to be true, B1 and B2 and ... and Bn must be true.

In the previous example, the constraints are Horn clauses, however, as we shall show later, there are many situations where negation in the body of clauses is required. Moreover, in some cases, allowing first order formulas in the body of clauses makes it easier to express the constraints. Our framework allows for the most general form of constraints, i.e. clauses which have a first-order formula in their bodies[2]. As is customary in logic programs, all variables in the clauses are considered to be universally quantified over their respective types at the outside. It is impossible for any such set of axioms to be inconsistent. On the other hand, in order for an axiom set to be complete, each

---

[2] The form of constraints is A :- W, where A is a term which involves a predicate method as the last invocation and W is a first-order formula involving terms that also have predicate methods as the last invocation

observer (i.e. predicate) should be defined for each mutator. In addition to that, the effect of constructors on the observers associated with the type of the constructed object must also be specified.

3 Parametric Polymorphism

The main language construct, the specification block, comes in general with a type parameter. That allows support of higher-order features, in spite of the fact that the language is still first order. A parametric specification block is in fact a function TYPE → TYPE, where TYPE is the collection of all types, each of which is expressed by a specification block. TYPE, however, is not explicitly present in the language. It is constructed starting with specification blocks for types such as Natural, Real, String etc. which are in fact pre-defined and thus have fixed interpretations. The next example is a polymorphic specification of the standard abstraction Bag.

Example 2. In the specification of Bag abstraction given below, the specification for Natural is assumed along with its associated methods succ, add, sub, max, and min.

```
Specification Bag[T];
Imports Natural;
Creators
    create();
Predicates
    belongs(T, Natural);
Mutators
    insert(T);
    delete(T);
Constructors
    union(MyType): MyType;
    intersect(MyType): MyType;
    difference(MyType): MyType;
Constraints
    create().belongs(X,0);
    B.insert(X).belongs(X,N.succ()) :- B.belongs(X,N);
    B.delete(X).belongs(X,N) :- B.belongs(X,N.succ());
    B1.union(B2).belongs(X,M.max(N)) :- B1.belongs(X,M),
                                        B2.belongs(X,N);
    B1.intersect(B2).belongs(X,M.min(N)) :-  B1.belongs(X,M),
                                             B2.belongs(X,N);
    B1.difference(B2).belongs(X,M.sub(N)) :- B1.belongs(X,M),
                                             B2.belongs(X,N);
Equality
    B.insert(X).delete(X) = B;
    B.insert(X).insert(Y) = B.insert(Y).insert(X);
    B1.union(create()) = B1;   B1.union(B1) = B1;
    B1.union(B2) = B2.union(B1);
    B1.union(B2.union(B3)) = B1.union(B2).union(B3);
    (* similar axioms for intersection and difference *)
End Bag.
```

This specification has a type parameter T and hence is an example of a polymorphic specification. It uses the type `Natural`, hence the `Imports` declaration. It defines a predicate `belongs`, two mutators (`insert` and `delete`) and a collection of constructors `union`, `intersect`, and `difference`. Constructors are methods that return new objects while preserving the state of the underlying object, whereas mutators are methods that modify the state of the underlying object. `MyType` is a distinguished type variable as in [13], denoting the type of the object defined by the underlying specification. The constraint section contains axioms that define the effect of mutators on observers. Additional constraints are provided defining the effects of the constructors on the observers (only one in this case, `belongs`). These constraints define what can be observed about the state of a newly created object. □

4 Inheritance and Subtyping

In this section, we present examples of specifications that are derived from other specifications. Such a technique is referred to as *inheritance*.

Example 3. The specification SavingsAccount and CheckingAccount can be derived from the specification Account by inheritance. Their specifications are given below:

```
Specification SavingsAccount;
Inherits Account; Imports Interest; Extends balance;
Creator
    open(Money,Interest);
Predicate
    interest_rate(Interest);
    interest(Money);
Mutators
    change_interest(Interest);
    add_interest();
Constraints
    A.deposit(M).interest_rate(I)  :-  A.interest_rate(I);
    A.withdraw(M).interest_rate(I)  :-  A.interest_rate(I);
    A.change_interest(M).interest_rate(M);
    A.change_interest(M).balance(B)  :-  A.balance(B);
    A.add_interest().balance(M.add(N))  :-  A.balance(M), A.interest(N)
End SavingsAccount.

Specification CheckingAccount;
Inherits Account; Imports Overdraft; Redefines balance;
Creator
    open(Money,Overdraft);
Predicate
    overdraft_amount(Overdraft);
Constraints
    A.deposit(M).overdraft_amount(I)  :-  A.overdraft_amount(I);
    A.withdraw(M).overdraft_amount(I)  :-  A.overdraft_amount(I);
```

```
            A.withdraw(M2).balance(M.sub(M2))  :-  A.balance(M),
                                                  overdraft_amount(N),
                                                  M.sub(M2).less_than(N)
End CheckingAccount.
```

□

In this paper the term *inheritance* refers to techniques for deriving one specification from another. In some cases the derived specification will produce a subtype of the initial one. The idea behind subtyping is substitutability [15]. We say that T2<:T1 (T2 is a subtype of T1) if an instance of T2 may be substituted any place an instance of T1 is expected. If S1 and S2 are specifications, then S2 will define a subtype of the type defined by S1 iff Methods(S1) ⊂ Methods(S2) (i.e. S2 has all the methods of S1) and for every method M(A1,A2, ..., An):A ∈ S1, S2 has a method M(B1,B2, ..., Bn):B such that Ai<:Bi for all i (contravariance) and B<:A (covariance). The subtyping relation is reflexive and transitive. If X2 is of type T2 and X1 is of type T1 then the predicate X2.project(X1) will be true if X1 is a projection of X2.

This is the usual definition of subtyping [15] which we call in this paper *syntactic*. A type system can only enforce syntactic subtyping in the sense that type errors will be detected if such substitutions are permitted. Although very important[3], syntactic subtyping addresses only a small portion of the substitutability issue. Since the object-oriented paradigm is a behavioral paradigm, a stronger and perfectly natural requirement is that if a substitution is performed, a user viewing an object of type T2 as an object of type T1 should see no behavioral difference [23]. Such a requirement can be addressed only in a paradigm that extends a sophisticated object-oriented type system with semantic (behavioral) specification facilities. This stronger form of subtyping is referred to as *behavioral* subtyping.

In our previous example, both SavingsAccount and CheckingAccount are subtypes of Account. CheckingAccount is not a behavioral subtype of Account since the semantics of the mutator withdraw on the observer balance has been redefined. SavingsAccount is a behavioral subtype of Account as the effect of the new mutator add_interest can be entirely described in terms of the existing mutator deposit [23].

5 Multiple Inheritance

In this section, we present an example of multiple inheritance where a specification is derived from more than one specification.

Example 4. The specification for Set is derived by multiple inheritance from the specifications SimpleSet and Bag. Sets differ from bags in that they may contain any element only once.

---

[3] It is, in general, impossible to check it completely at compile time in most non-trivial strongly typed, object-oriented languages.

```
Specification SimpleSet[T];
Predicates
    element(T);
Mutators
    insert(T);
    delete(T);
Constraints
    S.insert(X).element(X);
Equality
    S.insert(X).delete(X) = S
End Set.
```

Observe that the use of negation is avoided in specifying the effect of the `delete` mutator on the `element` observer by the equality axiom (`S.insert(X).delete(X)=S`).

```
Specification Set[T];
    Inherits SimpleSet[T]; Extends element;
    Inherits Bag[T];
Constraints
    S.element(X)          :- S.belongs(X,1);
    S1.union(S2).element(X)     :- S1.element(X);
    S1.union(S2).element(X)     :- S2.element(X);
    S1.intersect(S2).element(X) :- S1.element(X), S2.element(X);
    S1.difference(S2).element(X) :- S1.element(X), S2.belongs(X,0);
End Set.
```

Observe that the arguments and the result of union, intersect and difference are of type Set[T], as the type of these constructors was defined as MyType in the Bag[T] specification from which they are inherited. However, according to the subtyping rules stated above, Set[T] is not a subtype of Bag[T].

In the above specification, inheritance is used to avoid the use of negation in the body of the clause:

```
S1.difference(S2).element(X) :- S1.element(X), S2.belongs(X,0)
```

Otherwise, the most natural form of the above constraint would be:

```
S1.difference(S2).element(X) :- S1.element(X), ~S2.element(X)
```

We discuss this issue in more detail in the next section.   □

We now present an application-oriented example.

Example 5. Returning back to the Banking example, we could define a bank to be a set of accounts and perform meaningful operations as shown below:

```
let aBank,bBank,cBank: Set[Account];
let a,b: Account;
....
aBank.create();     bBank.create();
a.open($500);       aBank.insert(a);
```

```
    b.open($1000);     bBank.insert(b);
    ....
    (* merge banks *)
    let cBank=abank.union(bBank)
```

□

6 Non-Horn Constraints

So far, we have restricted our examples to include constraints which can be expressed in Horn clause logic. Now, we present more sophisticated examples which require more general forms of constraints. We first consider a restricted form of negation called stratified negation which prohibits recursion via negation. The semantics of such clauses is discussed. We provide examples of specifications where stratified negation is sufficient. Then, we present examples of specifications which require non-stratified negation in the constraint-clauses. The semantics of clauses with non-stratified negation is also addressed.

6.1 Stratified negation

A set of clauses is said to be *stratified* if the clauses can be partitioned into ordered sets of clauses such that if a negated atom appears in the body of a clause in a partition, then the definition of that atom appears in a previous partition and if a positive atom appears in the body of a clause in a partition, then its definition either appears in the same partition or a previous partition.

An example specification that requires stratified negation follows.

Example 6. Consider the specification of the proper_subset predicate of the Set abstraction. The signature for proper_subset predicate would have the form:

```
    proper_subset(Set[T]);
```

and the associated constraint is:

```
    S1.proper_subset(S2) :- S1.subset(S2), ~S1.difference(S2).empty()
```

The subset and empty predicates are defined later in Section 8. □

A collection of stratified clauses does have a minimal model semantics as described in [9]. The intended minimal model for a collection of stratified clauses is constructed in an intuitive manner as follows: starting from the first partition of clauses, compute the logical consequences of the clauses in a partition using only the consequences obtained in previous partitions. Since the clauses are stratified, the predicate that appears in a negated atom will have been completely computed (i.e. both its positive and negative ground instances would be known) in a previous partition and hence can be used in the current partition. The derivation of negative facts for a partition is done by complementation after all the positive facts have been computed for the partition.

6.2 Non-stratified negation

There are situations where stratified negation is not sufficient. We now present an example.

Example 7. The difference and symmetric_difference constructors for the Set abstraction have the following signatures:

```
difference(Set[T]): Set[T];
symmetric_difference(Set[T]): Set[T];
```

and the associated constraints are:

```
S1.difference(S2).element(X)          :- S1.element(X), ~S2.element(X);
S1.symmetric_difference(S2).element(X) :- S1.element(X),
                                          ~S2.element(X);
S1.symmetric_difference(S2).element(X) :- S2.element(X),
                                          ~S1.element(X);
```

As can be observed, the above constraints involve non-stratified negation. □

The semantics of non-stratified logical clauses is captured by means of a partial truth assignment on the Herbrand base. The *well-founded* semantics [35] of logic programs (with no restriction on negation) is a partial assignment of truth values obtained by two fixpoint operators, one to derive positive facts and the other to derive negative facts. The operator used to derive positive facts is the usual immediate-consequence operator. For the derivation of negative facts the notion of *unfounded sets* is required. Informally, an unfounded set A with respect to a partial interpretation I is a set of atoms of the Herbrand base of a logic program P which satisfy the following property:

> $p \in A$ iff for each ground instance of a clause whose head is p, either (1) some subgoal of the clause is inconsistent with I or (2) some positive subgoal occurs in A.

Intuitively, I is regarded as what is already known about the intended model of P. Condition (1) says that the rule instance cannot be used to derive p. Condition (2), referred to as the *unfoundedness condition*, states that of all the rules that still might be usable to derive some atom in set A, each requires an atom in A to be true. In other words, there is no first atom in A which can be established to be true. Consequently, all of the atoms in A are assumed to be false in the well-founded semantics. Of course, this process has to be iteratively performed to arrive at the final well-founded model.

7 Higher-order Polymorphism

A particularly important form of higher-order polymorphism for object-oriented languages is F-bounded polymorphism [14]. Although a fairly abstract and higher-level notion, it actually performs a very pragmatic role in our language.

Example 8. To specify an ordering we need at least a predicate, let us call it less_than. Its generic (parametric) definition is given below.

```
Specification Order[T];
Predicates
   less_than(T);
End Order.
```

A specific ordering will now be given by introducing appropriate constraints. So, for example, a preorder is just reflexive and transitive, as specified below. But the type parameter of the preorder abstraction must satisfy the condition T<:Order[T]. This condition guarantees that whatever the underlying type T is, it must have the predicate less_than. The form of subtyping is not just bounded by a particular specification. Rather, an F-bound is Order[T].

```
Specification PreOrder[T <: Order[T]];
Constraints
   X.less_than(X);
   X.less_than(Z) :- X.less_than(Y), Y.less_than(Z);
End PreOrder.
```

Although F-bounded polymorphism [14] is important for object-oriented type systems, as it allows some inheritance relationships to be captured within the type system, it is only within the framework of a constraint language that it assumes its full meaning. In the above example, it is only when the F-bounded subtyping condition is satisfied that the universal quantification of all variables (standard in logic programming and adopted in our language design) makes sense.

The following example specification of PartialOrder has equality in the head of a constraint clause:

```
Specification PartialOrder[T <: Order[T]];
Constraints
   X.less_than(Z) :- X.less_than(Y), Y.less_than(Z);
   X = Z :- X.less_than(Y), Y.less_than(X);
End PartialOrder.
```

This is a simple and easily tractable extension of our paradigm. For details, see also [20]. □

8 Programs: Sorting

A strictly more powerful paradigm allows constraints expressed as program statements of the form

$$A \ :- \ W$$

where A is a predicate and W is an arbitrary first-order formula [25]. The increase in expressivity is illustrated considering an object-oriented, polymorphic, high-level specification for sorting.

Example 9. In order to provide a high-level specification for sorting, we need to specify appropriately ordered sets. Specification OrderedSet will be derived by inheritance from the already introduced specification Set. OrderedSet has a type parameter expressed using F-bounded polymorphism which guarantees that the actual type parameter must be equipped with the method less_than. The mutator sort makes the underlying set object satisfy the well ordered property. A set S is well-ordered if every non-empty subset of S has a least element. Expressing this property requires logic program statements of the above form, as illustrated in the specification block that follows.

```
Specification OrderedSet[T <: Order[T]];
Inherits Set[T];
Predicates
    subset(MyType);
    empty();
    has_least_element();
    least_element(T);
    higher_than(T,MyType);
    well_ordered();
Mutators:
    sort();
Constraints:
    S1.subset(S2) :- ForAll(X)(S2.element(X) :- S1.element(X));
    S.empty() :- ForAll(X)(~S.element(X));
    S.has_least_element():- S.element(X),
                    ForAll(Y)(X.less_than(Y) :- S.element(Y));
    S.well_ordered() :- ForAll(S1)(S1.has_least_element() :-
                    S1.subset(S) and ~S1.empty());
    S.least_element(X) :- ForSome(X)(S.well_ordered() and S.element(X)
                    and ForAll(Y)(X.less_than(Y) :-
                    S.element(Y)));
    S.higher_than(X,R) :- R.subset(S),
                    ForAll(Y)(X.less_than(Y) :- R.element(Y));
    S.sort().well_ordered() :- ~S.empty();
    ...
Equality:
    S1=S2 :- S1.subset(S2), S2.subset(S1)
End OrderedSet.
```

□

9 Lower-level system abstractions

The typed object-oriented logic paradigm introduced in the previous section makes specifications of lower-level database system abstractions such as *indices*, *streams* and *files* possible. As an illustration, we present the most elaborate of those abstractions, essential for most database technologies.

Example 10. The specification Index has two type parameters. The type parameter T represents the underlying object type of the elements in the extent that is being indexed. T0 consists of the indexing attributes of T, hence T<:T0. The other constraint on the type parameters has the F-bounded form T0 :< Order[T0], which guarantees that

T0 is equipped with a method `less_than`. The underlying set is thus required to be well-ordered. Because of this, it becomes possible to search the underlying set using the mutator `next` of the Index abstraction. An application of `next` makes the next smallest element in the underlying set to become current. Such a search starts with the application of the mutator `reset` which makes the smallest element in the underlying set to become current.

Associative search is accomplished with the constructor `access`. It takes an argument X0 of type T0 and returns the set of all objects X of the underlying set satisfying the condition `X.project(X0)` as the result. The result set is not necessarily ordered in any way.

```
Specification Index[T,T0:T <: T0, T0 <:Order[T0]];
Imports OrderedSet[T,T0];
Creators
    connect(OrderedSet[T,T0]);
Predicates
    extent(OrderedSet[T,T0]);
    current(T);
    eos();
Mutators
    reset();
    next();
Constructors
    access(T0): Set[T];
Constraints
    connect(R).extent(R);
    connect(R).current(X) :- R.least_element(X);
    connect(R).eos() :- R.empty();

    I.reset().extent(R)    :- I.extent(R);
    I.reset().current(X)   :- I.extent(R), R.least_element(X);
    I.reset().eos()        :- I.extent(R), R.empty();

    I.next().extent(R)     :- I.extent(R);
    I.next().current(X)    :- I.current(Y), R.higher_than(Y,S),
                              S.least_element(X);
    I.next().eos()         :- I.current(X), R.higher_than(X,S), S.empty();

    I.access(X0).element(X) :- I.extent(R), R.element(X), X.project(X0)
End Index.
```

□

The reason for presenting the above object-oriented, strongly typed specification is that Index is as elaborate a database system component as they ever get. Furthermore, the above specification accommodates various particular implementations (such as various versions of B-trees, etc.). Our intention was to demonstrate that even lower-level system abstractions can be specified in the same framework. A further point that we would like to make is that in spite of the actual complexity of the Index abstraction, only

Horn clauses are sufficient to specify it, once specifications of more abstract, generic notions such as ordered sets are available.

While the presented generic high-level specification of the Index abstraction is appealing, generating a specific and efficient representation is admittedly a very difficult optimization problem, yet to be solved. But the system oriented relevance of the presented specifications is that they are executable so that a complete database management system can be designed and tested structurally and behaviorally. Evaluating efficiency of such a design will have to be postponed until the actual efficient representation is selected. But testing functionality of the system, both structurally and behaviorally, is possible with the presented technology. We are not aware of another comparable strongly typed semantic database system prototyping tool of this kind.

10 Comparisons with Related Research

Database research and development have largely ignored typed technologies. Adding abstract data types to extended relational systems is a modest exception [31]. Much more radical results are Galileo [6] and Machiavelli [30], both having advanced type systems, with Machiavelli also featuring a sophisticated type inference mechanism. Recent developments related to SQL3 also indicate considerable attention given to abstract data types, inheritance, parametric and subtype polymorphism.

Even if a type system is offered in an object-oriented database system, the level of sophistication of such a system is not sufficient for advanced database systems and applications. For example, O2 [22] does not support parametric polymorphism and neither does Ode [1]. Matching inheritance and subtyping in O2 creates well-known problems [18].

High-level semantic specification language integrated with an advanced type system is not offered by the current object-oriented database technology. Furthermore, most work in deductive and logic databases has been done for untyped paradigms.

Our high level constraint language is a major contribution. Possibly, the main problem in applying the object-oriented paradigm to database technology is the fact that the object-oriented paradigm comes from programming languages and its strongly typed versions are of procedural nature ([29, 32]). Our language is high-level, a significant step toward the goal to abandon procedural specification of methods altogether. Perhaps a more accurate statement is that we are accomplishing that goal by specifying methods in a very high-level procedural language.

In comparison with database type systems such as the one presented in [16], Galileo [7], Machiavelli [30], our paradigm is truly an object-oriented behavioral paradigm in the sense that it supports recently proposed behavioral subtyping [23]. This is only possible because of the logic-programming semantic-based extensions capturing behavioral properties of object types. Such facilities are missing from the above mentioned systems and languages.

Among the attempts to integrate logic, functional and some aspects of the object-oriented paradigm, an important place belongs to EQLOG [20] and MaudeLog [28]. The first is a programming language and the second a database programming language. Neither is really object-oriented. Both are based on modules. Although more general, modules are not object types. One of the implications is that MaudeLog represents object-identity in value-based style, which leads to well-known negative consequences [11].

In comparison with O-logic [27], the main difference is that our paradigm is based on an advanced object-oriented type system, whereas O-logic is largely untyped. F-logic [21] is typed, but our type system is strictly more powerful because of F-bounded polymorphism and reflection, the latter being the most significant difference. The type reflection part of our type system and its relevance to typed database technologies is presented in separate papers [5, 34].

In [20] Horn clause logic with equality is used and in [28] that logic is extended to the rewriting logic intended to capture state changes. We explored two strictly more expressive typed logic paradigms allowing negation in the body and an arbitrary first order formula in the body. This is precisely the main difference in comparison with our earlier paper [4].

We demonstrated that the expressive power of these paradigms is really required in order to provide strongly typed, polymorphic, high-level specifications of a variety of standard database abstractions, both system and application oriented. But our numerous examples lead to the following conjecture.

For application-oriented and system-oriented abstractions, Horn-clause logic with equality is largely sufficient, as long as the specifications of some more general mathematical abstractions (sets, various types of orderings, etc.) are available. Those definitely require more expressive logic paradigms, such as the ones used in the paper. Apart from the usual role that equality axioms play in the specification of abstract data types [20], a part of their role is to avoid some situations in which negation would otherwise be required.

On the implementation side of the matter, we have an implementation technique for a prototyping tool which is based on logic programming and run-time deductive architectures [4]. This tool is not a database management system. Rather, it represents a powerful assistant in designing complex database applications in strongly typed manner, together with the behavioral features of the object-oriented paradigm. That way complex design decisions may be tested structurally and behaviorally prior to the major database implementation efforts.

Our current work is directed toward a complete design and implementation of an object-oriented, logic-based, database management system, written entirely in terms of our executable specifications. The goal of that research effort is to allow experiments with various options in the underlying data model, its associated languages and the required database system support.

On the other hand, in order to produce an actual strongly typed object-oriented database technology based on the approach presented in the paper, the problem of compiling the presented specifications into efficient executable code must be solved. This involves major optimization research issues that we are working on at the moment. It is only with a good solution of the underlying optimization problems that the overall approach can produce a real object-oriented database typed technology. Otherwise, the result is a powerful prototyping tool which can be used to improve the quality and reliability of the database system design process.

References

1. R. Agrawal and N. Gehani. Ode: Object database and environment. In *Proceedings of ACM SIGMOD*, 1989.
2. S. Alagić. *Object-Oriented Database Programming*. Springer-Verlag, New York, 1989.
3. S. Alagić. Toward multiparadigm database interfaces. *Lecture Notes in Computer Science*, 504, 1991.
4. S. Alagić, R. Sunderraman, and R. Bagai. Declarative object-oriented programming: Inheritance, subtyping and prototyping. In *Proceedings of ECOOP-94, Lecture Notes in Computer Science, to appear*, 1994.
5. S. Alagić, R. Sunderraman, and R. Bagai. A typed object-oriented database technology with deductive capabilities. Submitted for Publication, 1994.
6. A. Albano, L. Cardelli, and R. Orsini. Galileo: A strongly typed interactive conceptual language. *ACM Transactions on Programming Languages and Systems*, 10(2):230–260, 1985.
7. A. Albano, G. Ghelli, and R. Orsini. Objects for a database programming language. In P. Kanelakis and J. Schmidt, editors, *Proceedings of the Workshop on Database Programming Languages*, pages 236–253. Morgan–Kaufman, 1991.
8. K. R. Apt. Logic programming. In J. van Leeuwen, editor, *Handbook of Theoretical Computer Science: Volume B (Formal Models and Semantics)*. MIT Press, 1990.
9. K. R. Apt, H. A. Blair, and A. Walker. Towards a theory of declarative knowledge. In Jack Minker, editor, *Foundations of Deductive Databases and Logic Programming*, pages 89–148. Morgan Kaufmann, Los Altos, 1988.
10. K. R. Apt and M. H. van Emden. Contributions to the theory of logic programming. *Journal of the ACM*, July 1982.
11. M. Atkinson, F. Bancilhon, D. DeWitt, K. Dittrich, and S. Zdonik. The object-oriented database system manifesto. In *Proceedings of the First Object-Oriented and Deductive Databases Conference*, 1989.
12. R. Bagai, S. Alagić, and R. Sunderraman. A prototyping technology for typed object-oriented software development. In *Proceedings of Software Quality Management Conference*, U.K., 1994.
13. K. Bruce. Safe type checking in a statically typed object-oriented programming language. In *Proceedings of the Conference on Functional Programming*, pages 285–298, 1993.
14. P. Canning, W. Cook, W. Hill, W. Olthoff, and J.C. Mitchell. F-bounded polymorphism for object-oriented programming. In *Proceedings of the Conference on Functional Programming and Computer Architecture*, pages 273–280, 1989.
15. L. Cardelli. A semantics of multiple inheritance. *Information and Computation*, 76:138–164, 1988.
16. L. Cardelli. Types for data oriented languages. In J.W. Schmidt, S. Ceri, and M. Missikoff, editors, *Advances in Database Technology, Lecture Notes in Computer Science, 303*, pages 1–15. Springer-Verlag, 1988.
17. W. F. Clocksin and C. S. Mellish. *Programming in Prolog*. Springer-Verlag, 1984.
18. W. Cook. A proposal for making Eiffel type safe. *The Computer Journal*, 32(4):305–311, 1989.
19. H. Gallaire and J. Minker. *Logic and Databases*. Plenum Press, New York, 1978.
20. J. Goguen and J. Meseguer. EQLOG: equality, types and generic modules for logic programming. In D. DeGroot and G. Lindstrom, editors, *Logic Programming: Functions, Relations and Equations*, pages 295–363. Prentice Hall, 1986.

21. M. Kifer and G. Laussen. F-logic: A higher-order language for reasoning about objects, inheritance, and scheme. In *Proceedings of ACM SIGMOD*, pages 134–146, 1989.
22. C. Lecluse and P. Richard. The O2 database programming language. In *Proceedings of the 15th International VLDB Conference*, pages 411–422. Morgan–Kaufmann, 1989.
23. B. Liskov and J.M. Wing. A new definition of the subtype relation. In *Proceedings of ECOOP-93*, 1993.
24. K.-C. Liu and R. Sunderraman. A generalized relational model for indefinite and maybe information. *IEEE Transactions on Knowledge and Data Engineering*, 3(1):65–77, 1991.
25. J. W. Lloyd. *Foundations of Logic Programming*. Springer-Verlag, second edition, 1987.
26. J.W. Lloyd and R.W. Topor. Making PROLOG more expressive. *J. Logic Programming*, 1:225–240, 1984.
27. D. Maier. A logic for objects. In *Proceedings of the Workshop on Deductive Databases and Logic Programming*, 1986.
28. J. Meseguer and X. Qian. A logical semantics for object-oriented databases. In *Proceedings of ACM-SIGMOD Conference*, 1993.
29. B. Meyer. *Eiffel: The Language*. Prentice Hall, 1992.
30. A. Ohori, P. Buneman, and V. Breazu-Tannen. Database programming in Machiavelli – A polymorphic language with static type inference. In *Proceedings of ACM SIGMOD Conference*, 1989.
31. M. Stonebraker and L.W. Rowe. The Postgres papers. Technical Report Memorandum No. UCB/ERL M86/85, University of California, Berkeley, 1987.
32. B. Stroustrup. *The C++ Programming Language*. Addison-Wesley, second edition, 1991.
33. R. Sunderraman. Deductive databases with conditional facts. *Lecture Notes in Computer Science*, 696:162–175, 1993.
34. M. Surendhar and S. Alagić. Object-oriented type evolution using reflection. In *Proceedings of TOOLS '94 (Technology of Object-Oriented Languages and Systems)*, pages 271–280. Prentice Hall, 1994.
35. A. van Gelder, K. A. Ross, and J. S. Schlipf. The well-founded semantics for general logic programs. *Journal of the ACM*, 38(3):621–650, 1991.

Algebraic Computation of the Weak Well-Founded Model for General Deductive Databases

Rajiv Bagai and Rajshekhar Sunderraman

Department of Computer Science
The Wichita State University
Wichita, KS 67260-0083, U.S.A.

Abstract. General logic programs are those that contain both positive and negative subgoals in their clause bodies. For such programs Fitting proposed an elegant 3-valued minimum model semantics that avoids some impracticalities of previous approaches. Here we present a method to compute this model for deductive databases. We introduce *partial relations*, which are the semantic objects associated with predicate symbols, and define algebraic operators over them. The first step in our model computation method is to convert the database rules into partial relation definitions involving these operators. The second step is to build the minimum model iteratively. We give algorithms for both steps and establish their termination and correctness. We also suggest extensions to our method for computing the well-founded model proposed by van Gelder, Ross and Schlipf.

Keywords. Deductive databases, Negation, Weak well-founded semantics.

1 Introduction

Deductive databases that allow both positive and negative subgoals in their clause bodies are commonly known as *general* deductive databases. Various semantics for such databases (in the context of logic programming) have been proposed in the past. Apt, Blair, and Walker [1] proposed a semantics for a subclass of general logic programs called *stratified* programs. The canonical model is defined by taking the least fixed points in order from lower to higher strata. Przymusinski [13] introduced "perfect models" for a subclass of general deductive databases called *locally stratified* databases. Every locally stratified database is shown to have a unique perfect model and the perfect model agrees with the stratified semantics of [1] for stratified databases. For more general deductive databases, van Gelder, Ross, and Schlipf [19] presented the "well-founded semantics" and Gelfond and Lifschitz [8] proposed the "stable model semantics". Fitting [7] gave a markedly different and a more uniform semantics for general logic programs by interpreting the program completion in a 3-valued constructive logic. The completion of every program has a unique minimum 3-valued model, which Fitting suggests as the semantics of the program. Fitting did not give a name to this semantics, but Bidoit [4] calls this the *weak* well-founded semantics.

Although most of the semantics issues have been studied in the context of logic programs, the results hold good for deductive databases as well. Some of the complexity issues get simplified in the context of deductive databases as function symbols are not allowed. A deductive database provides for extensional and intensional definitions of relations. Extensional definitions essentially contain only unit clauses (with no bodies), and intensional definitions contain arbitrary Horn clauses. Since it is customary to not use function symbols in the definitions and to use only a finite number of constant symbols, the relations defined may only be finite sets of tuples. It is thus, in principle, possible to generate all tuples contained in the relations by an effective procedure. While the complexity of the procedure clearly depends upon that of the intensional definitions contained in the database, the magnitude of the task of constructing such a procedure gets significantly reduced if some modules for algebraic operations on relations can be used to put the procedure together, since such modules normally exist in most relational database management systems.

Ullman in [17] described a method to convert the intensional definitions in a deductive database into *datalog equations*, which are essentially definitions of relations involving algebraic expressions over relations. These equations are then used for incremental construction of the entire data. Ullman also described a method for general deductive databases, in which negative subgoals are permitted in the clause bodies. However, the method is applicable only to stratified databases.

In this paper we present a more general method for arbitrary general deductive databases. Our method is capable of computing the model proposed by Fitting [7], which is a unique minimum 3-valued model for the completion of the given database. The model was originally proposed for general logic programs (finite number of function symbols allowed) and is known to be not always recursively enumerable. But in the deductive database setting (without any function symbols), it is in fact finite.

The central idea in arriving at the weak well-founded model for a given deductive database is to associate *partial relations* with the predicate symbols. A partial relation essentially contains two kinds of tuples: ones for which the predicate is believed to be true and ones for which it is believed to be false. Since beliefs are not always complete, a predicate's truth values for some tuples may well be unknown. Moreover, contradictory beliefs are provided by allowing a predicate to be believed both true as well as false for some tuples. We define algebraic operators over partial relations that extend the standard operators, such as selection, join etc., for ordinary relations. The intensional definitions in a given deductive database are first converted into algebraic definitions of partial relations, which are then used to incrementally construct the weak well-founded model in a bottom-up fashion.

The rest of this paper is organized as follows. Section 2 contains a brief overview of the weak well-founded model. Section 3 introduces partial relations and some algebraic operators over them. Section 4 presents the first part of the computation method, namely an algorithm to convert the intensional definitions into equations defining partial relations. It also establishes the termination of the algorithm and the equivalence of the immediate consequences in Fitting's semantics for the original database with the solution of the obtained equations. Section 5 presents the second part of the method, namely an algorithm to incrementally construct the partial relations defined by the equations. It also shows the termination and correctness of the algorithm. Finally, Section 6 contains some concluding remarks, related work and directions for future work.

2 The Weak Well-Founded Model

In this section we give a brief overview of the weak well-founded model. For a detailed exposition the reader is referred to [7]. We assume an underlying language with a finite set of constant, variable, and predicate symbols, but no function symbols. A *term* is either a constant or a variable. An *atom* is of the form $p(t_1, \ldots, t_n)$, where p is a predicate symbol and the $t_i's$ are terms. A *literal* is either a *positive literal* A or a *negative literal* $\neg A$, where A is an atom. For any literal l we let l' denote its complementary literal, i.e. if l is positive then $l' = \neg l$, otherwise $l = \neg l'$.

Definition 1. A *general deductive database* is a finite set of clauses of the form

$$a \leftarrow l_1, l_2, \ldots, l_m$$

where a is an atom, $m \geq 0$ and each l_i is a literal. □

A term, atom, literal, or clause is called *ground* if it contains no variables. The *Herbrand Base* of the underlying language is the set of all ground atoms. A *ground instance* of a term, atom, literal, or clause Q is the term, atom, literal, or clause, respectively, obtained by replacing each variable in Q by a constant. For any general deductive database P, we let P^* denote the set of all ground instances of clauses in P. Note that since the underlying language has no function symbols, unlike logic programs, P^* is always finite.

Definition 2. A *partial interpretation* is a pair $I = \langle I^+, I^- \rangle$, where I^+ and I^- are any subsets of the Herbrand Base. □

A partial interpretation I is *consistent* if $I^+ \cap I^- = \emptyset$. For any partial interpretations I and J, we let $I \cap J$ be the partial interpretation $\langle I^+ \cap J^+, I^- \cap J^- \rangle$, and $I \cup J$ be the partial interpretation $\langle I^+ \cup J^+, I^- \cup J^- \rangle$. We also say $I \subseteq J$ whenever $I^+ \subseteq J^+$ and $I^- \subseteq J^-$. While the collection of all consistent partial interpretations is clearly closed under arbitrary intersections, it is not closed under arbitrary unions. Therefore the collection, under the $\subseteq$ relation, does not form a complete lattice, but can be seen to meet the conditions of the following weaker structure.

Definition 3. $\langle S, \subseteq \rangle$ is a *complete semilattice* if

(a) The set S is partially ordered by $\subseteq$,
(b) every nonempty subset of S has a greatest lower bound in S, and
(c) every nonempty directed subset of S has a least upper bound in S. (A subset A is *directed* if, for any $X, Y \in A$, there is some $Z \in A$ such that $X \subseteq Z$ and $Y \subseteq Z$.) □

Complete semilattices are weaker structures than complete lattices, and monotonic maps on them are guaranteed to possess only unique least fixpoints, but not greatest fixpoints (see [12]). For our purposes, however, this property is sufficient.

Definition 4. Let S be partially ordered by $\subseteq$. A map $T : S \rightarrow S$ is *monotonic* if, for any $X, Y \in S$, $X \subseteq Y$ implies $T(X) \subseteq T(Y)$. □

The weak well-founded model of P is the least fixpoint of the immediate consequence function T_P^F on consistent partial interpretations defined as follows:

Definition 5. Let I be a partial interpretation. Then $T_P^F(I)$ is a partial interpretation, given by

$$T_P^F(I)^+ = \{a \mid \text{for some clause } a \leftarrow l_1, \ldots, l_m \text{ in } P^\star, \text{ for each } i, 1 \leq i \leq m,$$
$$\text{if } l_i \text{ is positive then } l_i \in I^+, \text{ and}$$
$$\text{if } l_i \text{ is negative then } l_i' \in I^-\},$$

$$T_P^F(I)^- = \{a \mid \text{for every clause } a \leftarrow l_1, \ldots, l_m \text{ in } P^\star, \text{ there is some } i, 1 \leq i \leq m,$$
$$\text{such that if } l_i \text{ is positive then } l_i \in I^-, \text{ and}$$
$$\text{if } l_i \text{ is negative then } l_i' \in I^+\}. \qquad \square$$

It is easily seen that T_P^F is monotonic and its application on a consistent partial interpretation always results in a consistent partial interpretation. It thus possesses a least fixpoint, which is the weak well-founded model for P. This least fixpoint is easily shown to be $T_P^F \uparrow \omega$, where the ordinal powers of T_P^F are defined as follows:

Definition 6. For any ordinal α,

$$T_P^F \uparrow \alpha = \begin{cases} \langle \emptyset, \emptyset \rangle & \text{if } \alpha = 0, \\ T_P^F(T_P^F \uparrow (\alpha - 1)) & \text{if } \alpha \text{ is a successor ordinal,} \\ \langle \cup_{\beta < \alpha}(T_P^F \uparrow \beta)^+, \cup_{\beta < \alpha}(T_P^F \uparrow \beta)^- \rangle & \text{if } \alpha \text{ is a limit ordinal.} \end{cases} \qquad \square$$

Example 1. Let P be the following general deductive database:

```
r(a,c)
r(b,b)
s(a,a)
p(X) ← r(X,Y), ¬p(Y)
p(Y) ← s(Y,a)
```

Then, $T_P^F \uparrow 0 = \langle \emptyset, \emptyset \rangle$. $T_P^F \uparrow 1$ is the following partial interpretation:

$(T_P^F \uparrow 1)^+ = \{$ r(a,c), r(b,b), s(a,a) $\}$,
$(T_P^F \uparrow 1)^- = \{$ r(a,a), r(a,b), r(b,a), r(b,c),
           r(c,a), r(c,b), r(c,c),
           s(a,b), s(a,c), s(b,a), s(b,b), s(b,c),
           s(c,a), s(c,b), s(c,c) $\}$.

And $T_P^F \uparrow 2 = I \cup T_P^F \uparrow 1$, where I is the partial interpretation $\langle \{p(a)\}, \{p(c)\} \rangle$. Furthermore, for every ordinal $\alpha > 2$, $T_P^F \uparrow \alpha$ can be seen to be the same as $T_P^F \uparrow 2$. Note that in the weak well-founded model the atom p(a) is *true* and the atom p(c) is *false*. No truth value is assigned to the atom p(b). $\qquad \square$

In [2], the *upward closure ordinal* of the immediate consequence function is defined as the least ordinal α such that $T_P^F \uparrow \alpha$ is a fixpoint of T_P^F. The following observation for deductive databases is relevant:

Proposition 7. *For any general deductive database P, the upward closure ordinal of T_P^F is finite, i.e. there is a number $n \geq 0$, such that $T_P^F \uparrow n = T_P^F \uparrow \omega$.*

Thus a mechanism that "computes" the ordinal powers of T_P^F can be employed to construct the weak well-founded model of P. In Sections 4 and 5 we present such a mechanism.

3 Partial Relations

In this section we construct a set-theoretic formulation of partial relations and some algebraic operators over them. Unlike ordinary relations that can model worlds in which every tuple is known to either hold a certain underlying predicate or to not hold it, partial relations provide a framework for incomplete or even inconsistent information about tuples. They are thus extensions of ordinary relations. Moreover, the algebraic operators on partial relations, such as union, join, projection, are also extensions of their ordinary counterparts. We reflect this fact by placing a dot over an operator on ordinary relations to obtain the corresponding extended operator on partial relations. For example, $\bowtie$ denotes the natural join among ordinary relations, and $\dot\bowtie$ denotes natural join on partial relations.

Let a *relation scheme* Σ be a finite set of *attribute names*, where for any attribute $A \in \Sigma$, $dom(A)$ is a non-empty *domain* of values for A. A *tuple* on Σ is any map $t : \Sigma \to \cup_{A \in \Sigma} dom(A)$, such that $t(A) \in dom(A)$, for each $A \in \Sigma$. We let $\tau(\Sigma)$ denote the set of all tuples on Σ.

Definition 8. A *partial relation* on scheme Σ is a pair $R = \langle R^+, R^- \rangle$, where R^+ and R^- are any subsets of $\tau(\Sigma)$. □

Intuitively, R^+ may be considered as the set of all tuples for which R is believed to be true, and R^- the set of all tuples for which R is believed to be false. We do not assume R^+ and R^- to be mutually disjoint, though this condition holds in the model that is ultimately computed. Also, R^+ and R^- may not together cover all tuples in $\tau(\Sigma)$.

Definition 9. A partial relation R on scheme Σ is *consistent* if $R^+ \cap R^- = \emptyset$. Moreover, R is *complete* if $R^+ \cup R^- = \tau(\Sigma)$. □

It should be observed that (the positive parts of) partial relations that are both consistent and complete are essentially the ordinary relations. Thus partial relations are a true generalization of ordinary relations, in that for every ordinary relation there exists a partial relation with the same information content, but not *vice versa*.

We now extend the usual operators on ordinary relations over this wider class of partial relations. For every such operator θ on ordinary relations we introduce its extension $\dot\theta$ on partial relations. The extended operators respect the belief model intuition underlying the partial relations.

Set-Theoretic Operators

We first introduce two fundamental set-theoretic algebraic operators on partial relations:

Definition 10. Let R and S be partial relations on scheme Σ. Then,

(a) the *union* of R and S, denoted $R \mathbin{\dot\cup} S$, is a partial relation on scheme Σ, given by

$$(R \mathbin{\dot\cup} S)^+ = R^+ \cup S^+, \qquad (R \mathbin{\dot\cup} S)^- = R^- \cap S^-;$$

(b) the *complement* of R, denoted $\mathbin{\dot-} R$, is a partial relation on scheme Σ, given by

$$(\mathbin{\dot-} R)^+ = R^-, \qquad (\mathbin{\dot-} R)^- = R^+. \qquad \square$$

A better understanding of the union operator may be obtained by recognizing that since R^+ and S^+ are the sets of tuples for which R and S, respectively, are believed to be true, the set of tuples for which "either R or S" is believed to be true is thus clearly $R^+ \cup S^+$. Moreover, since R^- and S^- are the sets of tuples for which R and S, respectively, are believed to be false, the set of tuples for which "either R or S" is believed to be false is similarly $R^- \cap S^-$. The definitions of all the other operators on partial relations defined later can (and should) be understood in the same way. For the sake of completeness, we define the following two related set-theoretic operators on partial relations:

Definition 11. Let R and S be partial relations on scheme Σ. Then,

(a) the *intersection* of R and S, denoted $R \mathbin{\dot\cap} S$, is a partial relation on scheme Σ, given by

$$(R \mathbin{\dot\cap} S)^+ = R^+ \cap S^+, \qquad (R \mathbin{\dot\cap} S)^- = R^- \cup S^-;$$

(b) the *difference* of R and S, denoted $R \mathbin{\dot-} S$, is a partial relation on scheme Σ, given by

$$(R \mathbin{\dot-} S)^+ = R^+ \cap S^-, \qquad (R \mathbin{\dot-} S)^- = R^- \cup S^+. \qquad \square$$

Though the above are independent definitions of intersection and difference, these two operators can be derived from the fundamental operators union and complement as expected.

Proposition 12. *For any partial relations R and S on a common scheme, we have*

$$R \mathbin{\dot\cap} S = \mathbin{\dot-}(\mathbin{\dot-} R \mathbin{\dot\cup} \mathbin{\dot-} S), \text{ and}$$
$$R \mathbin{\dot-} S = \mathbin{\dot-}(\mathbin{\dot-} R \mathbin{\dot\cup} S).$$

Relation-Theoretic Operators

If Σ and Δ are relation schemes such that $\Sigma \subseteq \Delta$, then for any tuple $t \in \tau(\Sigma)$, we let t^{Δ} denote the set $\{t' \in \tau(\Delta) \mid t'(A) = t(A), \text{ for all } A \in \Sigma\}$ of all extensions of t. We extend this notion for any $T \subseteq \tau(\Sigma)$ by defining $T^{\Delta} = \cup_{t \in T} t^{\Delta}$. We now define some relation-theoretic algebraic operators on partial relations.

Definition 13. Let R and S be partial relations on schemes Σ and Δ, respectively. Then, the *natural join* (or just *join*) of R and S, denoted $R \bowtie S$, is a partial relation on scheme $\Sigma \cup \Delta$, given by

$$(R \bowtie S)^+ = R^+ \bowtie S^+, \qquad (R \bowtie S)^- = (R^-)^{\Sigma \cup \Delta} \cup (S^-)^{\Sigma \cup \Delta},$$

where $\bowtie$ is the usual natural join among ordinary relations. □

It is instructive to observe that $(R \bowtie S)^-$ contains all extensions of tuples in R^- and S^-, because least one of R and S is believed false for these extended tuples.

Definition 14. Let R be a partial relation on scheme Σ, and Δ be any scheme. Then, the *projection* of R onto Δ, denoted $\dot{\pi}_{\Delta}(R)$, is a partial relation on Δ, given by

$$\dot{\pi}_{\Delta}(R)^+ = \pi_{\Delta}((R^+)^{\Sigma \cup \Delta}), \qquad \dot{\pi}_{\Delta}(R)^- = \{t \in \tau(\Delta) \mid t^{\Sigma \cup \Delta} \subseteq (R^-)^{\Sigma \cup \Delta}\},$$

where π_{Δ} is the usual projection over Δ of ordinary relations. □

It should be noted that, contrary to usual practice, the above definition of projection is not just for subschemes. However, if $\Delta \subseteq \Sigma$, then it coincides with the intuitive projection operation. In this case, $\dot{\pi}_{\Delta}(R)^-$ consists of those tuples in $\tau(\Delta)$, all of whose extensions are in R^-. We now define our last relation-theoretic operation.

Definition 15. Let R be a partial relation on scheme Σ, and let F be any logic formula involving attribute names in Σ, constant symbols (denoting values in the attribute domains), equality symbol $=$, negation symbol $\neg$, and connectives $\vee$ and $\wedge$. Then the *selection* of R by F, denoted $\dot{\sigma}_F(R)$, is a partial relation on scheme Σ, given by

$$\dot{\sigma}_F(R)^+ = \sigma_F(R^+), \qquad \dot{\sigma}_F(R)^- = R^- \cup \sigma_{\neg F}(\tau(\Sigma)),$$

where σ_F is the usual selection of tuples satisfying F from ordinary relations. □

Example 2. Strictly speaking, relation schemes are sets of attribute names, but in this example we treat them as ordered sequences of attribute names, so tuples can be viewed as the usual lists of values. Let $\{a, b, c\}$ be a common domain for all attribute names, and let R and S be the following partial relations on schemes $\langle X, Y \rangle$ and $\langle Y, Z \rangle$, respectively:

$$R^+ = \{(b,b),(b,c)\}, \quad R^- = \{(a,a),(a,b),(a,c)\},$$
$$S^+ = \{(a,c),(c,a)\}, \quad S^- = \{(c,b)\}.$$

Then, $R \bowtie S$ is the following partial relation on scheme $\langle X, Y, Z \rangle$:

$$(R \bowtie S)^+ = \{(b, c, a)\},$$
$$(R \bowtie S)^- = \{(a, a, a), (a, a, b), (a, a, c), (a, b, a), (a, b, b), (a, b, c),$$
$$(a, c, a), (a, c, b), (a, c, c), (b, c, b), (c, c, b)\}.$$

Observe how $(R \bowtie S)^-$ blows up to contain extensions of all tuples in R^- and S^-. Now, $\dot{\pi}_{\langle X,Z\rangle}(R \bowtie S)$ becomes the following partial relation on scheme $\langle X, Z \rangle$:

$$\dot{\pi}_{\langle X,Z\rangle}(R \bowtie S)^+ = \{(b, a)\}, \qquad \dot{\pi}_{\langle X,Z\rangle}(R \bowtie S)^- = \{(a, a), (a, b), (a, c)\}.$$

The tuples in the negative component of the projected partial relation are such that all their extensions were present in the negative component of the original partial relation. Finally, $\dot{\sigma}_{\neg X=Z}(\dot{\pi}_{\langle X,Z\rangle}(R \bowtie S))$ becomes the following partial relation on the same scheme:

$$\dot{\sigma}_{\neg X=Z}(\dot{\pi}_{\langle X,Z\rangle}(R \bowtie S))^+ = \{(b, a)\},$$
$$\dot{\sigma}_{\neg X=Z}(\dot{\pi}_{\langle X,Z\rangle}(R \bowtie S))^- = \{(a, a), (a, b), (a, c), (b, b), (c, c)\}.$$

All tuples that do not satisfy the selection condition always make it to the negative component of the selected partial relation. □

We end our brief introduction to partial relations by defining the following "type-conversion" operation.

Definition 16. Let $\Sigma = \{A_1, \ldots, A_n\}$ and $\Delta = \{B_1, \ldots, B_n\}$ be any schemes, such that $dom(A_i) = dom(B_i)$, for all i, $1 \leq i \leq n$. Then, for any tuple $t \in \tau(\Sigma)$, $\delta_{A_1,\ldots,A_n \to B_1,\ldots,B_n}(t)$ is the tuple $t' \in \tau(\Delta)$, such that $t(A_i) = t'(B_i)$, for all i, $1 \leq i \leq n$. We extend this notion for any $T \subseteq \tau(\Sigma)$ by defining

$$\delta_{A_1,\ldots,A_n \to B_1,\ldots,B_n}(T) = \{\delta_{A_1,\ldots,A_n \to B_1,\ldots,B_n}(t) \mid t \in T\}.$$

Furthermore, for any partial relation R on scheme Σ, we let

$$\delta_{A_1,\ldots,A_n \to B_1,\ldots,B_n}(R) = \langle \delta_{A_1,\ldots,A_n \to B_1,\ldots,B_n}(R^+), \delta_{A_1,\ldots,A_n \to B_1,\ldots,B_n}(R^-) \rangle. \quad \square$$

4 From Database Rules to Relational Expressions

We now describe our method for computing the weak well-founded model for a given general deductive database P. In this model, partial relations are the semantic objects associated with the predicate symbols occurring in P.

Our method involves two steps. The first step is to convert P into a set of partial relation definitions for the predicate symbols of P. These definitions are of the form

$$\mathrm{p} = D_\mathrm{p},$$

where p is a predicate symbol of P, and D_p is an algebraic expression involving predicate symbols of P and partial relation operators. The second step is to iteratively evaluate the expressions in these definitions to incrementally construct the partial relations associated with the predicate symbols.

The schemes of these partial relations are set internally. Let $\Gamma = \langle \nu_1, \nu_2, \ldots \rangle$ be an infinite sequence of some distinct attribute names. For any $n \geq 1$, let Γ_n be the scheme $\{\nu_1, \ldots, \nu_n\}$. We use the following two scheme renaming operators.

Definition 17. Let $\Sigma = \{A_1, \ldots, A_n\}$ be any scheme. Then,

(a) for any partial relation R on scheme Γ_n, $R(A_1, \ldots, A_n)$ is the partial relation

$$\delta_{\nu_1, \ldots, \nu_n \to A_1, \ldots, A_n}(R)$$

on scheme Σ, and

(b) for any partial relation R on scheme Σ, $R[A_1, \ldots, A_n]$ is the partial relation

$$\delta_{A_1, \ldots, A_n \to \nu_1, \ldots, \nu_n}(R)$$

on scheme Γ_n. □

In the remaining part of this section we describe our method to convert the given database P into a set of definitions for the predicate symbols in P. Before presenting the actual algorithm, let us look at an example. In the intensional portion of the database of Example 1, the following are the only clauses with the predicate symbol p in their heads:

$$p(X) \leftarrow r(X, Y), \neg p(Y)$$
$$p(Y) \leftarrow s(Y, a)$$

From these clauses the algebraic definition constructed for the symbol p is the following:

$$p = (\dot{\pi}_{\{X\}}(r(X, Y) \bowtie \dot{\neg} p(Y)))[X] \; \dot{\cup} \; (\dot{\pi}_{\{Y\}}(\dot{\sigma}_{Z=a}(s(Y, Z))))[Y] \tag{1}$$

Such a conversion exploits the close connection between attribute names in relation schemes and variables in clauses, as pointed out by Ullman in [17]. The expression thus constructed can be used to arrive at a better approximation of the partial relation p from some approximations of p, r and s.

The algebraic expression for the predicate symbol p is a union ($\dot{\cup}$) of the expressions obtained from each clause containing the symbol p in its head. It therefore suffices to give an algorithm for converting a clause into an expression.

Algorithm CONVERT.
INPUT: A general deductive database clause $l_0 \leftarrow l_1, \ldots, l_m$. Let l_0 be of the form $p_0(A_{01}, \ldots, A_{0k_0})$, and each l_i, $1 \leq i \leq m$, be either of the form $p_i(A_{i1}, \ldots, A_{ik_i})$, or of the form $\neg p_i(A_{i1}, \ldots, A_{ik_i})$. For any i, $0 \leq i \leq m$, let V_i be the set of all variables occurring in l_i.
OUTPUT: An algebraic expression involving partial relations.
METHOD: The expression is constructed by the following steps:

1. For each argument A_{ij} of literal l_i, construct argument B_{ij} and condition C_{ij} as follows:
   (a) If A_{ij} is a constant a, then B_{ij} is any brand new variable and C_{ij} is $B_{ij} = a$.
   (b) If A_{ij} is a variable, such that for each k, $1 \leq k < j$, $A_{ik} \neq A_{ij}$, then B_{ij} is A_{ij} and C_{ij} is *true*.
   (c) If A_{ij} is a variable, such that for some k, $1 \leq k < j$, $A_{ik} = A_{ij}$, then B_{ij} is a brand new variable and C_{ij} is $A_{ij} = B_{ij}$.

2. Let $\hat{l}_i$ be the atom $p_i(B_{i1},\ldots,B_{ik_i})$, and F_i be the conjunction $C_{i1} \wedge \cdots \wedge C_{ik_i}$. If l_i is a positive literal, then let Q_i be the expression $\dot{\pi}_{V_i}(\dot{\sigma}_{F_i}(\hat{l}_i))$. Otherwise, let Q_i be the expression $\dot{-}\dot{\pi}_{V_i}(\dot{\sigma}_{F_i}(\hat{l}_i))$.
   As a syntactic optimization, if all conjuncts of F_i are *true* (i.e. all arguments of l_i are distinct variables), then both $\dot{\sigma}_{F_i}$ and $\dot{\pi}_{V_i}$ are reduced to identity operations, and are hence dropped from the expression. For example, if $l_i = \neg p(X,Y)$, then $Q_i = \dot{-}p(X,Y)$.
3. Let E be the natural join ($\bowtie$) of the Q_i's thus obtained, $1 \leq i \leq m$. The output expression is $(\dot{\sigma}_{F_0}(\dot{\pi}_V(E)))[B_{01},\ldots,B_{0k_0}]$, where V is the set of variables occurring in $\hat{l}_0$.
   As in step 2, if all conjuncts in F_0 are *true*, then $\dot{\sigma}_{F_0}$ is dropped from the output expression. However, $\dot{\pi}_V$ is never dropped, as the clause body may contain variables not in V. □

From the algebraic expressions obtained by Algorithm **CONVERT** for clauses in the given general deductive database, we construct a system of equations defining partial relations as follows.

Definition 18. For any general deductive database P, $EQN(P)$ is a set of all equations of the form $\mathtt{p} = D_\mathtt{p}$, where p is a predicate symbol of P, and $D_\mathtt{p}$ is the union ($\dot{\cup}$) of all expressions obtained by Algorithm **CONVERT** for clauses in P with symbol p in their head. The algebraic expression $D_\mathtt{p}$ is also called a *definition* of p. □

It is evident that a predicate symbol may have many definitions. We now establish that the above method for converting a general deductive database P into definitions for its predicate symbols terminates, and that the definitions produced mimic the T_P^F map defined by Fitting.

Proposition 19. (Termination) *The above procedure for constructing the set $EQN(P)$ terminates for any general deductive database P.*

In order to establish correctness with respect to the Fitting approach we need to define the following transformations between Fitting's partial interpretations and our partial relations.

Definition 20. Let I be any partial interpretation and $\mathtt{r}(X_1,\ldots,X_n)$ be any atom, where the X_i's are distinct variables. Then, $I \triangleright \mathtt{r}$ is the following partial relation

$$\langle \{t \in \tau(\Sigma) \mid \mathtt{r}(t(X_1),\ldots,t(X_n)) \in I^+\},$$
$$\{t \in \tau(\Sigma) \mid \mathtt{r}(t(X_1),\ldots,t(X_n)) \in I^-\} \rangle$$

on scheme $\Sigma = \{X_1,\ldots,X_n\}$. Moreover, for any partial relation R on scheme Σ, $\mathtt{r}\lfloor R \rfloor$ is the following partial interpretation

$$\langle \{\mathtt{r}(t(X_1),\ldots,t(X_n)) \mid t \in R^+\}, \{\mathtt{r}(t(X_1),\ldots,t(X_n)) \mid t \in R^-\} \rangle. \quad \square$$

Proposition 21. (Correctness) *Let $a_1, \ldots, a_n$ be the atoms occurring in the definition of some equation $p = D_p$ in EQN(P), for any general deductive database P. Let k_0 be the arity of p and each a_i be of the form $p_i(B_{i1}, \ldots, B_{ik_i})$. For all i, $1 \leq i \leq n$, let R_i be any partial relation on scheme Γ_{k_i}, such that if for any i, j, $p_i = p_j$, then $R_i = R_j$. Then, the partial relation R on scheme Γ_{k_0} obtained by evaluating D_p by interpreting each p_i as the partial relation R_i is*

$$T_P^F\left(\left\langle \bigcup_{i=1}^n p_i \lfloor R_i \rfloor^+, \bigcup_{i=1}^n p_i \lfloor R_i \rfloor^- \right\rangle\right) \triangleright p.$$

As with all other results in this paper, the proof of the above proposition can be found in [3]. It essentially establishes equivalence between the T_P^F function and single step evaluation of the algebraic equations produced by the algorithm **CONVERT**.

5 Computation of the Weak Well-Founded Model

The second and final step in our model computation process is to incrementally construct the partial relations defined by the given database. For any general deductive database P, we let P_E and P_I denote its extensional and intensional portions, respectively. P_E is essentially the set of clauses of P with empty bodies, and P_I is the set of all other clauses of P. Without loss of generality, we assume that no predicate symbol occurs both in P_E as well as in P_I. Let us recall that $P_E^\star$ is the set of all ground instances of clauses in P_E.

The overall computation algorithm is rather straightforward. It treats the predicate symbols in a given database as imperative "variable names" that may contain a partial relation as value. Thus, any variable p has two set-valued fields, namely p^+ and p^-.

Algorithm COMPUTE
INPUT: A general deductive database P.
OUTPUT: Partial relation values for the predicate symbols of P.
METHOD: The values are computed by the following steps:

1. *(Initialization)*
   (a) Compute $EQN(P_I)$ using Algorithm **CONVERT** for each clause in P_I.
   (b) For each predicate symbol p in P_E, set

   $$p^+ = \{\langle a_1, \ldots, a_k \rangle \mid p(a_1, \ldots, a_k) \leftarrow\, \in P_E^\star\}, \text{ and}$$
   $$p^- = \{\langle b_1, \ldots, b_k \rangle \mid k \text{ is the arity of p, and } p(b_1, \ldots, b_k) \leftarrow\, \notin P_E^\star\}.$$

   (c) For each predicate symbol p in P_I, set $p^+ = \emptyset$, and $p^- = \emptyset$.
2. For each equation of the form $p = D_p$ in $EQN(P_I)$, compute the expression D_p and set p to the resulting partial relation.
3. If step 2 involved a change in the value of some p, goto 2.
4. Output the final values of all predicate symbols in P_E and P_I. □

Proposition 22. (Termination) *Algorithm **COMPUTE** terminates for all general deductive databases.*

We now present our main result that the above algorithm computes the weak well-founded model for the given database.

Theorem 23. (Correctness) *A tuple $\langle a_1,\ldots,a_k \rangle$ is in p^+ computed by Algorithm* **COMPUTE** *iff $p(a_1,\ldots,a_k) \in (T_P^F \uparrow \omega)^+$. Also, $\langle a_1,\ldots,a_k \rangle \in p^-$ iff $p(a_1,\ldots,a_k) \in (T_P^F \uparrow \omega)^-$.*

It is instructive to execute Algorithm **COMPUTE** on the database of Example 1, which we reproduce here.

```
r(a,c)
r(b,b)
s(a,a)
p(X) ← r(X,Y), ¬p(Y)
p(Y) ← s(Y,a)
```

After step 1, the predicate variables have the following values:

$$r^+ = \{\langle a,c \rangle, \langle b,b \rangle\},$$
$$r^- = \{\langle a,a \rangle, \langle a,b \rangle, \langle b,a \rangle, \langle b,c \rangle, \langle c,a \rangle, \langle c,b \rangle, \langle c,c \rangle\},$$
$$s^+ = \{\langle a,a \rangle\},$$
$$s^- = \{\langle a,b \rangle, \langle a,c \rangle, \langle b,a \rangle, \langle b,b \rangle, \langle b,c \rangle, \langle c,a \rangle, \langle c,b \rangle, \langle c,c \rangle\},$$
$$p^+ = \emptyset,$$
$$p^- = \emptyset.$$

Step 1 can be seen to mimic the production of $T_P^F \uparrow 1$. Each iteration of step 2 uses only equation (1), reproduced below.

$$p = (\dot{\pi}_{\{X\}}(r(X,Y) \bowtie \dot{\neg} p(Y)))[X] \; \dot{\cup} \; (\dot{\pi}_{\{Y\}}(\dot{\sigma}_{Z=a}(s(Y,Z))))[Y] \qquad (1)$$

By applying the definitions of the various operators introduced earlier,

$$(\dot{\pi}_{\{X\}}(r(X,Y) \bowtie \dot{\neg} p(Y)))[X]$$

can be seen to be the partial relation $\langle \emptyset, \{\langle c \rangle\} \rangle$, and

$$(\dot{\pi}_{\{Y\}}(\dot{\sigma}_{Z=a}(s(Y,Z))))[Y]$$

the partial relation $\langle \{\langle a \rangle\}, \{\langle b \rangle, \langle c \rangle\} \rangle$. So their union is the partial relation $\langle \{\langle a \rangle\}, \{\langle c \rangle\} \rangle$ assigned by step 2 to the variable p. Further iterations of step 2 do not change the value of p. Step 2 can be seen to mimic an application of the T_P^F function.

6 Conclusions and Future Work

We have presented an algorithm to compute the weak well-founded model for a general deductive database. The algorithm is based on an extension of the relational model of data, called *partial relations*, in which negative facts are explicitly represented. Partial relations were defined to consist of two components, a set of positive tuples and a set of negative tuples. A suitable set of relational operators were defined on partial relations. The extension to the relational model for explicit negation was motivated by the generalized relational model for disjunctive databases of [11], for which a bottom-up computation method is described in [16]. The intensional portion of the deductive database was used in the construction of equations for the derived partial relations which involved the extended relational operators. An iterative procedure to solve these equations was presented. Finally, the correctness of our algorithm was established.

Recently there has been some research in providing efficient algorithms to compute the semantics of general deductive databases. Leone and Rullo [10] present a bottom-up method to compute the well-founded semantics of Datalog queries. The answers to queries are evaluated without having to compute the entire greatest unfounded set. The computation of false facts is limited to only those that contribute to derive new positive facts. However, their method works only for a given query. Kemp, Stuckey and Srivastava [9], on the other hand, provide a method for computing the entire well-founded model for *allowed* Datalog programs (these are programs in which all variables appearing in a clause also appear in a positive body literal). Their method is based on van Gelder's alternating fixpoint semantics presented in [18]. Chen and Warren [6] present a goal-oriented method for computing the well-founded semantics of general logic programs. It has the practical advantages of top-down evaluation and integration with Prolog. Another top-down procedure for constructing the well-founded semantics is presented by Bidoit and Legay in [5]. Ross [14] adapts the magic-sets rewriting technique for a subclass of logic programs called *modularly stratified programs*.

Our approach differs from all of these in its algebraic nature. It is applicable to arbitrary general deductive databases (including non-range restricted ones), and is essentially bottom-up in nature. The method requires explicit carrying around of *definitely true* and *definitely false* facts (the latter are usually large in number). However, if our method is restricted to some of the subclasses of programs considered by others, such as allowed, stratified etc., a simple modification can eliminate the need for maintaining the *definitely false* facts.

As has been noted in [19], the Fitting semantics is based on the first of two conditions used in the definition of unfounded sets in the development of the well-founded semantics for general deductive databases. The second condition, which states that at least one positive literal of the body of the ground rule belongs to the unfounded set being defined, allows us to infer additional negative facts at each iteration of the bottom-up computation. This second condition has also been addressed by Ross and Topor [15] in which "closed sets" were defined using this condition. There are two possible ways by which the algorithm presented in this paper can be extended to capture the second condition and in effect compute the well-founded semantics of general deductive databases. The first possibility is to introduce an inner-level iteration in our algorithm **COMPUTE** which will construct the greatest unfounded set of the database for the interpretation of the outer iteration. The other possibility is to wait until our algorithm COMPUTE terminates and then compute the greatest unfounded set with respect to the final interpretation. We are currently investigating both these possibilities.

7 Acknowledgements

The authors would like to thank Mary Flagg for her useful comments.

References

1. K. R. Apt, H. A. Blair, and A. Walker. Towards a theory of declarative knowledge. In Jack Minker, editor, *Foundations of Deductive Databases and Logic Programming*, pages 89–148. Morgan Kaufmann, Los Altos, 1988.
2. R. Bagai, M. Bezem, and M. H. van Emden. On downward closure ordinals of logic programs. *Fundamenta Informaticae*, XIII(1):67–83, March 1990.
3. R. Bagai and R. Sunderraman. Algebraic computation of the Fitting model for general deductive databases. Technical Report WSUCS-93-2, Department of Computer Science, Wichita State University, April 1993.
4. N. Bidoit. Negation in rule-based database languages: a survey. *Theoretical Computer Science*, 78:3–83, 1991.
5. N. Bidoit and P. Legay. Well!: An evaluation procedure for all logic programs. In *Proceedings of International Conference on Database Theory*, pages 335–345. Lecture Notes in Computer Science, 470, Springer-Verlag, 1990.
6. W. Chen and D. S. Warren. A goal-oriented approach to computing well founded semantics. In *Proceedings of the Joint International Conference and Symposium on Logic Programming, Washington, D.C.* MIT Press, 1992.
7. M. Fitting. A Kripke-Kleene semantics for logic programs. *Journal of Logic Programming*, 4:295–312, 1985.
8. M. Gelfond and V. Lifschitz. The stable model semantics for logic programming. In *Proceedings of the 5th International Conference and Symposium on Logic Programming*, pages 1070–1080, Seattle, WA, August 1988.
9. D. B. Kemp, P. J. Stuckey, and D. Srivastava. Magic sets and bottom-up evaluation of well-founded models. In *Proceedings of the 1991 International Symposium on Logic Programming*, pages 337–354, San Diego, USA, 1991. The MIT Press.
10. N. Leone and P. Rullo. The safe computation of the well-founded semantics of datalog queries. *Information Systems*, 17(1):17–31, 1992.
11. K.-C. Liu and R. Sunderraman. A generalized relational model for indefinite and maybe information. *IEEE Transactions on Knowledge and Data Engineering*, 3(1):65–77, 1991.
12. Z. Manna and A. Shamir. The theoretical aspect of the optimal fixed point. *SIAM Journal of Computing*, 5:414–426, 1976.
13. T. C. Przymusinski. On the declarative semantics of deductive databases and logic programs. In Jack Minker, editor, *Foundations of Deductive Databases and Logic Programming*, pages 193–216. Morgan Kaufmann, Los Altos, 1988.
14. K. A. Ross. Modular stratification and magic sets for datalog programs with negation. In *Proceedings of the Ninth Annual ACM Symposium on Principles of database systems*. ACM, 1990.

15. K. A. Ross and R. W. Topor. Inferring negative information from disjunctive databases. *Journal of Automated Reasoning*, 4:397–424, 1988.
16. R. Sunderraman. Deductive databases with conditional facts. In M. Worboys and A. F. Grundy, editors, *Advances in Databases*, pages 162–175. Lecture Notes in Computer Science, 696, Springer-Verlag, 1993. (Proceedings of the 11th British National Conference on Databases).
17. J. D. Ullman. *Principles of Database and Knowledge-Base Systems*, volume 1. Computer Science Press, 1988.
18. A. van Gelder. The alternating fixpoint of logic programs with negation. In *Proceedings of the 8th ACM Symposium on Principles of Database Systems*, pages 1–10, Philadelphia, USA, 1989. ACM Press.
19. A. van Gelder, K. A. Ross, and J. S. Schlipf. The well-founded semantics for general logic programs. *Journal of the ACM*, 38(3):621–650, 1991.

Benchmarking Parallel SQL Database Machines

Innes Jelly*, Jon Kerridge+, Chris Bates†

* Computing Research Centre, Sheffield Hallam University, Sheffield, UK
+ Department of Computer Science, Sheffield University, Sheffield, UK
† National Transputer Support Centre, Sheffield, UK
I.E.Jelly@shu.ac.uk, J.Kerridge@dcs.shef.ac.uk

Abstract. New parallel database systems are being developed to support the data processing needs of large commercial organisations: these offer increased performance in terms of processing throughput and enhanced support for both on-line transaction processing and management information provision. In order to evaluate the performance of these systems a new SQL benchmark has been developed which models the requirements for real database applications. Based on a large commercial database the benchmark system includes the specification of the test or "mimic" database and sets of transactions and queries, and the data/transaction generation tools. The benchmark uses synthetic data which closely resembles real world data and provides for evaluation of the scalability of system under test.

1 Introduction

The ability to store and manipulate large volumes of information is a crucial requirement for the operation of most large commercial organisations. These rely upon their database systems to provide the effective implementation of tasks such as order processing, invoicing and ledger maintenance. Most current databases systems are able to support this role without providing sufficiently detailed management information which could be extracted from the data if there was sufficient spare processing capacity. Projects such as IDIOMS [1,2] have demonstrated the feasibility of building a parallel relational database machine which can support both the transaction processing capability and the management information needs of an organisation at the same time on the same data. Increasingly parallel hardware will be needed to meet the demands for this enhanced functionality and to provide better performance for large data volumes. We have already seen the emergence of parallel implementations of Oracle on a number of different parallel platforms such as N-cube, Meiko and Parsys, and new parallel systems such as the recently announced database machine Goldrush from

ICL. In order to evaluate the performance of this new generation of database machines, appropriate benchmarks are required. These must reflect the different modes of operation of the systems and indicate how well they scale to a range of database sizes.

We report on the development of a new benchmark suite targeted towards SQL [4] parallel databases. The work arises from the ESPRIT PEPS (Performance Evaluation of Parallel Systems) project [3, 13] and has resulted in the design of a benchmark which realistically models a commercial database, both in terms of data structures and volume. The new benchmark system includes the definition of the test or "mimic" database, on-line transaction processing operations and management information system query specifications, and the software tools required for generating the large volumes of data, transactions and queries needed to carry out the benchmarking.

The paper contains an evaluation of current database benchmarks, and discusses their limitations. Requirements for a more effective benchmark are described and details given of the structure of the new test system and the support tools developed for it. The benchmarking process is presented and the methods of timing and reporting the results outlined. It is worth noting that because the mimic database, transactions and queries are all specified in SQL, the benchmark provides an architecture-independent performance evaluation system, and thus is equally applicable to relational database systems running on conventional hardware as well as parallel platforms.

1.1 Database Usage and Operation

Commercial databases are increasingly required to support two different modes of operation: first, on-line transaction processing (OLTP), in which a typically small request for work is received in an on-line environment. The result of that request is usually reported back immediately it has been completed. Such requests tend to access either a single or at most a very few records and carry out a very simple operation. In a banking environment, for example, a transaction could comprise a debit or credit or request for a balance. For many organisations the ability to respond to such transactions is paramount because this is the normal interface with their customers. Hence a great deal of effort has been expended ensuring that the transaction processing system has a performance commensurate with the needs of the organisation.

The second mode of operation is commonly referred to as management information (MIS) or decision support. This mode of access generally involves accessing a large number of records to find out some piece of information from all the data that is stored in the database. The information that is generated is often statistical in nature. In more modern systems we are moving to a situation where data satisfying some set of predicates is extracted from the database to be processed using genetic algorithms or neural networks, to determine patterns within the data rather than mere statistics. Such queries access many rows and are thus very long running. They impose a totally different overhead on the database machine to that presented by transaction processing.

The relational database model supports both types of operation and allows the users to interact with the system at a high level using a standard (SQL) interface. However good overall performance is difficult to obtain with relational systems and, because of this, most conventional systems have to be optimised towards either efficient OLTP or MIS functionality.

1.2 The Impact of Parallel Database Machines

The use of parallel hardware as the underlying platform for large relational database systems produces not only increased performance in terms of system response and throughput, but provides the potential for concurrent OLTP and MIS operations [16]. The advantage that a parallel implementation can bring is that it is possible to place processing resource much closer to data storage so that only the required data is manipulated. In terms of enhanced performance, gains can be made in the expensive process of index maintenance: by partitioning data over a number of discs, each with their own processor then the index maintenance function can also be distributed as well as data accessing.

Such a partitioning of the data also gives a hint as to how transaction processing can be improved by distributing the data over a number of discs. Each disc has its own associated transaction processor which carries out transactions for those parts of tables held on that disc. Thus the transaction processing load is distributed over as many processors as there are discs used to hold the data. A simple partitioning strategy would partition the data by account number. Teradata [5] adopt a different approach in which accounts are distributed using a round-robin allocation and an index is constructed giving the location of each account row and which disc it is stored on. From this brief description it can be seen that there are many different ways in which a parallel database machine can be organised and thus any benchmark has to be sufficiently flexible to accommodate these variations.

1.3 Benchmark Requirements

The aim of benchmarking is to produce performance data that can be used to make meaningful comparisons between the systems under test. This means that a valid database benchmark must model the functionality of a real commercial system, and in particular it must support both OLTP and MIS operations. More importantly, as the need for high quality management information is given a higher profile, it will become necessary to have both styles of interaction available at the same time. The benchmark mimics a real application environment and therefore can be used as an aid to the design of an actual database implementation. Further more, the benchmark must also be able to measure the scalability of a database system.

Scalability manifests itself in a number of different ways. First, the system has to be scaled to meet the initial operating needs of the organisation. This is commonly referred to as sizing the application. Subsequently the organisation will wish to increase the performance of the database system on an as-required basis. It should be possible to measure the performance of the database system to determine this scalability. For example, if we have a given data set size and the amount of hardware is doubled will the database performance be twice that it was before? The answer is unlikely to be *yes* but it is important to be able to quantify the improvement factor.

2 Current Database Benchmarks

There have been a number of recognised database benchmarks developed over the last ten years to test different aspects of performance. Normally either OLTP or MIS operations on their own are involved, reflecting the situation that for most conventional databases the system is only geared to one type of functionality. A full account of database benchmarks can be found in [6] and [7].

Of the currently available benchmarks, the tests developed by the Transaction Processing Council are widely quoted in vendors' literature. Driven by the need to get some standardisation into the performance evaluation of database systems, the Transaction Processing Council was established in 1988. Today it represents a body of over 40 major international system and database vendors. Its formation led to the definition of the benchmarks, TPC-A, TPC-B, which are now the only generally recognised benchmark for database systems [8]. These measure OLTP operations in a similar fashion to the DebitCredit [8] set, results being given as the single measurements, transactions per second and transactions per US $. However criticism of the TPC suite of tests has focused on their lack of realistic functionality, and recent studies on typical transaction profiles from a number of large public and commercial database systems has confirmed this deficiency [9].

Two benchmarks specifically address the performance of MIS operations. Of these, the Wisconsin tests are designed to test the major components of the system rather than model a real world application [10]. The relations are "easy to understand" so that extra queries can be added. It uses synthetic data as this can be easily scaled and allows queries with known selectivity factors. It is worth noting that the Wisconsin tests have been used to measure the speedup and scalability of parallel database implementations. The Set Query suite has been developed specifically to test MIS functionality [11]. The query set is based upon the experience and advice of a number of commercial users and so tries to simulate the way in which databases are actually used. Unfortunately the data sets used for this test are unrealistically small.

The only current database benchmark that incorporates any notion of mixed OLTP and MIS functionality is the AS^3AP set of tests [12]. Use of this benchmark produces a single figure metric known as the equivalent database ratio. This is defined as the maximum size of database that the system can run all of the AS^3AP tests on in under 12 hours. However the AS^3AP benchmark suffers from some serious limitations which undermine its standing as a useful performance evaluation vehicle for modern commercial systems. These limitations can be summarised as: unrealistically small row lengths in the table definitions, atypical mix of queries and transactions with no attempt to model realistic database functionality, and finally the use of integer data in the key and other frequently accessed fields. This use of integer data represents a failure to understand the typical characteristics of real databases where information such as "account-number" is always specified in the form of character strings. It can lead to considerable error in the timing of database functions as the duration of fundamental CPU operations on integer and character data differs widely.

These examples demonstrate some of the problems with the existing benchmarks and serve to highlight the detailed consideration that must be given to the production of a realistic model on which to base the performance testing. From this brief outline it can be seen that current benchmarks for database systems are in the main over-simplistic in their model of real world applications and too specific in the functionality they test.

3 Requirements for an Application Mimic

One of the key features of a well respected benchmark is that it mimics current practice in an application environment. As shown in the previous section there are a number of limitations in database benchmarks. This section identifies the important features that must be incorporated if a realistic database benchmark is to be achieved. In order to provide a good model as a basis for testing, the benchmark must mimic a typical "real" database in the following features:
- database structure
- data volumes
- mix and volume of OLTP operations
- mix of MIS queries
- maintenance of audit information

In addition the design must take account of aspects such as the manner of data representation. It has already been seen in Section 2 that most current benchmark systems do not manipulate symbolic data and it is necessary to rectify this.

3.1 Realistic Database Structure

The IDIOMS project built a database machine that mimicked the operation of the TSB Bank plc Common Banking System. This is the system which maintains the cheque account balances for their customers. The project built both a transaction processing interface and a management information system. The database design developed for that project is representative of a large class of commercial systems, ranging from banking, insurance, mail order and public/private monopoly utilities. As these systems comprise some of the largest databases currently in operation, the decision to base the mimic benchmark system on a banking model appears to be sensible. The benchmark has been designed to include information on customers, their accounts and standing orders.

3.2 Realistic Data Volumes

A major problem in any benchmark that is based upon a mimic of a real system is that it is difficult to generate synthetically realistic data volumes. For a realistic benchmark the typical data scaling requirements run from 100,000 to 10 million row per table. In order to support the production of this amount of synthetic data a software tool has been developed to generate these for the benchmarking system. However it is not sufficient merely to generate data in volume: it must also model real data if the benchmark is to be a marked improvement on current systems. The manner in which synthetic data can be made to appear as close to real world data is discussed in Section 5.

3.3 Coherent Set of Transaction and Queries

Previous work on the IDIOMS project has already provided an analysis of the most commonly used banking transactions and the profile of their distribution by transaction type. By incorporating this information into the benchmark OLTP set, the benchmark system provides a realistic test of normal database usage. One important aspect of the benchmark is the inclusion of the creation/deletion operations as part of the normal OLTP functionality: this means that the ability of the system under test to manipulate indexes will be tested because invariably the creation of a new account or customer will cause index modification.

In order to achieve an equivalent set of realistic MIS queries, an analysis has been carried out of the exiting MIS type benchmarks and the current (and projected) requirements of commercial users. This has resulted in a categorisation of MIS queries from which a typical mix of individual queries can be generated. Categories include such management requirements as statistical reporting, and security checking.

3.4 Maintenance of Audit Information

A further aspect of real database systems is that they generally include some aspect of auditing and security and it is thus necessary to ensure that any benchmark contains a realistic representation of these features. By including the requirement to maintain audit information during transaction processing and query response, the benchmark not only mimics the accepted commercial practice but provides information at completion of testing that can be used to validate that the tests have been correctly conducted.

4 System Specification

This section considers the specification for the benchmark mimic database and the associated processing operations. One of the advantages that the database benchmark possesses is that SQL can be used both as a specification language and as an implementation language: not only does this extend its applicability to all relational database platforms but it means that the method of low level implementation can be left to the system designer. No requirements are laid down for indexing methods, query optimisation inclusion and other system dependent factors. In other words, the benchmark reflects performance as viewed from the end user's perspective and permits direct comparison between systems whose underlying implementation policies and hardware may be quite different. It also reflects the move to the client-server architecture for database systems. The benchmark discussed in this paper is designed to evaluate performance of the server.

4.1 Database Structure

```
CREATE TABLE CUSTOMER_ACCOUNTS
(        ACCOUNT_NUMBER        CHARACTER(12) NOT NULL,
         CUSTOMER_NUMB         CHARACTER(12) NOT NULL,
PRIMARY KEY (ACCOUNT_NUMB, CUSTOMER_NUMB),
FOREIGN KEY ACCOUNT_NUMB REFERENCES ACCOUNT,
FOREIGN KEY CUSTOMER_NUMB REFERENCES CUSTOMER  )


CREATE TABLE ACCOUNT
(        ACCOUNT_NUMBER        CHARACTER(12) NOT NULL,
         CURRENT_BALANCE       DOUBLE PRECISION NOT NULL,
         NO_OF_STAT_LINES      INTEGER DEFAULT 0,
         STAT_REQ_FLAG         CHARACTER(1) DEFAULT 1
PRIMARY KEY (ACCOUNT_NUMBER),
CHECK (NO_OF_STAT_LINES BETWEEN 0 AND 25),
CHECK (STAT_REQ_FLAG IN ( '0', '1' )  )

CREATE TABLE CUSTOMER
(        CUSTOMER_NUMB    CHARACTER(12) NOT NULL,
         TITLE            CHARACTER(8)  DEFAULT ' ',
         INITIALS         CHARACTER(3)  DEFAULT ' ',
         FORENAME         CHARACTER(24) DEFAULT ' ',
         SURNAME          CHARACTER(25) DEFAULT ' ',
         ...
         AREA_CODE        CHARACTER(7)  DEFAULT ' ',
         PHONE_NUMBER     CHARACTER(8)  DEFAULT ' ',
         ...
         POST_CODE        CHARACTER(8)  DEFAULT ' ',
         ...
PRIMARY KEY ( CUSTOMER_NUMB ),
CHECK ( AREA_CODE LIKE '0%')   )

CREATE TABLE STATEMENT_LINE
(        ACCOUNT_NUMBER   CHARACTER(12) NOT NULL,
         LINE_NUMBER      INTEGER NOT NULL,
         AMOUNT           DOUBLE PRECISION NOT NULL,
         TRANS_CODE       CHARACTER(4) NOT NULL,
         DATE             CHARACTER (6) NOT NULL,
         CURRENT_BALANCE  DOUBLE PRECISION NOT NULL,

PRIMARY KEY ( ACCOUNT_NUMBER, LINE_NUMBER ),
FOREIGN KEY ACCOUNT_NUMBER REFERENCES ACCOUNT  )
```

Figure 1 - SQL Table Definitions

The mimic database comprises six tables: customers, accounts, customer-accounts, statement-line, history and standing-order. Figure 1 shows a fragment of the SQL specification required to set up these tables. In these examples only the columns which will be used in the transaction specification are shown. Such a definition could normally be processed by the data definition language parser of an SQL system. It is worth noting that the key fields. eg CUSTOMER_NUMB, ACCOUNT_NUMBER etc, are realistically specified as character data, and the rows sizes represent the actual data requirements based on the TSB system (see Figure 2).

Table Name	Key Type	No of Fields	Row Size in bytes	Comments
CUSTOMER	CHAR[12]	12	250	
ACCOUNT	CHAR[12]	17	78	
CUSTOMER-ACCOUNT	CHAR[24]	2	24	
STATEMENT-LINE	CHAR[12]	12	80	Up to 25 entries per account
HISTORY	CHAR[12]	12	80	Same as STATEMENT-LINE
STANDING-ORDER	CHAR[12]	10	51	

Figure 2 - SQL Tables Sizes

4.2 Transaction Specification

A transaction is specified using a style of pseudo code which mixes an ordinary sequential programming language (lower case) with SQL statements (upper case). The pseudo code shown in Figure 3 gives the transaction which represents the deposit of money into an account. As such this code can not be directly executed but needs modification to a particular host language environment. Conversely an implementor of the benchmark could implement the whole transaction in another language which does not invoke SQL statements in the way indicated. This is not unreasonable as many systems have evolved their transaction processing system to a high degree and would expect to use no SQL in the transaction processing part of the system. We do not believe that the benchmark should indicate the way in which the transactions are implemented but the result should indicate the style of processing used. It should be noted that a SELECT which specifies ACCOUNT_NUMBER implicitly involves, due to its specification as a PRIMARY KEY, an index access which is hidden from the specification and only becomes apparent in the implementation. We do not intend to specify which indexes a system maintains but such information should be reported when the benchmark results are presented.

```
var
        string: acc_no, date, s_req_flag
        real: balance, deposit
        integer: line_no, n_s_l
input ( acc_no, date, deposit )

SELECT CURRENT_BALANCE, NO_OF_STAT_LINES, STAT_REQ_FLAG
        INTO balance, n_s_l, s_req_flag
        FROM ACCOUNT
        WHERE ACCOUNT_NUMBER = acc_no.
balance := balance + deposit
line_no := n_s_l + 1

INSERT INTO STATEMENT_LINE
        VALUES ( acc_no, line_no, deposit, '0113', date, balance, ...).
if line_no = 25 then
        n_s_l := 0
        s_req_flag := '1'
else
        n_s_l := n_s_l + 1

UPDATE ACCOUNT
        SET CURRENT_BALANCE = balance
        SET NO_OF_STAT_LINES = n_s_l
        SET STAT_REQ_FLAG = s_req_flag
        WHERE ACCOUNT_NUMBER = acc_no.
```

Figure 3 - Transaction Specification

4.3 Query Specification

A range of MIS queries has been included in the benchmark representing the type of functionality required by large commercial organisations. The coding in Figure 4, gives an example specification: this is a query which accesses all the accounts that have a negative balance and also calculates the average negative balance and the number of such accounts grouped by telephone area code. The query first constructs a cursor which is a view of the database comprising those accounts which have a negative balance. This view is then used to produce the desired results. It should be noted that the view requires a join of three tables. The resulting view is then subject to a GROUP BY operation which can either be implemented by a sort operation or by index access if such an index on the column AREA_CODE has been maintained.

```
var
        string: area
        integer: n
        real: mean
DECLARE NEG_BY_AREA CURSOR FOR
        SELECT AREA_CODE, COUNT (CURRENT_BALANCE), AVG (CURRENT_BALANCE)
            FROM CUSTOMER, CUSTOMER_ACCOUNT, ACCOUNT
            WHERE    ACCOUNT.CURRENT_BALANCE < 0
            AND      ACCOUNT.ACCOUNT_NUMBER =
                                    CUSTOMER_ACCOUNT.ACCOUNT_NUMBER
            AND      CUSTOMER_ACCOUNT.CUSTOMER_NUMBER =
                                    CUSTOMER.CUSTOMER_NUMBER
            GROUP BY AREA_CODE.
OPEN NEG_BY_AREA.
while not endof ( NEG_BY_AREA )
        FETCH NEG_BY_AREA INTO area, n, mean.
        /* process these values in some way */
```

Figure 4 - Query Specification

5 Benchmark Generation Support Tools

The support environment is provided by four main software tools; Data Generation, Transaction Generation, Information System and Results Analysis. Of these, the Information System and Results Analysis are used to provide the benchmarker with information regarding the generated system and an analysis of the output of the tests, and are at present in the design stage. The benchmark generation tools have been implemented and are described in this section. It is vital that these tools are as portable as possible to different environments so that they can be implemented as easily as possible. To this end all the tools have been implemented in ANSI C. The interaction between the tools is shown in Figure 5 and is taken from [15].

5.1 Database Generation

The main problem in creating reasonable synthetic data for a real application is that the real world data contains relationships between data items which are not explicitly stated. For example, in a customer record there is an informal relationship between town name, postcode and telephone area code. Thus queries can be formulated which access the data using each of these fields separately. The responses should in some way be consistent. It is therefore critical that fields which contain symbolic data maintain some degree of correlation. Similarly, the initial balance of an account is dependent upon the type of account, business or personal. Subsequently, the way in which the accounts are manipulated will vary. For example, a business account will have a much larger number of credits than a personal account which will tend to have a single monthly credit followed by a number of much smaller debits. For the purposes of benchmarking a database with a large number of default parameters is created. It is also possible to set the size of

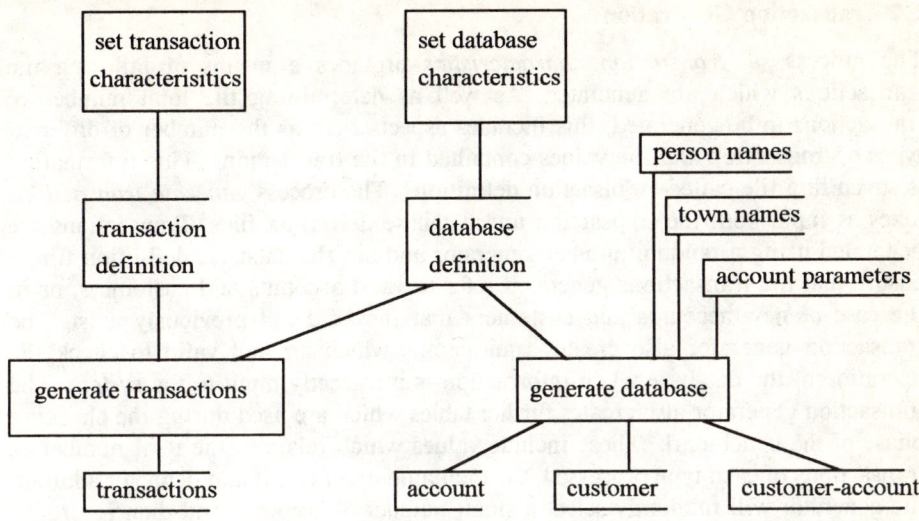

Figure 5 - Interaction Between the Benchmark Generation Tools

the database. The database definition file contains a specification of how each customer, account and standing order record is to be constructed. The *set database characteristics* function provides a machine independent means of creating a database definition file.

The *generate database* process takes as input the database definition and a number of other files which allow the parameterisation of the generated database. The "person names" file contains a set of typical first and last names for customers of the country for which the benchmark is being created. Similarly, the "town names" file contains typical road and town names for the country for which the benchmark is being created. Finally, the "account parameters" file contains values which represent initial starting values for accounts of different types. The *generate database* process can be configured so that it generates the database load files "account", "customer" and "customer-account" in the format required by the bulk data load facility of the database system being evaluated. An important feature of the database generation mechanism is that the data is generated in a completely computed manner, rather than using a random number generator. This aspect is used subsequently when transactions are generated because it is known absolutely what the parameters of an account or customer are directly from the database definition file. Thus there is no need when creating a transaction to determine whether or not a particular customer or account exists. For audited benchmarks the creation of test databases can easily be controlled by providing 'standard' definition and parameter files which can be guaranteed to produce the same set of data every time.

5.2 Transaction Generation

The process *set transaction characteristics* provides a means of tailoring the transactions which are generated. As well as determining the total number of transactions to be generated, this includes aspects such as the number of different types of transaction and the values contained in the transactions. This information is saved in a file called "transaction definition". The process *generate transactions* takes as input both the transaction and database definition files. Transactions are generated using a random number generator and use the database definition file to ensure that the transactions generated refer to valid accounts and customers, or in the case of new accounts and customers that they did not previously exist. The transaction generator also creates transactions which are not valid to check the operation of the database when information is incorrectly input to the system. The transaction generator also creates further tables which are used during the checking phase of the benchmark. These include values which relate to the total number of transactions of each type processed, the total amount of credit and debit. In addition the generator will randomly select a small number of accounts and then record all subsequent operations that are undertaken on that account. This information is used at the end of the benchmarking process for validation purposes. The transactions can be generated so that they can comply with the input requirements of the database system under test. The generation system also permits the creation of a number of different streams of transactions, each of which is put into a separate file. This allows the database system under test to be driven by any number of transaction streams. In the same way as there are standard database definition files for the benchmark suite there are also standard transaction definition files.

The MIS queries do not need to be generated in the same way because the aim is to run a set of queries which capture typical queries in such an environment. The same queries when executed against different size databases will naturally reflect the scaling factor which has been applied to the database generation.

5.3 Information System

The information system is intended to provide a means of determining the likely effect of a particular query. It takes as input the transaction and database definition files and because the system has been constructed in a computable manner will allow extraction of statistics about the generated data. This part of the system will be of more use when the benchmark is being used as a design aid, rather than for benchmarking.

6 Running the Benchmark

As well as defining the mimic benchmark database, OLTP and query operations, it is necessary to specify the manner in which the benchmarking tests are to be carried out. This involves consideration of the testing programme including timing methods and data scalability, as well as validation and reporting of results and enforcement of testing protocols.

6.1 Testing Programme

In order to test the database system under normal conditions of usage the benchmarking programme includes two test runs for each data set as shown in Figure 6.

First Run	Second Run
Load database	Load database
OLTP operations	OLTP operations ‖ MIS queries
MIS queries	"End of Day" processing
"End of Day" processing	

Figure 6 - Testing Strategy

In each run several operational phases are included. Loading the database according to the benchmark protocol ensures an "level playing field" start, but allows different system manufacturers to incorporate their own data placement and indexing strategies. During the first run, transaction and query processing are tested consecutively whereas the second run requires that these operations occur concurrently where the system can provide this functionality. The "End of Day" processing follows the procedure normally adopted in most large commercial systems. It comprises two stages: the handling of standing order payments and statement production, and the production of audit information from the audit trail maintained throughout the interactive phase. This "batch" processing stage not only mimics real database operation but provides the information for the validation of the benchmark process.

6.2 Data Scalability and System Cost

One important aspect of the new benchmark is its ability to measure performance as the data volumes increase. It is proposed that data volumes ranging from 100,000 to 10 million rows per table should be tested where the database platform can support these. The proportion of the data that can be stored in main memory will alter as the volumes increase, and the ratio between memory and disk storage will also be reflected in the overall system cost. In order to make valid comparisons between the systems under test, the relationship between disk utilisation and memory storage must be included in the reporting of benchmarking results.

The tests will be run for data sets increasing by factors of ten and results generated for each set. For each size of generated database a corresponding set of transactions is required but there is no need to scale the MIS queries. The intention is that the benchmarking process should mimic the daily processing of a commercial organisation and thus the volume of transactions and MIS queries should be of sufficient volume to ensure a run in the region of 10 to 12 hours. Information is available from TSB on the average number of transactions per account per day and this will be used to check on the number of transactions specified for each database size.

6.3 Performance Measurement

Previous benchmarks have incorporated two approaches to timing: measurements based on throughput either at a micro or macro level, eg transactions/second [8], equivalent database ratio [12], or length of time for a specified number and mix of operations [10]. This reflects the different interests of those concerned with benchmarking. A system user is likely to be concerned with such aspects as query response time, transaction residency time; the database manager may focus on throughput over a longer period of time and the platform manufacturer may wish to emphasise such figures as transaction execution time. This divergence of interests is a problem for all benchmarking, and leads to the general conclusion that the production of a benchmark as a single figure value is inappropriate and may be misleading. Work is currently being undertaken to specify the set of measurements that will appropriately represent the performance of the database system and provide a valid basis for comparison for users and manufacturers. Provisionally it is proposed that each stage in the test runs, ie the database load, the OLTP operations, the MIS responses and End of Day processing are all separately timed and these results are available for all database sizes. However further consultation is required before these become the established performance measurements for the benchmark.

6.4 Validation of Benchmark Output

The maintenance of an audit trail during the on-line phase of the benchmarking process allows the correctness of the test implementation to be checked. Two forms of information are to be stored during testing: first, a running total of debits and credits relating to customers' accounts is kept, and is matched to the final state of the database at completion of on-line operations. The second validation procedure involves the flagging of a small number of accounts: this is done randomly at the time of transaction generation, and thus selects accounts in a completely unpredictable manner. During the OLTP operations all accesses to those selected accounts are logged, and this information compared with the values separately monitored by the transaction generator.

6.5 Reporting of Results

The move away from a "single figure" benchmark to one which is capable of delivering different categories of performance data also gives rise for opportunities for misrepresentation of results. It is our policy to ensure that reporting of the benchmark includes the full set of results. This will include results obtained from each data set and will also involve a cost function. In order to support this a certification procedure is being considered under the auspices of SOSIP (Standards Organisation of Special Interest in Parallel Systems) [14]. This multi-national group was formed as part of the PEPS project and represents the major standards organisations with Europe.

7 Benchmarking for Design

It is worth noting that the benchmarking system forms an important design aid for the development of new parallel database machines, and we believe that this aspect of its usage will complement its role as a standard for benchmarking.

The importance of the benchmark as a design tool lies in the flexibility built into the database generator. The "default" mimic database produced for the standard benchmark represents a model of real world data; however by inclusion of appropriate parameterisation, it is easy to produce skewed data, either in terms of modelling different "social" conditions (eg. range of names) or "technical" conditions (eg. data values with a high index clustering). This means that the platform manufacturers can experiment with the mimic database in order to test out aspects of their design and relate high level functionality to aspects such as CPU usage, communication and I/O bandwidths. In order to support these investigations, appropriate monitoring of these operational aspects is required. This is likely to involve additional timing of the progress of the testing process, as it will be necessary to obtain data on the performance of individual transactions and queries.

8 Conclusions

The emergence of new parallel database machines provides the potential for increased performance in large commercial systems, not only can these systems handle large data volumes and provide good operational throughput but they support enhanced functionality in the form of management information or decision support provision. In order to evaluate their performance a new benchmark system is under development. The strengths of this benchmark lie in its ability to model normal database operations on realistic data, the inclusion of data volume sizing and the production of a set of results which form a valid and unambiguous basis for comparison between the systems under test. Because of the manner in which the benchmark mimic has been designed, it can in addition be used as a design tool for future high performance systems.

The database definition, the transactions and queries have been specified, prototype generation tools have been implemented, and the development of the full versions is nearing completion. Further consideration is being given to the detailed specification of timing and reporting arrangements and experience is required on the usage of the benchmark with realistically sized systems.

Acknowledgements

The contribution of John Cook was invaluable, as he implemented a prototype version of the database generation system.

References

1. JM Kerridge, "The Design of the IDIOMS Parallel Database Machine", Proc. British National Conf. on Databases 9 (Wolverhampton, 1991), pub. Aspects of Databases, eds. M.S. Jackson and A.E. Robinson Oxford: Butterworth - Heinemann, 1991.
2. R England et al, "The Performance of the IDIOMS Parallel Database Machine", Parallel Computing and Transputer Applications '92 (PACTA '92), eds M. Valero, M.R. Jane and E Onate IOS Press Amsterdam, 1992.
3. E Brocklehurst, T Chambers, C Francis, A Mansfield, M Stevens, H Symm, "PEPS Benchmark Methodology - Draft 5.1", NPL Report, April 1992
4. International Standards Organisation, Database Language SQL, ISO 9075:1987(E), 1987.
5. J Page, "High Performance Database for Client/Server Systems", in Parallel Processing and Data Management, ed. P. Valduriez, Chapman and Hall, 1992.
6. "The Benchmark Handbook" Ed J Gray, Morgan Kaufmann, 1991
7. S Dietrich, M Brown, E Cortes-Rello and S Wunderlin "A Practitioners Introduction to Database Performance Measurement" in Computer Journal,, Vol 35, No. 4, August 1992
8. O Serlin "The History of DebitCredit and TPC, TPC-A and TPC-B" in [6]
9. N Revell and M W Youssef "Database Performance Evaluation: A Methodological Approach" in Proc DEXA '93, Database and Expert Systems Applications, Sept 1993, Prague, Czeck Republic, LNCS, Springer Verlag (1993)
10. D DeWitt "The Wisconsin Benchmark: Past, Present and Future" in [6]
11. P E O'Neil " The Set Query Benchmark" in [6]
12. C Turbifill, C Orji and D Bitton "AS^{3}AP: An ANSI SQL Standard Scalable and Portable Benchmark for Relational Database Systems" in [6]
13. Jon Kerridge, Innes Jelly, Chris Bates and Yannis Tsitsogiannis, "Towards a Benchmark for Scalable Parallel Database Machines" Proceedings of PEPS Workshop on Performance Evaluation of Parallel Systems, ESPRIT/BCS, November 1993, Warwick University, UK
14. A Mansfield "SOSIP and the PEPS Benchmarking Methodology" Proceedings of PEPS Workshop on Performance Evaluation of Parallel Systems, ESPRIT/BCS, November 1993, Warwick University, UK
15. RJ Cook "Performance Testing of the IDIOMS Parallel Database Machine", MSc Thesis, University of Sheffield, 1993
16. P Valduriez "Parallel Database Systems: Open Problems and New Issues" in Distributed and Parallel Databases 1 (1993)

Branching Transactions: A Transaction Model for Parallel Database Systems

Albert Burger and Peter Thanisch

Department of Computer Science,
University of Edinburgh, Scotland

Abstract. In order to exploit massively parallel computers, database management systems must achieve a high level of concurrency when executing transactions. In a high contention environment, however, parallelism is severely limited due to transaction blocking, and the utilisation of hardware resources, e.g. CPUs, can be low.

We propose a transaction model, *Branching Transactions*, together with an appropriate concurrency control algorithm, which, in case of data conflicts, avoids unnecessary transaction blockings and restarts by executing alternative paths of transactions in parallel. Our approach uses additional hardware resources, mainly CPU — which would otherwise sit idle due to data contention — to improve transaction response time and throughput.

1 Introduction

In recent years, multi-processor systems based on fast and inexpensive microprocessors have become widely available. The total performance/price ratio of such systems is usually higher than that of traditional mainframe computers. We, therefore, see a trend towards the replacement of mainframes by parallel systems in high performance transaction processing environments.

In general, high transaction throughput and short transaction response time are the primary performance design goals for a database management system. In parallel transaction processing systems, *interference* [2] — the slowdown each new process imposes on all others when accessing shared resources — limits speedup and scaleup. In fact, data contention can be the limiting factor for performance in a shared-nothing parallel database machine [3] [5]; under such conditions the utilisation of CPUs and disks is relatively low.

The component of a database management system dealing with synchronisation of access to shared data, and therefore responsible for issues of data contention, is the *concurrency control manager*. All existing algorithms resolve conflicts either by *blocking* or *restarting* transactions at the time of conflict (pessimistic algorithms) or when a transaction tries to commit (optimistic algorithms). Common to both groups, the decision made at the time of conflict may not be the right one. In a pessimistic algorithm, for example, the roll-back of a transaction is frequently caused by a situation that *might* have led to a deadlock; or a transaction is blocked because it *might* have violated serializability. In an optimistic algorithm, a conflict that was ignored during the execution may require the restart of a transaction. The key problem is that at the time of conflict we usually don't know which is the right decision to make. Contrary to all CC algorithms known to us, we propose an approach where a transaction, instead of making a particular decision, follows up alternative paths of execution concurrently. Once it is known which was the right path to pursue, all others can be aborted. This approach allows us to avoid many unnecessary blockings and restarts of transactions which lead to performance problems in all existing CC algorithms.

Executing alternative paths of a transaction concurrently increases demand on hardware resources, in particular, CPUs. However, as we pointed out earlier, in a parallel database system data contention can lead to low CPU utilisation, and it seems appropriate to use this idle CPU time to reduce the problem caused by sharing data. The idea of "sacrificing" hardware resources to improve concurrency in a database system is not entirely new: multi-version algorithms [6] use additional memory and disk space — to store multiple versions of the same data item — to improve the level of concurrency.

The remainder of the paper is organised as follows: in Section 2 we present the branching transaction model; Section 3 contains a two-phase locking algorithm for branching transactions; Section 4 presents a formal proof of correctness for the two-phase locking algorithm presented before; Section 5 discusses aspects of logging and recovery; Section 6 briefly introduces the idea of branching restrictions; and Section 7 gives a conclusion and summary of future work.

2 The Branching Transaction Model

Existing concurrency control algorithms resolve a conflict by either blocking or restarting one of the transactions involved. We will use the following three transactions, T_1, T_2 and T_3, to illustrate this point, and to describe the principles of branching transactions. ($r[x]$ denotes a read operation on data item x; $w[x]$ denotes a write operation on data item x.)

T_1: $r[z]$, $r[x]$, $r[y]$, $r[t]$, $w[t]$, $r[m]$, $r[n]$, $w[n]$
T_2: $w[x]$, $r[z]$, $r[u]$, $w[u]$
T_3: $w[y]$, $r[l]$, $r[k]$, $w[k]$, $r[u]$, $w[u]$, $r[p]$

If these transactions were executed under a two-phase locking algorithm, the schedule in Table 1 would be a possible interleaving of their execution. ($r_i[x_j]$ denotes T_i reading the value of data item x written by T_j; $w_i[x_i]$ denotes T_i updating x; c_i denotes the Commit operation of T_i. The values of data items prior to the execution of this schedule are indicated by subscript 0.) At step (2), when T_1 tries to read data item x, it is blocked by T_2's lock on x; T_2 has written to x at step (1), and must therefore hold an exclusive lock on it. T_1 remains blocked until T_2 releases its lock on x. Similarly, T_1 gets blocked again at step (7), because of T_3's lock on y.

The scheduler blocks T_1 at step (2), since it cannot decide whether T_1 should read the value written to x by T_2, or the value x had prior to step (1). In case T_2

aborts, or commits after T_1, T_1 should read x_0, otherwise it should read x_2. Since T_2's fate is not know at the time of conflict, the scheduler delays its decision — blocks T_1 — until it has sufficient information to decide.

Step	T_1	T_2	T_3
1	$r_1[z_0]$	$w_2[x_2]$	
2	blocked	$r_2[z_0]$	$w_3[y_3]$
3	blocked	$r_2[u_0]$	$r_3[l_0]$
4	blocked	$w_2[u_2]$	$r_3[k_0]$
5	blocked	c_2	$w_3[k_3]$
6	$r_1[x_2]$		$r_3[u_2]$
7	blocked		$w_3[u_3]$
8	blocked		$r_3[p_0]$
9	blocked		c_3
10	$r_1[y_3]$		
11	$r_1[t_0]$		
12	$w_1[t_1]$		
13	$r_1[m_0]$		
14	$r_1[n_0]$		
15	$w_1[n_1]$		
16	c_1		

Table 1. Schedule under Two-phase Locking (No Branching)

In case T_2 commits before T_1, blocking of T_1, and the delay of its response time that follows from it, is unnecessary. Other concurrency control algorithms have similar problems: optimistic algorithms, for example, need to abort a transaction and restart it, if the certification of it fails; timestamp ordering algorithms maintain serializability by enforcing the timestamp order on conflicting operations, even though not all aborted transactions would have violated serializability.

To overcome the problems of these "wrong decisions" by the scheduler, we propose to pursue alternative paths of execution of a transaction until it is known which was the correct path to follow. In other words, at the time of conflict a transaction branches into two or more alternative copies of itself which then continue to execute concurrently.

Table 2 shows a schedule in which T_1 is executed as a branching transaction. This time when T_1 tries to read data item x, it branches into two components: $T_{1,1}$ and $T_{1,2}$, the first proceeds using the original value of x, the second reads x_2. At step (3), further branching is necessary since y has been updated by T_3 at step (2). At step (6), it has become clear — since T_2 just committed — that the correct decision at step (2) was to read x_2. Therefore, it is not necessary to pursue further those components that were started under the assumption that x_0 should be read, and $T_{1,3}$ and $T_{1,4}$ abort.

When a particular path of a branching transaction has executed all operations, it is not allowed to commit until it is known whether all assumptions made by it are fulfilled: $T_{1,5}$ and $T_{1,6}$ are blocked at step (9) since they cannot commit until after T_3 committed (or aborted). Since T_3 indeed commits, $T_{1,5}$ aborts and $T_{1,6}$ commits at step (10).

Running T_1 as a branching transaction allowed the scheduler to commit the transaction action within 10 steps, as opposed to 16 in the previous case.

Step	Branching Transaction T_1				T_2	T_3
1	$T_{1,0}$: $r_{1,0}[z_0]$				$w_2[x_2]$	
2	$T_{1,1}$: $r_{1,1}[x_0]$		$T_{1,2}$: $r_{1,2}[x_2]$		$r_2[z_0]$	$w_3[y_3]$
3	$T_{1,3}$: $r_{1,3}[y_0]$	$T_{1,4}$: $r_{1,4}[y_3]$	$T_{1,5}$: $r_{1,5}[y_0]$	$T_{1,6}$: $r_{1,6}[y_3]$	$r_2[u_0]$	$r_3[l_0]$
4	$r_{1,3}[t_0]$	$r_{1,4}[t_0]$	$r_{1,5}[t_0]$	$r_{1,6}[t_0]$	$w_2[u_2]$	$r_3[k_0]$
5	$w_{1,3}[t_{1,3}]$	$w_{1,4}[t_{1,4}]$	$w_{1,5}[t_{1,5}]$	$w_{1,6}[t_{1,6}]$	c_2	$w_3[k_3]$
6	$a_{1,3}$	$a_{1,4}$	$r_{1,5}[m_0]$	$r_{1,6}[m_0]$		$r_3[u_2]$
7			$r_{1,5}[n_0]$	$r_{1,6}[n_0]$		$w_3[u_3]$
8			$w_{1,5}[n_{1,5}]$	$w_{1,6}[n_{1,6}]$		$r_3[p_0]$
9			blocked	blocked		c_3
10			$a_{1,5}$	$c_{1,6}$		

Table 2. Schedule for Branching Transaction

Transaction Graphs and Components: We represent the branching hierarchy of a branching transaction T_i by a *transaction graph* (a rooted, directed tree), with T_i's transaction components as nodes ($T_{i,0}$ as root), and an edge $T_{i,j} \rightarrow T_{i,k}$, if $T_{i,j}$ created $T_{i,k}$. The transaction graph for T_1 in our example is shown in Figure 1. A transaction component $T_{i,j}$ is a *descendant* of transaction component $T_{i,k}$, if there exists a path from $T_{i,j}$ to $T_{i,k}$ in T_i's transaction graph.

Figure 2 shows the state transition diagram of transaction components. After a component has been created it is *ACTIVE*, i.e. it is executing the operations of the corresponding transaction. (We include the temporary blocking of a component in this state.) If the component is involved in a conflict, and branching is necessary, it creates two or more descendant components and enters the *BRANCHED* state. In this state no more operations are executed by the component. If all descendants of a component eventually abort, then it must be aborted as well. An active transaction component can be aborted either by the system (such as $T_{1,3}$ and $T_{1,4}$ in our example), or by an explicit abort command issued by the component itself. If a component is active and has executed the last operation of its transaction, and if no unresolved dependencies exist, it can

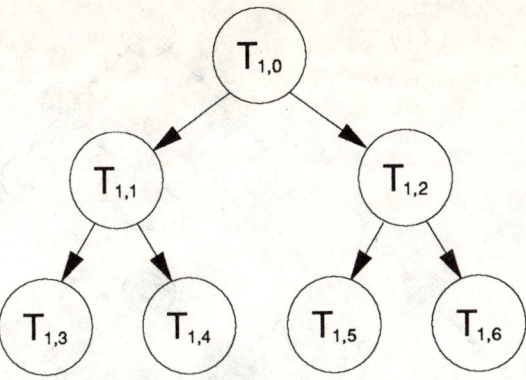

Fig. 1. Transaction Graph

commit. If a component commits, so do all its ancestors. We show the state changes for transaction components in our example in Figure 3.

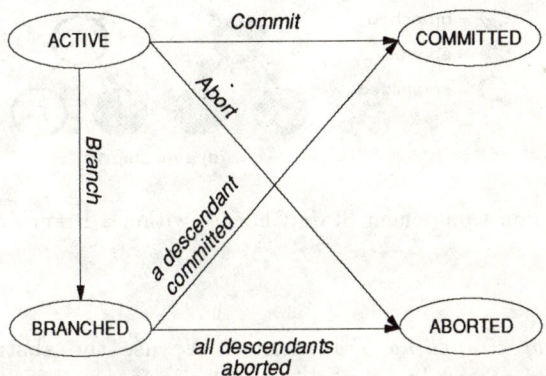

Fig. 2. Transaction Component State Transition Diagram

It is a key property of branching transactions that only one path in every transaction graph can commit, and all components not part of this path are aborted. Any updates on the database performed by aborted transaction components are rolled-back.

Any two transaction components of the same transaction tree can be executed in parallel, unless there exists a path in the tree between them. Components from different paths execute in isolation: they do not read any updates made by the other and are allowed to update the same data items independently. To be able to maintain the ACID properties [1] of transactions, multiple versions of data items must be maintained.

---

[1] A=Atomicity, C=Consistency, I=Isolation, and D=Durability [4]

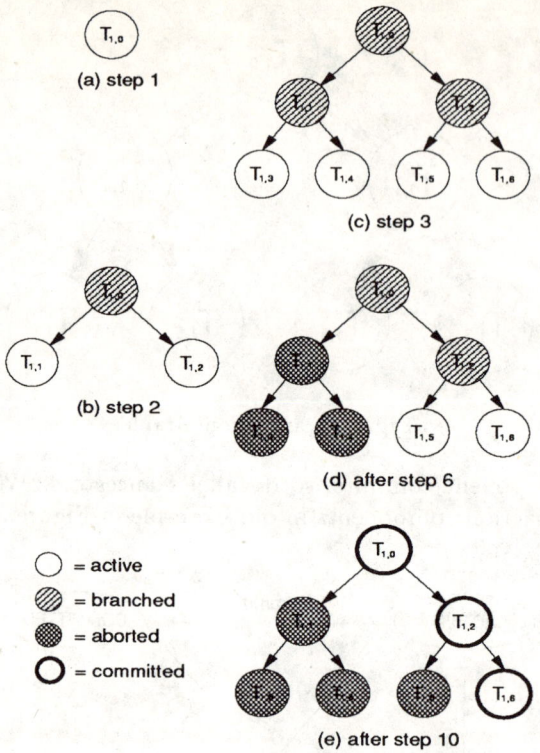

Fig. 3. Transaction Component State Changes within a Branching Transaction

Implementation of Branching Transactions: We use the abstract model of a database system depicted in Figure 4 to describe some aspects of implementing branching transactions [2]. A user submits a transaction for execution to the transaction manager (TM), which creates a new transaction component for it. The TM maintains the transaction graph for each transaction and submits database operations (Read and Write) to the scheduler. The scheduler implements a concurrency control policy, and therefore decides when branching should occur. Although we only describe a locking policy in this paper, other mechanisms are possible. The scheduler is also responsible for preventing a transaction component from committing, if there exist some unresolved dependencies for it. Once a branching transaction has committed (or aborted), the TM reports back to the user. Branching of transactions is transparent to the user.

---

[2] The model ignores the distributed nature of a parallel database system. A detailed discussion of this, however, would be beyond the scope of this paper.

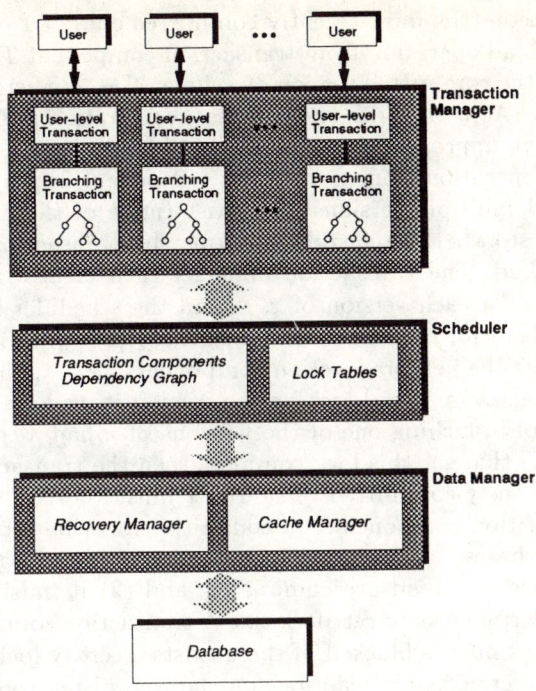

Fig. 4. DBMS Model for Branching Transactions

3 Two-Phase Locking for Branching Transactions

In this section we describe a multi-version two-phase locking algorithm for branching transactions (hereafter referred to as BT_MV2PL). Our algorithm is based on Bernstein, etal.'s [1] description of multi-version two-phase locking.

As mentioned earlier, branching transactions require a multi-version (MV) environment to enable the concurrent execution of alternative paths. Under BT_MV2PL the data manager has to store one or more versions of a data item, of which only one was created by a committed transaction. When a transaction component that created a new version of an item commits, its version overrides the previously committed one.

When the scheduler receives a Write from transaction component $T_{i,j}$ ($w_{i,j}[x]$), it translates it into $w_{i,j}[x_{i,j}]$, immediately schedules it for execution — the data manager creates a new version: $x_{i,j}$ — and sets a write lock ($wl_{i,j}[x_{i,j}]$) on this new version.

A transaction component $T_{i,j}$ cannot access versions of x created by another component, $T_{i,k}$, of the same transaction, unless $T_{i,j}$ is a descendant of $T_{i,k}$. In this case, or when $T_{i,j}$ itself has previously written to x, the scheduler translates a Read operation from $T_{i,j}$ ($r_{i,j}[x]$) into a version Read on $x_{i,k}$ or $x_{i,j}$, respectively (irrespective of any other existing versions of x).

If only one version (the most recently committed one) of x exists, the scheduler translates a Read operation from transaction component $T_{i,j}$, ($r_{i,j}[x]$), into a version Read on the committed version of x, i.e. $r_{i,j}[x_{k,l}]$, where $x_{k,l}$ is the committed version of x. As with Write operations, the operation (Read) is scheduled immediately, and an appropriate lock is set ($rl_{i,j}[x_{k,l}]$).

When a Read operation from transaction component $T_{i,j}$ ($r_{i,j}[x]$) arrives at the scheduler, and multiple versions of x exist (none of them created by $T_{i,j}$ or one of its ancestors), the scheduler informs the transaction manager that branching is required. The transaction manager then creates new transaction components — one for each version of x — and the scheduler immediately executes a version Read for each new component: $r_{i,k_l}[x_{m_l,n_l}]$, for $l = 1..$number of versions (T_{i,k_l} are the new transaction components, $[x_{m_l,n_l}]$ the versions of x). Each new component sets a read lock on the version it read.

If at the time of branching one of the versions of x had a certify lock on it, and the transaction that set this lock commits, then the transaction component that read the previously committed version of x must abort.

Before a transaction component can commit, it must be certified. *Certification* involves two phases: (1) a transaction component must wait until all data it or one of its ancestors read are committed, and (2) it must upgrade all its and its ancestors' write locks to certify locks. A transaction component trying to acquire a certify lock on x is blocked, if there exists a certify lock on any version of x already, or if there exists a read lock on the committed version of x.

As with other locking protocols, deadlocks may occur. Traditional deadlock detection and resolution techniques can be applied. Some (or possibly all — this is subject of further investigation) deadlocks can be resolved by aborting only some transaction components without having to roll-back any transaction completely.

Note that there are no conflicts between read locks and write locks, and between write locks and write locks. Transactions only conflict through read locks and certify locks, as described above. Write locks are simply markers to remember on which items a transaction needs to obtain a certify lock.

4 Correctness Proof

To prove the correctness of our new concurrency control algorithm, we will now formalise the concept of branching transactions, and show that a BT_MV2PL scheduler only allows serializable schedules of concurrent transactions. Our proof is based on the serializability theorem of Bernstein, etal. ([1]). We will present some of their theorems here to keep our paper as self contained as possible; proofs of their theorems are, however, omitted. The interested reader is referred to their book.

4.1 Branching Transaction Multi-Version Histories

As described earlier, the branching of transactions is solely the responsibility of the scheduler and is transparent to the user. Hence, at the user level, we consider a transaction as a sequence of operations on the database.

Definition 1. *(from [1], page 27)* **A user-level transaction** UT_i **is a partial order with ordering relation** $<_i^U$, **where**

1. $UT_i \subseteq \{r_i[x], w_i[x] \mid x \text{ is a data item}\} \cup \{a_i, c_i\}$.
2. $a_i \in UT_i$ iff $c_i \notin UT_i$.
3. if t is c_i or a_i (whichever is in UT_i), for any other operation $p \in UT_i$, $p <_i^U t$.
4. if $r_i[x], w_i[x] \in UT_i$, then $r_i[x] <_i^U w_i[x]$ or $w_i[x] <_i^U r_i[x]$.

Condition (1) states that the only operations on the database are either Reads ($r_i(x)$) or Writes ($w_i(x)$) and that a transaction either Commits [3] (c_i) or Aborts (a_i). Condition (2) says that a transaction can either Commit or Abort, but not both. Condition (3) states that a Commit or Abort is the last operation of a transaction. Condition (4) requires the partial order $<_i^U$ to specify an order of execution on a Read and Write if they access the same data.

Since user-level transactions are described in terms of these 4 operations: $r_i[x]$, $w_i[x]$, c_i and a_i, we need some mapping function h that captures the fact that one user-level operation may be translated into a set of BT operations. The following BT operations are defined:

$r_{i,j}[x_{k,l}]$: transaction component $T_{i,j}$ reads the version of data item x written by transaction component $T_{k,l}$.
$w_{i,j}[x_{i,j}]$: transaction component $T_{i,j}$ creates a new version of data item x.
$b_{i,j}(i,k)$: transaction component $T_{i,j}$ spawns a new transaction component $T_{i,k}$.
$a_{i,j}$: transaction component $T_{i,j}$ aborts.
$c_{i,j}$: transaction component $T_{i,j}$ commits.

The mapping from user-level to BT operations depends on the concurrency control policy used by the scheduler. The following mapping rules, however, hold independently of what policy is used.

1. Mapping of Read operations:
    $h(r_i[x]) = \{r_{i,j}[x_{l,m}] \mid T_{i,j} \text{ is a transaction component}$
      executing in behalf of T_i and reading some version of $x\} \cup$
    $\{b_{i,j}(i,k) \mid T_{i,j} \text{ created transaction component } T_{i,k}\}$
    A user-level Read operation may require multiple BT Read operations and the creation of new transaction components.
2. Mapping of Write operations:
    $h(w_i[x]) = \{w_{i,j}[x_{i,j}] \mid T_{i,j} \text{ is a transaction component updating } x\}$
    A user-level Write operation on x may be executed by more than one transaction component, although only one of these versions will ultimately be committed.

---
[3] The Commit here means that a transaction actually commits, not merely that it requests to commit, since in the latter case a transaction may still be aborted.

3. Mapping of Abort operations:
   $$h(a_i) = \{a_{i,j} \mid T_{i,j} \text{ is a leaf node in } T_i\text{'s transaction graph }\}$$
   A user-level transaction aborts, if all leaf nodes in the corresponding BT's transaction graph abort.
4. Mapping of Commit operations:
   $$h(c_i) = \{c_{i,j}\} \cup$$
   $$\{a_{i,k} \mid T_{i,k} \text{ is an active transaction component of } T_i, \text{ and } j \neq k\}$$
   If a user-level transaction T_i commits, then one of the active components commits, but all others abort.

A *branching transaction* T_i is the result of mapping the operations of a user-level transaction UT_i onto BT operations. Before we give a formal definition of branching transactions, we must present formal definitions for some of the terminology introduced earlier.

Definition 2. Two BT operations, p and q, **conflict** with each other if p is a Read operation ($r_{i,j}[x_{m,n}]$), reading the version of a data item ($x_{m,n}$) which was written by q ($w_{k,l}[x_{k,l}]$, where $m = k$, $n = l$), and p and q are operations of different transactions ($i \neq k$).

Definition 3. A **transaction component** $T_{i,j}$ of branching transaction T_i is obtained by deleting all operations $p_{i,k}$ of T_i for which $k \neq j$.

Definition 4. A transaction component $T_{i,d}$ is a **descendant** of transaction component $T_{k,a}$ in history H, if $k = i$ and either (1) operation $b_{k,a}(k,d) \in H$, or (2) $\exists \ b_{k,\alpha_1}(k,\alpha_2), b_{k,\alpha_2}(k,\alpha_3), \ldots, b_{k,\alpha_{n-1}}(k,\alpha_n) \in H$, such that $\alpha_1 = a$, $\alpha_n = d$ and $n \geq 2$ The set of all descendants of transaction component $T_{k,a}$ is denoted by $desc(k,a)$.

Definition 5. A transaction component $T_{i,a}$ is an **ancestor** of transaction component $T_{k,d}$ in history H, if $k = i$ and either (1) operation $b_{k,a}(k,d) \in H$, or (2) $\exists \ b_{k,\alpha_1}(k,\alpha_2), b_{k,\alpha_2}(k,\alpha_3), \ldots, b_{k,\alpha_{n-1}}(k,\alpha_n) \in H$, such that $\alpha_1 = a$, $\alpha_n = d$ and $n \geq 2$ The set of all ancestors of transaction component $T_{k,d}$ is denoted by $anc(k,a)$.

Definition 6. A **transaction graph** (TG) for branching transaction T_i in history H, denoted $TG(H,i)$, is a rooted directed tree whose nodes are the transaction components of T_i in H, and whose edges are all $T_{i,j} \rightarrow T_{i,k}$, such that $b_{i,j}(i,k) \in H$. The root node is labelled $T_{i,0}$.

Definition 7. A **transaction path** in branching transaction T_i is a path in $TG(H,i)$ between the root node ($T_{i,0}$) and one of its leaf nodes.

Definition 8. A **branching transaction** T_i is obtained by translating the operations of a user-level transaction UT_i into BT operations according to some mapping function h. T_i is a partial order with ordering relation $<_i$, where

1. let $q \in UT_i$; if $c_{i,j} \in H$, then there exists some $p_{i,k} \in H$, such that $p_{i,k} \in h(q)$, and $j = k$ or $T_{i,k} \in anc(i,j)$.

2. let $p, q \in h(o)$, where o is a user-level operation of UT_i. If $p \in T_{i,j}$ and $q \in T_{i,k}$, and there exists a transaction path which contains both, $T_{i,j}$ and $T_{i,k}$, then $j = k$ and $p = q$, unless $p = b_{i,j}(i,k)$ and $q = r_{i,k}[x_{m.n}]$ (for some $x_{m.n}$).
3. if p_i and q_i are operations in UT_i and $p_i <_i^U q_i$, then for any $s_{i,j}, t_{i,k} \in T_i$, where $s_{i,j} \in h(p_i)$, $t_{i,k} \in h(q_i)$: if there exists a transaction path P in $TG(H, i)$ that contains transaction components $T_{i,j}$ and $T_{i,k}$, then $s_{i,j} <_i t_{i,k}$.
4. if $c_{i,j} \in T_i$, then for any transaction component $T_{i,k}$ where $k \neq j$, $a_{i,k} \in T_{i,k}$ or $b_{i,k}(i,l) \in T_{i,k}$ (for some l).
5. $c_{i,j} \in T_{ij}$ iff $a_{i,j}, b_{i,j}(i,k) \notin T_{i,j}$, $a_{i,j} \in T_{ij}$ iff $c_{i,j}, b_{i,j}(i,k) \notin T_{i,j}$, $b_{i,j}(i,k) \in T_{ij}$ iff $c_{i,j}, a_{i,j} \notin T_{i,j}$ (for some k).
6. let $p, q \in H$ be two Branch operations: $p = b_{i,j}(i,k)$ and $q = b_{l,m}(l,n)$. If $i = l$ and $k = n$, then $p = q$.
7. if t is $c_{i,j}$ or $a_{i,j}$ (whichever is in $T_{i,j}$), then for any other operation $p_{i,j} \in T_{i,j}$, $p_{i,j} <_i t$. If t is $b_{i,j}(i,k)$ (for some k), then all operations $p_{i,j}$, such that $t <_i p_{i,j}$, are Branch operations $b_{i,j}(i,l)$, where $l \neq k$.

Condition (1) states that all operations requested by the user-level transaction are translated into the appropriate BT operations, i.e. all user-level operations are executed at least once along the successful transaction path of the corresponding BT transaction. Condition (2) states that each user-level operation is executed at most once along each transaction path. Condition (3) says that all orderings given in user-level transactions are preserved within branching transactions. Condition (4) states that only one branch (path) of a BT transaction is allowed to commit. Each transaction component either branches, commits or aborts (condition (5)). Condition (6) guarantees that all newly created transaction components are uniquely identified by their two indices. Condition (7) says that a transaction component either terminates with a Commit, an Abort, or a number of Branch operations.

Similar to histories and multi-version histories described in [1], we use the notion of a BT history to describe the interleaved execution of branching transactions.

Definition 9. A complete BT history H over a set of top-level transactions $UT = \{UT_1, \ldots, UT_n\}$ is a partial order on the corresponding set of branching transactions $T = \{T_0, \ldots, T_n\}$ with ordering relation $<_H$, where

1. $H = h(\bigcup_{i=1}^n UT_i)$, for some translation function h.
2. $<_H \supseteq \bigcup_{i=1}^n <_i$.
3. for any two conflicting operations $p, q \in H$, either $p <_H q$ or $q <_H p$.
4. if $r_{i,j}[x_{k,l}] \in H$, then $w_{k,l}[x_{k,l}] <_H r_{i,j}[x_{k,l}]$.
5. if $w_{i,j}[x_{i,j}] <_i r_{i,k}[x_{l,m}]$, and $k = j$ or $T_{i,k} \in desc(i,j)$, then $i = l$ and $j = m$.
6. if $r_{i,j}[x_{k,l}] \in H$ and $i \neq k$, then if $c_{i,j} \in H$ or $c_{i,d} \in H$ and $T_{i,d} \in desc(T_{i,j})$, then it also holds that either $c_{k,l} \in H$ or $c_{k,m} \in H$ and $T_{k,m} \in desc(T_{k,l})$, and that $c_{k,x} <_H c_{i,y}$, for some x, y.

Condition (1) states that all operations submitted by user-level transactions are translated into appropriate BT operations. Condition (2) states that the execution of branching transactions maintains all orderings defined on BT operations. Condition (3) states that the scheduler must determine an order on all pairs of conflicting BT operations. Condition (4) states that a BT transaction cannot read a version before it was created. Condition (5) states that if a transaction component wants to read a data item which it or any of its ancestors has previously created a version of that data item, then it must read that version. Condition (6) states that if a transaction component wants to commit, then all versions read by it or one of its ancestors must be committed, i.e. the transaction component that created the version, or one of its descendants, must have committed.

To prove serializability for $BTMV$ histories we need only be concerned with those operations that were executed by transaction components which committed, or which have a descendant that committed. We use the notion of a *committed projection* to represent the committed part of a BT history.

Definition 10. The **committed projection** of a BT history is obtained through the following three steps, and is denoted by $C(H)$.

1. Delete all operations $p_{i,j} \in T_{i,j}$ from H for which it is not the case that $c_{i,j} \in H$ or $c_{i,d} \in H$ and $T_{i,d} \in desc(T_{i,j})$.
2. Delete all $b_{i,j}(i,k)$ operations from H.
3. Map each $r_{i,j}[x_{k,l}]$ into $r_i[x_k]$, each $w_{i,j}[x_{i,j}]$ into $w_i[x_i]$, and each $c_{i,j}$ into c_i.

Step (1) eliminates all operations which were not executed by those components that are part of the committed BT transactions. We have now effectively pruned all transaction graphs to one particular transaction path. To determine whether our history is serializable, we don't need the information about which operation was executed by what transaction component, but only by which transaction. Hence, we can delete all BT Branch operations and map all remaining operations $o_{i,j}$ to o_i (steps (2) and (3)). The latter implicitly leads to a mapping of data versions $x_{i,j}$ to x_i.

Proposition 11. *The committed projection of a BT history is a multi-version history (as defined in [1]).*

Proof: omitted for space reasons; □

4.2 Correctness of BT_MV2PL

To prove that all committed projections of histories produced by a BT_MV2PL scheduler are serializable, we first need to describe certain properties of these projections, i.e. an algorithm implementing BT_MV2PL policy guarantees the following properties of the committed projections of histories allowed by this algorithm. The certification of a transaction T_i is denoted by f_i.

BT_MV2PL_1: For every T_i, f_i follows all of T_i's Reads and Writes and precedes T_i's commitment. ($r_i[x_j], w_i[x_i] <_{C(H)} f_i <_{C(H)} c_i$, for all j)

The certification of a transaction, i.e. a transaction component and all of its ancestors in H, takes place after all of its Reads and Writes are executed; and only after successful certification can a transaction commit.

BT_MV2PL_2: For every $r_j[x_i]$ in $C(H)$, if $j \neq i$, then $c_i <_{C(H)} f_j$.

A Read of a transaction cannot be certified until the transaction that created the read version has committed.

BT_MV2PL_3: If $r_k[x_j]$ and $w_i[x_i]$ are in $C(H)$, then either $c_i <_{C(H)} r_k[x_j]$ or $r_k[x_j] <_{C(H)} f_i$.

A transaction's Read on x is either ordered after the Commit or before the certification of another transaction that creates a new version of x. This is because of the conflicts between Read Locks and Certify Locks.

BT_MV2PL_4: For every $r_k[x_j]$ and $w_i[x_i]$ (i, j, k distinct), if $f_i <_{C(H)} r_k[x_j]$, then $f_i <_{C(H)} f_j$.

A Read operation is only certified if it read the most recently certified version of x. This is because a Read cannot be certified until the version it read has been committed; and since the transaction does not release its Read Lock until commit time, it prevents any other transaction from overwriting x — to overwrite the last certified version of x, a transaction needs to obtain a Certify Lock, which is not possible before the Read Lock on the last certified version has been released.

BT_MV2PL_5: For every $r_k[x_j]$ and $w_i[x_i]$, where $i \neq j$ and $i \neq k$, if $r_k[x_j] <_{C(H)} f_i$ and $f_j <_{C(H)} f_i$, then $f_k <_{C(H)} f_i$.

A transaction can only certify an update of x after all transactions that have read a previously certified version have certified their Read. This is because of the same reason as in BT_MV2PL_4: a transaction does not release its Read Locks until after it was certified.

BT_MV2PL_6: For every $w_i[x_i], w_j[x_j]$ ($i \neq j$), either $f_i <_{C(H)} f_j$ or $f_j <_{C(H)} f_i$.

The certification of every two transactions that write the same data item are ordered with respect to each other. This is because Certify Locks conflict with each other.

The proof of serializability of BT_MV2PL histories is based on two theorems by Bernstein, etal. [1]; we will present these theorems here, but omit their proofs. Furthermore, we shall use their notion of *serialization graphs*, denoted $SG(H)$ and *multi-version serialization graphs*, denoted $MVSG(H, \ll)$. In brief, a serialization graph describes transaction dependencies due to conflicting operations. In addition, a multi-version serialization graph, also describes transaction dependencies due to the ordering of versions in a multi-version system. For more details on these graphs and the omitted proofs, we refer the reader to [1].

Theorem 12. (Theorem 5.3 in [1]) *Let H be a MV history over a set of transactions T. $C(H)$ is equivalent to a serial, 1V history over T iff H is 1SR.*

Theorem 13. (Theorem 5.4 in [1]) *An MV history H is 1SR iff there exists a version order $\ll$ such that $MVSG(H, \ll)$ is acyclic.*

Theorem 14. *Every committed projection $C(H)$ of a BT history produced by a BT_MV2PL scheduler is serializable, i.e. is equivalent to a serial, 1V history.*

Proof: [4] To prove above theorem, we will show that all edges in $MVSG(C(H), \ll)$ are in certification order, i.e. if $T_i \rightarrow T_j$ in $MVSG(C(H), \ll)$, then $f_i <_{C(H)} f_j$. Because of BT_MV2PL_6, $\ll$ is indeed a version order.

Let $T_i \rightarrow T_j$ be in $SG(C(H))$, then T_j must read a version created by T_i: $r_j[x_i] \in C(H)$. By BT_MV2PL_2, we know that $c_i <_{C(H)} f_i$, and since $f_i <_{C(H)} c_i$ (by BT_MV2PL_1), it follows that $f_i <_{C(H)} f_j$.

Let $w_i[x_i], w_j[x_j], r_k[x_j] \in C(H)$, where i, j, k are distinct. Then either $x_i \ll x_j$ or $x_j \ll x_i$. If $x_i \ll x_j$, then the version order edge is $T_i \rightarrow T_j$. $f_i <_{C(H)} f_j$ follows directly from the definition of $\ll$. If $x_j \ll x_i$, then the version order edge is $T_k \rightarrow T_i$. By BT_MV2PL_3, either $c_i <_{C(H)} r_k[x_j]$ or $r_k[x_j] <_{C(H)} f_i$. In the first case, by BT_MV2PL_1, if follows that $f_i <_{C(H)} r_k[x_j]$, and then by BT_MV2PL_4 $f_i <_{C(H)} f_j$. But this contradicts $f_j <_{C(H)} r_k[x_i]$ (given by the definition of the version order), and therefore it follows that $r_k[x_j] <_{C(H)} f_i$; and since $f_j <_{C(H)} f_i$, it follows by BT_MV2PL_5 that $f_k <_{C(H)} f_i$, as desired.

We have shown that all edges in $MVSG(C(H), \ll)$ are in certification order; and since the certification is embedded in a history which is acyclic by definition, $MVSG(C(H), \ll)$ is acyclic, too. By theorems 12 and 13 it follows that $C(H)$ is equivalent to a serial 1V history. □

5 Logging and Recovery

The component of a DBMS responsible for maintaining transaction atomicity is called the *recovery manager (RM)* [5]. A RM has to write log records to disk to allow transaction roll-backs in case of transaction or system failures. To avoid excessive I/O overhead under BT, we suggest the following logging and recovery strategy. During execution of a transaction component, all updates to the database are kept as new versions of an item in main memory only; the database on disk is not updated and no log records are written. If a transaction component aborts, all data versions created by it are simply discarded; no I/O is necessary

---

[4] This proof is based on Bernstein, Hadzilacos and Goodman's proof of correctness for 2-Version 2-Phase-Locking; Theorem 5.6 in their book.

[5] An overview of existing recovery techniques can be found in [1].

for aborting transaction components. To commit a component, for each item to be written, first a log record is written and then the database is updated on disk. Assuming that log records and the database are stored on different disks, I/O to log disks and database disks can proceed in parallel (as long as for each item the log record is written before updating the database). Recovery from a system crash works as with traditional recovery techniques (see [1]). Since no log records are written until commit time — the time at which it is known which path of execution of a branching transaction is correct — logging is only required for one path of a branching transaction, and hence, the BT model does not impose any extra I/O overhead for logging on the system; in both cases, branching and non-branching, two I/O accesses (one for logging and one to update the database) are required per database update.

6 Branching Restriction Policies

If unlimited branching of transactions is allowed, the number of transaction components may grow exponentially and the system suffer from thrashing. We, therefore, need a policy to regulate the branching of transactions, a policy which will only allow transactions to branch if sufficient system resources are available. A function *branch_control* must be defined which determines whether branching should be permitted. Since BT requires primarily additional CPU time, *branch_control* may allow branching only, if the average CPU utilization is below a certain threshold x. The value to which x should be set and what other *branch_control* functions may be applied, are open questions. Simulation studies will help to clarify this issue.

In case branching of a transaction component is denied by *branch_control*, the corresponding read operation follows the (non-branching) $MV2PL$ policy as described in [1], i.e. the component tries to set a read-lock on the last committed version of the item to be read. Serializability is still maintained the same way as before (read-locks conflict with certify-locks).

Using such a policy, branching of transactions is controlled dynamically. It is adapted to the current system workload in the sense that branching is only allowed as long as enough resources are available.

7 Conclusion and Future Work

In this paper we have presented a transaction model which aims to reduce the problem of data contention in a parallel database system. Our approach takes advantage of low resource utilisation, which is frequently the result of data contention. Using a simple example we have shown the potential performance advantage of branching transactions. We also presented a two-phase locking algorithm for our new transaction model, and proved that it guarantees serializability. Although we used 2PL as a concrete example, branching transactions is a more general concept, and other algorithms, e.g. timestamp ordering, can be adapted to work with it.

More information is needed about the performance of branching transactions. In particular, we must investigate how various transaction workloads and hardware environments influence the performance of BTs. We also need a performance comparison with already existing transaction models/concurrency control algorithms. For this work, we are currently preparing a comprehensive simulation study. This study will also be used to investigate various branching restriction policies.

References

1. P.A. Bernstein, V. Hadzilacos, and N. Goodman. *Concurrency Control and Recovery in Database Systems*. Addison-Wesley, 1987.
2. D. DeWitt and J. Gray. Parallel Database Systems: The Future of High Performance Database Systems. *Communications of the ACM*, 35,6:85–98, 1992.
3. P. Franaszek and J.T. Robinson. Limitations of Concurrency in Transaction Processing. *ACM Transactions on Database Systems*, 10(1):1–28, March 1985.
4. J.N. Gray. A transaction model. In G. Goos and J. Hartmanis, editors, *Lecture Notes in Computer Science 85*, pages 282–298. Springer Verlag, Berlin, 1980.
5. B-C Jenq, B.C. Twitchell, and T.W. Keller. Locking Performance in a Shared Nothing Parallel Database Machine. *IEEE Transactions on Knowledge and Data Engineering*, 1(4):530–543, December 1989.
6. R. Reed. *Naming and Synchronization in a Decentralized Computer System*. PhD thesis, Massachusetts Institute of Technology, Cambridge, MA, 1978.

A Strategy for Semantic Integrity Enforcement in a Parallel Database Machine

Niall McCarroll, Jon Kerridge

Department of Computer Science
University of Sheffield
Regent Court, 211 Portobello Street
Sheffield S1 4DP, UK
e-mail: N.McCarroll@dcs.shef.ac.uk

Abstract. Semantic integrity constraints represent knowledge about data with which a relational database must be consistent. To enforce semantic integrity we must ensure that transactions which alter the database will preserve database consistency by accompanying each transaction with integrity tests. In this paper we address two problems. Firstly, how can we choose integrity tests that are correct and efficient? Secondly, how do we schedule and control the execution of integrity tests in the context of a parallel database machine? We use a theorem-proving method for deriving integrity tests to prove the integrity of the database which takes into account knowledge about the transaction, the partitioning strategy, and the truth of all constraints in the initial database state. Our method can derive, at schema compilation time, a range of possible sufficient or necessary tests as well as complete tests for transaction safety with respect to a constraint, and can generate separate sub-tests to independently verify changes to a section of the database. When a transaction is to be executed, tests or sub-tests are selected (from the range of alternatives generated at compile time) in order to maximise parallelism, minimise the amount of data accessed in integrity enforcement activity, and allow testing to commence as soon as possible.

1 Introduction

Static integrity constraints are an example of meta-data. Only database states which are *consistent* with the set of integrity constraints (all constraints are true) can be accurate models of the 'real world'. For a given consistent initial database state, a transaction is said to be safe if and only if the new state resulting from its execution is consistent. Integrity enforcement is carried out by ensuring that only safe transactions are executed on the database. Transaction safety is evaluated by integrity tests. Integrity tests will nearly always be much cheaper to evaluate than the original constraints because they need only search for inconsistencies arising out of alterations made by a transaction. In this paper we are not concerned with the fate of transactions found to be unsafe, but concentrate instead on finding ways of automatically generating integrity tests and of reducing the costs and delays incurred by integrity enforcement.

The context of the work is that of a scalable shared nothing parallel relational database machine, constructed using INMOS transputers. The machine provides on-line transaction processing (OLTP) services, for processing transactions and allows management information system (MIS) queries to read OLTP data [8]. We must try to keep within soft real time constraints on OLTP transaction execution time when considering how to implement semantic integrity enforcement.

This paper describes a strategy for enforcing semantic integrity in a parallel database machine. We construct integrity tests to use with a range of transaction templates, at compile time (at the time the database schema is defined). However, we do not simply insert tests into the transaction. A number of alternative (sufficient, necessary or complete) tests can often be employed to check a constraint, and so test selection and scheduling is handled separately from the management of the rest of the transaction at execution time. In particular, we propose the use of integrity sub-tests where applicable. Each sub-test independently verifies the safety of changes to a section of the database without accessing data outside that section. Sub-tests are made possible if an appropriate partitioning strategy is adopted in the database. Sub-tests allow us to exploit parallelism in integrity enforcement, minimise the amount of data that needs to be accessed and allow testing to start as soon as possible.

In section 2, previous work in this area is acknowledged. In section 3, the notation for describing partitioning information, transactions and integrity constraints is explained, and an example is given which illustrates the motivation for this work. In section 4 the methods for deriving integrity tests and sub-tests are given. In section 5 we explain in more detail how the test compiler is integrated into the DBMS architecture and how integrity tests and sub-tests are scheduled. Finally, the conclusion summarises the contribution of this work and suggests some problems which will require further investigation.

2 Previous Work

Early work by Nicolas on deriving integrity tests from constraints [13] showed the importance of the fact that the database is consistent before a transaction is executed, in the search for efficient integrity tests to prove the safety of the transaction.

Subsequent work by Henschen, McCune and Naqvi provides much of the inspiration for and starting point of this work. They present an integrity test derivation method which relies upon a theorem prover [6]. Transactions are defined by 'transaction axioms' which relate the original and updated states of relations. The transition axiom, the assertion that the constraint was satisfied in the original database state and the assertion that the constraint is not satisfied in the updated database state, form a set of clauses that are given to the theorem prover. The aim is to derive a contradiction, proving that the transaction will be safe with respect to the constraint, or a set of simplified tests on the database which may be used to prove or disprove the transaction's safety. Further work on this method has provided proof of its correctness [5] and described its application for complicated transactions [10].

Simon and Valduriez realise the importance of local testing in distributed data bases, and aim to reduce the amount of data that needs to be transferred across the network for the purposes of integrity checking [16]. Although data communication between nodes will be cheaper in a parallel database machine, reducing these costs is still an important goal.

Qian's aim is also to minimise the costs of inter-site communication by processing constraints locally as far as possible[14]. An integrity constraint C may be transformed to a set of local constraints $T_1, ..., T_n$ which are distributed to the n sites at which data referenced by C is stored. Each local constraint provides either a sufficient or a complete test of integrity for local data. If local data fails a sufficient local test, the global constraint C must be evaluated. The partitioning (horizontal or vertical) and placement of data is used in the transformation process.

Wang, Fiddian and Gray have constructed a knowledge based transaction design assistant [18] which re-writes transactions with extra operations to ensure that transaction safety is maintained.

Qian and Smith look at the advantages of deriving sematically stronger statements (which they term antecedents) from integrity constraints by the process of integrity constraint reformulation [15]. The antecedents chosen are cheaper to evaluate than the original constraints from which they are derived, and are used in place of the original constraint until it is found that they have to be withdrawn (the antecedent fails but the original constraint remains true).

Gupta and Widom also consider localising integrity tests for changes to partitions to just the contents of the partition itself [4]. They present an algorithm to generate 'local constraints'.

Grefen and Flokstra investigate the checking of integrity constraints within the parallel database machine PRISMA, and recognise the importance of localising constraint testing in order to reduce the workload imposed by integrity checking [3]. They term the execution of complete local tests as implicit constraint enforcement. In cases where no local testing can be carried out, the enforcement must be explicit - with testing being handled by global queries. An interesting case here is that of hybrid enforcement, with sufficient local tests being used to verify some changes and the remainder of the changes being verified by global tests.

We will describe integrity constraints, partitioning rules and properties of transactions using the class of function free predicate logic formulae with equality which have the range restricted property and are thus 'useful' in the database context [13] [2]. We use the following precedence ordering (from highest to lowest) where parenthesis are omitted: $\neg, \wedge, \vee, \Leftrightarrow, \Leftarrow, \Rightarrow, \forall_{var-list}, \exists_{var-list}$.

3 Notation and Motivating Example

3.1 Example Database

Consider a simple bank database comprising two relations, ACC which stores information on individual accounts, and AUTH which relates the bank's customers to the accounts to which they are authorised access.

$$\text{ACC(acc-nr, balance, limit)} \qquad \text{AUTH(cust-nr, acc-nr)}$$

The account number (acc-nr) is the primary key for the ACC relation. The balance attribute records the current balance of the account, while the limit attribute holds the authorised overdraft limit. The AUTH relation relates customers identified by their customer number (cust-nr) to the account numbers (acc-nr) for accounts to which they have authorised access. The set of database relations is termed DB, and will be the set {ACC,AUTH} in our example.

3.2 Data Partitioning and Placement

The strategy adopted for data partitioning in the context of this work is horizontal partitioning [17]. Assume that each relation R is partitioned into N partitions $R_1, ..., R_N$. $R_{\neg i}$ denotes the relation formed by the union of all partitions of relation R other than partition R_i. For a relation R, the partitioning strategy used can be described by a set of partitioning rules P(R), with the general form:

$$\forall \bar{v} \; R_i(\bar{v}) \Leftrightarrow R(\bar{v}) \wedge \text{some-condition}_i(\bar{v})$$

In the example we choose the following partitioning strategy:

Range partition ACC on primary key (acc-nr):
$P(ACC) \equiv \bigcup_{i=1}^{N}$
$\{ \; \forall x,y,z \; ACC_i(x,y,z) \Leftrightarrow (ACC(x,y,z) \wedge ((i-1)*100000) \leq x < (i*100000)) \; \}$

Range partition AUTH on the (acc-nr) attribute:
$P(AUTH) \equiv \bigcup_{i=1}^{N}$
$\{ \; \forall x,y \; AUTH_i(x,y) \Leftrightarrow (AUTH(x,y) \wedge ((i-1)*100000) \leq y < (i*100000)) \; \}$

We can also infer additional information from these rules, for instance:

$\forall x,y \; AUTH_i(x,y) \Rightarrow \neg \exists v,w \; ACC_{\neg i}(y,v,w)$

$\forall x,y \ AUTH(x,y) \Leftrightarrow AUTH_i(x,y) \vee AUTH_{\neg i}(x,y)$

$\forall x,y,z \ ACC(x,y,z) \Leftrightarrow ACC_i(x,y,z) \vee ACC_{\neg i}(x,y,z)$

$\forall x1,y1,z1,x2,y2,z2 \ ACC_i(x1,y1,z1) \wedge ACC_{\neg i}(x2,y2,z2) \Rightarrow x1 \neq x2$

We divide the database logically into N disjoint sections which we term *regions*. The ith region contains the ith partition of each relation in DB. We also define region $\neg i$ as the part of the database not contained in region i. So for the example database:

region $i = \{ACC_i, AUTH_i\}$
region $\neg i = \{ACC_{\neg i}, AUTH_{\neg i}\}$

In this paper make the assumption that updates to partitions comply with partitioning rules - the responsibility for ensuring this is outside the jurisdiction of the semantic integrity enforcement system.

3.3 Integrity Constraints

We adopt the set $\{C1,C2,C3,C4\}$ of integrity constraints for the example database.

Key Constraint: Each account must have a unique account number:
$C1 \equiv \forall x,y1,z1,y2,z2 \ ACC(x,y1,z1) \wedge ACC(x,y2,z2) \Rightarrow (y1 = y2 \wedge z1 = z2)$

Referential constraint, customers may only have access to registered accounts:
$C2 \equiv \forall x,y \ AUTH(x,y) \Rightarrow (\exists v,w \ ACC(y,v,w))$

An account cannot be overdrawn beyond the authorised limit:
$C3 \equiv \forall x,y,z \ ACC(x,y,z) \Rightarrow (y \geq z)$

No more than two customers may access an account:
$C4 \equiv \forall v,x,y,z \ AUTH(x,y) \wedge AUTH(z,y) \wedge AUTH(v,y) \Rightarrow (x=z \vee x=v \vee z=v)$

3.4 Transactions

Changes to the database are made by transactions. The set of tuples inserted into (deleted from) the relation R by a transaction is denoted ΔR (∇R). We have the property $\nabla R \subseteq R$.

Each transaction T can apply one of four basic operations to each relation in the database. If tuples can only added to (respectively, only deleted from) a relation or partition R by T, we refer to this as an R^{Δ} operation (respectively an R^{∇} operation). If both insertions and deletions can be made to R (respectively, no changes are made) by T, this is an $R^{\diamond}$ operation (respectively, an $R^{\square}$ operation).

Each operation is defined by a logical statement relating the pre-transaction and post-transaction states of relation or partition (respectively denoted R and R') and the sets ΔR and ∇R. If R is an n-ary relation, $\bar{v}$ is a vector of n variables, then each operation is defined as a logic formula:

$R^\Delta \equiv (\forall \bar{v}\ R'(\bar{v}) \Leftrightarrow R(\bar{v}) \vee \Delta R(\bar{v}))$

$R^\nabla \equiv (\forall \bar{v}\ R'(\bar{v}) \Leftrightarrow R(\bar{v}) \wedge \neg\ \nabla R(\bar{v})) \wedge (\forall \bar{v}\ \nabla R(\bar{v}) \Rightarrow R(\bar{v}))$

$R^\diamond \equiv (\forall \bar{v}\ R'(\bar{v}) \Leftrightarrow ((R(\bar{v}) \wedge \neg\ \nabla R(\bar{v})) \vee \Delta R(\bar{v})) \wedge (\forall \bar{v}\ \nabla R(\bar{v}) \Rightarrow R(\bar{v}))$

$R^\square \equiv (\forall \bar{v}\ R'(\bar{v}) \Leftrightarrow R(\bar{v}))$

A transaction T is described logically by a set TF(T) of transaction formulae. For every database relation R in DB, TF(T) will contain either formula $R^\diamond$, R^∇, R^Δ or $R^\square$ depending on the potential effects T may have on R. In addition, TF(T) can contain formulae ranging over database relations and their Δ- and ∇-sets which describe the transaction in more detail. The transaction formulae for two example transactions {T1,T2} are given below.

T1: Insert tuples into both AUTH and ACC relations:
$TF(T1) \equiv \{\ AUTH^\Delta,\ ACC^\Delta\ \}$

T2: Modify the balance of account A:
$TF(T2) \equiv \{\ AUTH^\square,\ ACC^\diamond,\ \forall x,y,z\ \Delta ACC(x,y,z) \Rightarrow x=A,$
$\qquad \forall x,y,z\ \Delta ACC(x,y,z) \Rightarrow \exists v\ \nabla ACC(x,v,z),$
$\qquad \forall x,y,z\ \nabla ACC(x,y,z) \Rightarrow \exists v\ \Delta ACC(x,v,z)\ \}$

Note that the transaction formulae will present a partial rather than a full specification of the effects of the transaction.

3.5 I-Tests

Integrity tests (I-Tests) are used to prove the safety of changes made by a transaction. An I-Test is specific to a transaction T and constraint C, and is either a complete test denoted $C_{comp}(T)$, a sufficient test denoted $C_{suff}(T)$, or a necessary test, denoted $C_{nece}(T)$. A complete test will indicate the safety of changes. Sufficient and necessary tests are related to complete tests in the following way:

$$(C_{suff}(T) \Rightarrow C_{comp}(T)) \wedge (\neg C_{nece}(T) \Rightarrow \neg C_{comp}(T))$$

I-Tests will be generally simpler than the original constraint, because we know that the constraint will be satisfied before the transaction is executed. I-Tests can range over pre- and post- transaction relation states and the Δ- and ∇- sets. I-Tests for the example transactions and constraints are listed in Table 1.

Table 1: Integrity Tests for Example Constraint Set and Transactions	
I-Test	Expression
$C1_{comp}(T1)$	$\forall x,y,z,v,w \; \Delta ACC(x,y,z) \wedge ACC'(x,v,w) \Rightarrow (y=v \wedge z=w)$
$C1_{nece}(T1)$	$\forall x,y,z,v,w \; \Delta ACC(x,y,z) \wedge \Delta ACC(x,v,w) \Rightarrow (y=v \wedge z=w)$
$C2_{comp}(T1)$	$\forall x,y \; \Delta AUTH(x,y) \Rightarrow \exists v,w \; ACC'(y,v,w)$
$C2_{suff}(T1)$	$\forall w,x \; \Delta AUTH(w,x) \Rightarrow \exists v \; AUTH(v,x)$
$C3_{comp}(T1)$	$\forall x,y,z \; \Delta ACC(x,y,z) \Rightarrow y \geq z$
$C4_{comp}(T1)$	$\forall x,y \; \Delta AUTH(x,y) \Rightarrow$ $\neg \; (\exists v,w \; AUTH'(v,y) \wedge AUTH'(w,y) \wedge x \neq v \wedge x \neq w \wedge v \neq w \;)$
$C4_{nece}(T1)$	$\forall x,y \; \Delta AUTH(x,y) \Rightarrow$ $\neg \; (\exists v,w \; \Delta AUTH(v,y) \wedge \Delta AUTH(w,y) \wedge x \neq v \wedge x \neq w \wedge v \neq w \;)$
$C1_{comp}(T2)$	TRUE
$C2_{comp}(T2)$	TRUE
$C3_{comp}(T2)$	$\forall x,y,z \; \Delta ACC(x,y,z) \Rightarrow y \geq z$
$C4_{comp}(T2)$	TRUE

3.6 I-SubTests

Once an integrity test (I-Test) has been formulated it can possibly be divided into a number of independent integrity sub-tests (I-SubTests) using knowledge about how relations are partitioned in the database, where each I-SubTest proves the consistency of changes to a specific region and *each I-SubTest accesses data from its own region only*. A complete, sufficient or necessary I-SubTest for constraint C, transaction T and region i is written, respectively, $C^i_{comp}(T)$, $C^i_{suff}(T)$ or $C^i_{nece}(T)$. In table 2, some integrity SubTests are listed which may be employed to test the safety of transaction T1. Note that the partitioning strategy chosen means that no complete SubTest for transaction T1 and constraint C4 can be constructed.

Table 2: Integrity SubTests for Example Constraints and Transaction T1	
I-SubTest	Expression
$C1^i_{comp}(T1)$	$\forall x,y,z,v,w \; \Delta ACC_i(x,y,z) \wedge ACC'_i(x,v,w) \Rightarrow (y=v \wedge z=w)$
$C2^i_{comp}(T1)$	$\forall x,y \; \Delta AUTH_i(x,y) \Rightarrow \exists v,w \; ACC'_i(y,v,w)$
$C2^i_{suff}(T1)$	$\forall w,x \; \Delta AUTH_i(w,x) \Rightarrow \exists v \; AUTH_i(v,x)$
$C3^i_{comp}(T1)$	$\forall x,y,z \; \Delta ACC_i(x,y,z) \Rightarrow y \geq z$

If an I-Test can be divided into a set of I-SubTests, then rather than issuing a single I-Test once modifications have been carried out, we may issue an I-SubTest immediately whenever alterations to a specific region have been completed. By employing I-SubTests, we are also minimising the portion of the database which needs to be accessed to check the safety of changes.

4 Generating Integrity Tests and SubTests

I-Tests and I-SubTests are generated at compile time in two main stages. The first stage is closely based on the method of Henschen, McCune and Naqvi [6], [12]. We aim to derive I-Tests for a pair of constraint C and transaction T, using the set of transaction formulae TF(T) and the fact that all constraints in the database are satisfied prior to transaction execution. In the second stage, we attempt to identify I-SubTests for an I-Test by considering the partitioning rules.

4.1 Stage 1: Deriving I-Tests

Consider the example constraint C2 and transaction T1 (which inserts tuples into the ACC relation). How do we derive integrity tests? We attempt to infer a contradiction from the assertion A that the constraint will be false after the database has been updated, using clauses representing the truth of relevant integrity constraints prior to database updates, and the transaction's effects, as a set-of-support.

We use the set of support clauses as the truth of C2 prior to T1's execution (clause 1) and the transaction formulae TF(T1) (clauses 2 - 7).

(1) $\neg$AUTH(x,y) $\vee$ ACC(y,f1(y),f2(y))
(2) $\neg$ACC(x,y,z) $\vee$ ACC'(x,y,z)
(3) $\neg\Delta$ACC(x,y,z) $\vee$ ACC'(x,y,z)
(4) $\neg$ACC'(x,y,z) $\vee$ ACC(x,y,z) $\vee$ ΔACC(x,y,z)
(5) $\neg$AUTH(x,y) $\vee$ AUTH'(x,y)
(6) $\neg\Delta$AUTH(x,y) $\vee$ AUTH'(x,y)
(7) $\neg$AUTH'(x,y) $\vee$ AUTH(x,y) $\vee$ ΔAUTH(x,y)

The set of input clauses will be the assertion A:

(8a)   AUTH'(a,b)
(8b) $\neg$ACC'(b,x,y)

Using an acceptable deletion strategy [1], we infer all possible clauses.

(9)(2,8b) $\neg$ACC(b,x,y)
(10)(3,8b) $\neg\Delta$ACC(b,x,y)
(11)(8a,7) AUTH(a,b) $\vee$ ΔAUTH(a,b)
(12)(1,9) $\neg$AUTH(x,b)

Clauses 8a and 8b can be deleted from the set, as they are derivable from 9,10,11. We then continue:

(13)(11,1) $\triangle$AUTH(a,b) $\vee$ ACC(b,f1(b),f2(b))
(14)(12,11) $\triangle$AUTH(a,b)

Because (14) subsumes (13) and (11), (13) and (11) can be deleted. (12) is redundant with (9,1) and can be deleted. We then unskolemise [11] the remaining clauses (9),(10),(14) to obtain the predicate logic formula:

$\exists x,y \ \forall v,w \ \triangle$AUTH(x,y) $\wedge \neg$ ACC(y,v,w) $\wedge \neg \triangle$ACC(y,v,w)

This is negated to form integrity test $C2_{comp}(T1)$:

$\forall x,y \ \triangle$AUTH(x,y) $\Rightarrow (\exists v,w$ ACC(y,v,w) $\vee \triangle$ACC(y,v,w))

This is equivalent to $\forall x,y \ \triangle$AUTH(x,y) $\Rightarrow \exists v,w$ ACC'(y,v,w)

According to Henschen et. al's method [12] we can turn any subset S of the inferred clauses into a sufficient test if S can be unskolemised into a range restricted formula F (which is negated to produce the test). A sufficient test in this case is derived by undeleting clause (12) and combining with (14), by first unskolemising to obtain:

$\exists x,y \ \triangle$AUTH(x,y) $\wedge (\forall z \ \neg$AUTH(z,y))

This formula is then negated to obtain $C2_{suff}(T1)$:

$\forall x,y \ \triangle$AUTH(x,y) $\Rightarrow$ ($\exists z$ AUTH(z,y))

We can also generate necessary tests by unskolemising all clauses (but first omitting one or more disjuncts).

If at this stage we infer a contradiction, then we've proved that the transaction cannot invalidate the constraint. This is the case in our example when we consider constraints C1,C2 and C4 and transaction T2. In such cases the resulting I-Test is simply 'TRUE'.

4.2   Stage 2: Identifying I-SubTests

Suppose we have an I-Test $C_{comp}(T)$, which references either or both of $\triangle R$ and $\triangledown R$, where R is some database relation. We can attempt to construct an I-SubTest $C^i_{comp}(T)$ to check the alterations made to region i by T. The I-SubTest for region i will have the same structure as the original test, except that it will range over the partitions in region i rather than over whole database relations.

We must prove that: $(\bigwedge_{i=1}^{N} C^i_{comp}(T)) \Leftrightarrow C_{comp}(T)$

We therefore propose two candidate I-SubTests, the first to check changes to region i, the second to check all the changes to the rest of the database (region $\neg i$). These are obtained by replacing all instances of R, R', $\triangle$R and $\triangledown$R for each relation R in the original I-Test formula F by R_i, R_i', $\triangle R_i$ and $\triangledown R_i$ to produce the first SubTest ST_i, and by $R_{\neg i}$, $R_{\neg i}$', $\triangle R_{\neg i}$ and $\triangledown R_{\neg i}$ to produce the second

SubTest $ST_{\neg i}$. We then attempt to show that $ST_i \wedge ST_{\neg i}$ is equivalent to the original test F by proving that:

$\neg$ F $\wedge$ ST_i $\wedge$ $ST_{\neg i}$ is inconsistent (sufficiency criteria)

F $\wedge$ $\neg(ST_i \wedge ST_{\neg i})$ is inconsistent (necessity criteria)

The theorem prover then attempts to find a contradiction for each assertion expressed in clause form. For the set-of-support, we use the extended transaction formulae describing the transaction T and the assertion that the partitioning rules will be satisfied in the updated database. The extended transaction formulae ETF(T) describe the effects of transaction T on partitions R_i and $R_{\neg i}$, as well as on R as a whole. Each formulae of type $R^\square$, $R^\triangle$, $R^\triangledown$ and $R^\diamond$ in TF(T) generates a set of formulae to be added to ETF(T) according to table 3.

Table 3: Deriving Extended Transaction Formulae (ETF)	
Formula from TF(T)	Formulae to be added to ETF(T)
$R^\square$	$\{R_i^\square, R_{\neg i}^\square\}$
$R^\triangle$	$\{R_i^\triangle, R_{\neg i}^\triangle, \forall \bar{v}\ \triangle R(\bar{v}) \Leftrightarrow \triangle R_i(\bar{v}) \vee \triangle R_{\neg i}(\bar{v})\}$
$R^\triangledown$	$\{R_i^\triangledown, R_{\neg i}^\triangledown, \forall \bar{v}\ \triangledown R(\bar{v}) \Leftrightarrow \triangledown R_i(\bar{v}) \vee \triangledown R_{\neg i}(\bar{v})\}$
$R^\diamond$	$\{R_i^\diamond, R_{\neg i}^\diamond, \forall \bar{v}\ \triangledown R(\bar{v}) \Leftrightarrow \triangledown R_i(\bar{v}) \vee \triangledown R_{\neg i}(\bar{v}),$ $\forall \bar{v}\ \triangle R(\bar{v}) \Leftrightarrow \triangle R_i(\bar{v}) \vee \triangle R_{\neg i}(\bar{v})\}$

To illustrate this method, consider again the example test $C2_{comp}(T1)$ as the candidate formula F for division into SubTests:

$F \equiv \forall x,y\ \triangle AUTH(x,y) \Rightarrow \exists v,w\ ACC'(y,v,w)$

The two candidate I-SubTests are:

$ST_i \equiv \forall x,y\ \triangle AUTH_i(x,y) \Rightarrow (\exists v,w\ ACC_i(y,v,w) \vee \triangle ACC_i(y,v,w))$

$ST_{\neg i} \equiv \forall x,y\ \triangle AUTH_{\neg i}(x,y) \Rightarrow (\exists v,w\ ACC_{\neg i}(y,v,w) \vee \triangle ACC_{\neg i}(y,v,w))$

The relevant set-of-support clauses will represent the extended transaction formulae ETF(T1) (clauses A-G) and clauses representing the truth of the partitioning rules in the updated database state (clauses H-L):

(A) $\neg \triangle AUTH(x,y)$ $\vee\ \triangle AUTH_i(x,y)$ $\vee\ \triangle AUTH_{\neg i}(x,y)$
(B) $\neg \triangle AUTH_i(x,y)$ $\vee\ \triangle AUTH(x,y)$
(C) $\neg \triangle AUTH_{\neg i}(x,y)$ $\vee\ \triangle AUTH(x,y)$
(D) $\triangle ACC(x,y,z)$ $\vee\ \neg \triangle ACC_i(x,y,z)$
(E) $\triangle ACC(x,y,z)$ $\vee\ \neg \triangle ACC_{\neg i}(x,y,z)$
(F) $\neg \triangle AUTH_i(x,y)$ $\vee\ AUTH_i'(x,y)$
(G) $\neg \triangle AUTH_{\neg i}(x,y)$ $\vee\ AUTH_{\neg i}'(x,y)$

(H) $ACC(x,y,z)$ $\vee\ \neg ACC_i(x,y,z)$
(I) $ACC(x,y,z)$ $\vee\ \neg ACC_{\neg i}(x,y,z)$

(J)　　　　　¬ACC'(x,y,z)　　　∨ ACC$_i$'(x,y,z)　　　∨ ACC$_{\neg i}$'(x,y,z)
(K)　　　　　¬AUTH$_i$'(x,y)　　∨ ¬ACC$_{\neg i}$'(y,v,w)
(L)　　　　　¬AUTH$_{\neg i}$'(x,y)　∨ ¬ACC$_i$'(y,v,w)

To test for sufficiency, the input clauses represent ¬F (1,2,3), ST$_i$ (4) and ST$_{\neg i}$ (5):

(1)　　　　　△AUTH(a,b)
(2)　　　　　¬ ACC(b,v,w)
(3)　　　　　¬ △ACC(b,v,w)
(4)　　　　　ACC$_i$(y,f(y),g(y))　　∨ △ACC$_i$(y,f(y),g(y))　∨ ¬△AUTH$_i$(x,y)
(5)　　　　　ACC$_{\neg i}$(y,f(y),g(y))　∨ △ACC$_{\neg i}$(y,f(y),g(y))　∨ ¬△AUTH$_{\neg i}$(x,y)

(6)(1,A)　　△AUTH$_i$(a,b)　　∨ △AUTH$_{\neg i}$(a,b)
(7)(2,H)　　¬ ACC$_i$(b,v,w)
(8)(2,I)　　 ¬ ACC$_{\neg i}$(b,v,w)
(9)(3,D)　　¬ △ACC$_i$(b,v,w)
(10)(3,E)　　¬ △ACC$_{\neg i}$(b,v,w)
(11)(4,7)　　△ACC$_i$(b,f(b),g(b))　∨ ¬ △AUTH$_i$(x,b)
(12)(11,9)　¬ △AUTH$_i$(x,b)
(13)(5,8)　　△ACC$_{\neg i}$(b,f(b),g(b))∨ ¬ △AUTH$_{\neg i}$(x,b)
(14)(13,10)　¬ △AUTH$_{\neg i}$(x,b)
(15)(14,6)　△AUTH$_i$(x,b)
(16)(15,12)　□

To test for necessity, the input clauses represent F (1) and ¬ST$_i$ ∨ ¬ST$_{\neg i}$ (2,3,4):

(1)　　　　　¬△AUTH(x,y)　　∨ ACC'(y,f(y),g(y))
(2)　　　　　△AUTH$_i$(a,b)　　∨ △AUTH$_{\neg i}$(a,b)
(3)　　　　　¬ ACC$_i$'(b,x,y)　　∨ ¬ △AUTH$_i$(a,b)
(4)　　　　　¬ ACC$_{\neg i}$'(b,x,y)　∨ ¬ △AUTH$_{\neg i}$(a,b)

(6)(1,J)　　ACC$_{\neg i}$'(y,f(y),g(y))　∨ ACC$_i$'(y,f(y),g(y))　∨ ¬△AUTH(x,y)
(7)(6,B)　　ACC$_{\neg i}$'(y,f(y),g(y))　∨ ACC$_i$'(y,f(y),g(y))　∨ ¬△AUTH$_i$(x,y)
(8)(6,C)　　ACC$_{\neg i}$'(y,f(y),g(y))　∨ ACC$_i$'(y,f(y),g(y))　∨ ¬△AUTH$_{\neg i}$(x,y)
(9)(7,3)　　¬△AUTH$_i$(x,b)　　∨ ACC$_{\neg i}$'(b,f(b),g(b))
(10)(8,4)　　¬△AUTH$_{\neg i}$(x,b)　∨ ACC$_i$'(y,f(b),g(b))
(11)(9,K)　　¬△AUTH$_i$(x,b)　　∨ ¬ AUTH$_i$'(v,b)
(12)(10,L)　¬△AUTH$_{\neg i}$(x,b)　∨ ¬ AUTH$_{\neg i}$'(v,b)
(13)(11,F)　¬△AUTH$_i$(x,b)
(14)(12,G)　¬△AUTH$_{\neg i}$(x,b)
(15)(14,2)　△AUTH$_i$(a,b)
(16)(15,13)　□

We have proved that the SubTest proposed will be suitable - the effects of transaction T1 on region i can be checked for consistency with constraint C2 using the SubTest:

$C2^i_{comp}(T1) \equiv \forall x,y \; \triangle AUTH_i(x,y) \Rightarrow (\exists v,w \; ACC_i'(y,v,w))$

We can also derive SubTests which are sufficient or necessary rather than complete. A sufficient SubTest is derivied from a sufcient or complete original test and must meet the sufficiency criteria. A necessary SubTest is derived from a necessary or complete original test, and must meet the necessity criteria. For example, a necessary SubTest for C4 and T1 can be constructed, based on the original test $C4_{comp}(T1)$. This SubTest meets the necessity criteria but not the sufficiency criteria.

$C4^i_{nece}(T1) \equiv \forall x,y \; \triangle AUTH_i(x,y) \Rightarrow$
$\quad \neg \; (\exists v,w \; AUTH'_i(v,y) \wedge AUTH'_i(w,y) \wedge x \neq v \wedge x \neq w \wedge v \neq w \;)$

5 Controlling Test Execution

At database schema compilation time (compile time) we wish to create integrity test templates to deal with 'transaction templates' (generic transactions). We would construct transaction templates describing all predefined transactions that we anticipate will be used on the database, and also some very basic templates (detailing different combinations of inserts/deletes and modifications to relations) with which we can try to match any 'ad hoc' (unanticipated) transactions on the database (though basic templates may, admittedly, not describe important properties of such transactions). The transaction template contains the code for the transaction, plus the transaction formulae which declaratively describe some of its properties.

We assign the task of finding test templates to a DBMS component called the Test/SubTest Compiler. Each pair of transaction template and constraint are retrieved from libraries which form part of the database's data dictionary, and a range of suitable I-Test and I-SubTest templates are generated and placed in the Test Template Library using the methods described in the preceeding section. Fig. 1 shows the essential processes and flows of information involved in compiling integrity tests and appending them to transactions.

At run time, when a DBMS user requests transaction execution, the name of a predefined transaction and the required parameters (or the specification of an 'ad hoc' transaction) are supplied to the run time preprocessor. This component retrieves the transaction template and relevant test templates from libraries, subsitutes any parameters for generic values and performs any simplifications that are made possible as a result. The run time preprocessor delivers the transaction and tests ready to be executed.

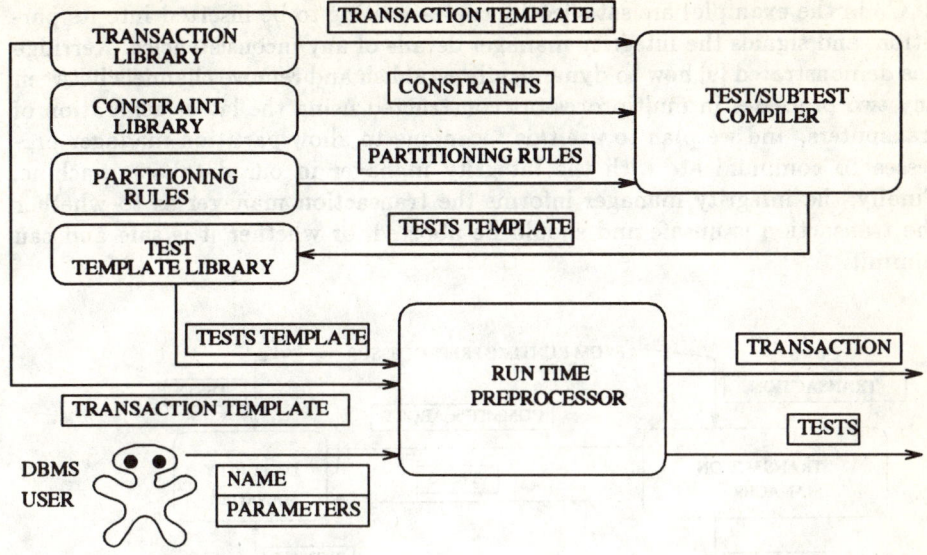

Fig. 1: A Framework for Generating Integrity Tests For Transactions

The transaction is passed from the run time preprocessor to a transaction manager process which is allocated to control the execution of the transaction on the database. The test portion is sent to an integrity manager process which is allocated to prove or disprove the safety of the transaction. Fig. 2 illustrates the processes involved in executing the transaction and associated tests. Both transaction manager and integrity manager use the facilities provided by the database's processing subsystem, which executes logically formulated queries or update operations which range over relations or specific partitions.

Partitions are held in a logically separate part of the database - the storage subsystem, and tuple streams carry relevant data to the processing subsystem and return data to be written back to partitions. Each partition is managed by a partition manager process. Note that a number of transaction and integrity manager processes will be handling different transactions at the same time - in Fig. 2 we show only one transaction executing. Consideration of concurrency control and recovery facilities are outside the scope of this paper, except to say that integrity tests must be subject to the same concurrency control procedure as normal read operations.

When a partition has been altered, the partition manager signals the integrity manager to indicate the type of alteration (insert,delete or modify). In response, the integrity manager can schedule the appropriate I-SubTests to prove the safety of the alterations to specific region or I-Tests to verify changes to the database as a whole. The integrity manager must choose between various sufficient, necessary or complete I-Tests and I-SubTests in order to check a constraint. The partition manager will be given responsiblty for checking that 'simple' constraints (such as C3 in the example) are satisfied by tuples waiting to be inserted into its partition, and signals the integrity manager details of any inconsistencies. Kerridge has demonstrated [9] how to dynamically establish and remove channels between any two processes in multiprocessors constructed using the latest generation of transputers, and we plan to use this technique to allow partition manager processes to communicate with the integrity manager in our database machine. Finally, the integrity manager informs the transaction manager as to whether the transaction is unsafe and should be aborted, or whether it is safe and can commit.

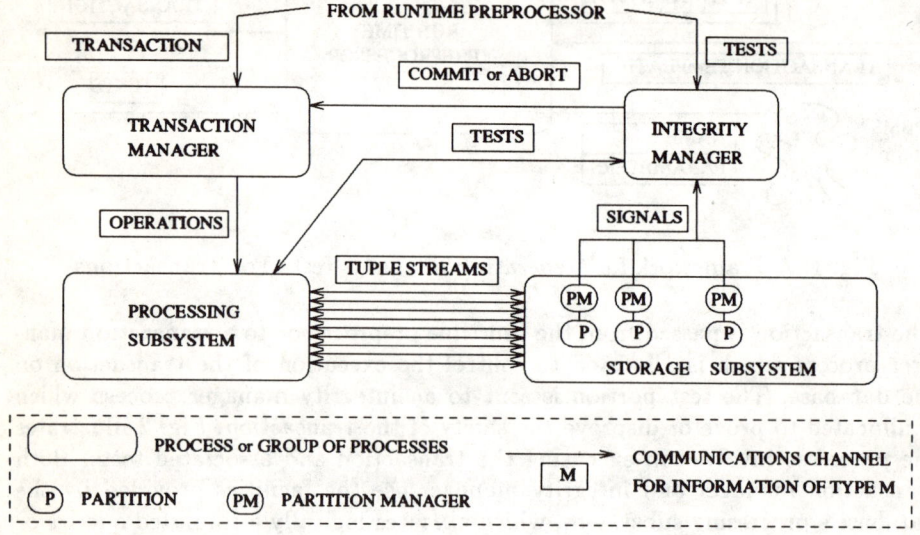

Fig. 2: Controlling Integrity Test Execution

The advantages of using integrity SubTests (rather than by just allowing the processing subsystem to optimally organise joins using the partitioning rules anyway) lie in the fact that a SubTest can begin execution as soon as changes to a region have completed, that SubTests only need to be executed when a region is actually changed, and that different types of SubTests (sufficient or complete, for example) can be issued in different regions according to the circumstances in each region (for instance, what parts of the region are locked by other transactions). Our methods allow *fine grained* and *dynamic* control of semantic integrity enforcement.

6 Conclusions and Future Work

A method has been presented which derives integrity tests for a transaction, given the details of a set of integrity constraints, the transaction being considered and the partitioning strategy adopted in the database. Integrity tests may be either complete, sufficient or necessary.

The novel feature of our method is the automatic division of integrity tests into SubTests (if the partitioning strategy allows). SubTests, which independently investigate the safety of changes to disjoint sections of the database, are useful because their execution can commence as soon as the changes to the partitions have been defined. This allows us to commence integrity testing as soon as possible. Using SubTests also allows us to minimise the amount of data that needs to be accessed to verify integrity, by ignoring irrelevant partitions, and maximise parallelism. We believe that the use of SubTests is essential if we wish to build scalable transaction processing systems which offer support for integrity constraints. Further investigation is required to study how optimal partitioning strategies (which enable SubTests to be used) can be decided. We are currently fine-tuning the Test/SubTest compiler (which has been implemented in PROLOG).

We consider that an important aim is to reduce the amount of data which needs to be accessed in integrity testing. Further work is required to formalise the order in which we apply various types (sufficent,complete,necessary) of available tests, by considering the tests' respective costs and accuracies. We expect to estimate these costs and accuracies by monitoring the database during a trial period in which we try different testing strategies.

We outlined a DBMS architecture incorporating a semantic integrity subsytem which enables the dynamic selection of tests from a range of alternatives according to the progress of a transaction, preceeding test results, and the current workload on the database. Each transaction is associated with an integrity manager process, which coordinates the execution of tests. We are currently extending the prototype parallel database system IDIOMS [7] with integrity enforcement facilities, in order to gain some practical insights into the usefulness of our approach.

Acknowledgements

This research has been supported by a SERC studentship.

References

1. C Chang and R C Lee. *Symbolic Logic and Mechanical Theorem Proving.* Academic Press, 1973.
2. A Van Gelder and R W Topor. Safety and the correct translation of relational calculus formulas. In *Proceedings of the 6th ACM PODS*, pages 313–327, 1987.
3. P W P J Grefen and J Flokstra. Parallel handling of integrity constraints. In *Parallel Database Systems, Proceedings of the Prisma Workshop, Noordwijk*, pages 242–258, 1990.

4. A Gupta and J Widom. Local verification of global integrity constraints in distributed databases. In *Proceedings, 1993 ACM SIGMOD*, pages 49–58, 1993.
5. L J Henschen and W W McCune. Maintaining state constraints in relational databases: A proof theoretic basis. *Journal of the ACM*, 36(1):46–68, jan 1989.
6. L J Henschen, W W McCune, and S A Naqvi. Compiling constraint-checking programs from first order formulas. In *Advances in Database Theory Volume II*, pages 145–169. Plenum Press, 1984.
7. J M Kerridge. The design of the idioms parallel database machine. In *Proceedings of the 9th British National Conference on Databases*, pages 128–147, 1991.
8. J M Kerridge. The implementation of large parallel database machines on T9000 and C104 networks. In *Networks, Routers and Transputers: Function, Performance and Application*, pages 133–149. IOS Press, 1993.
9. J M Kerridge. Dynamic allocation of processes and channels in T9000/C104 networks using occam3. In *Proceedings of the 17th World occam and Transputer User Group (WoTUG) Technical Meeting*, 1994.
10. S H Lee, L J Henschen, M H Kim, and Y Lee. Enforcement of integrity constraints against transactions with transition axioms. In *Proceedings, COMPSAC'92*, pages 162–167, 1992.
11. W W McCune. Un-skolemising clause sets. *Information Processing Letters*, 29(5):257–263, 1988.
12. W W McCune and L J Henschen. Maintaining state constraints in relational databases: A proof theoretic basis. *Journal of the Association for Computing Machinery*, 36(1):46–67, 1989.
13. J M Nicolas. Logic for improving integrity checking in relational databases. *Acta Informatica*, 18:227–253, 1982.
14. X Qian. Distribution design of integrity constraints. In *2nd International Conference on Expert Database Systems*, pages 205–226, 1989.
15. X Qian and D R Smith. Integrity constraint reformulation for efficient validation. In *Proceedings of the 13th VLDB*, pages 417–425, 1987.
16. E Simon and P Valduriez. Integrity control in distributed database systems. In *Proceedings of the 19th Hawaii International Conference on System Sciences*, pages 622–632, 1986.
17. M Unwalla and J M Kerridge. Control of a large massively parallel database machine using SQL catalogue extensions and a DSDL in preference to an operating system. In *Proceedings of the 10th British National Conference on Databases*, pages 138–155, 1992.
18. X Y Wang, N J Fiddian, and W A Gray. The development of a knowledge based transaction design assistant. In *Proceedings, Database and Expert Systems Applications (DEXA'91)*, pages 356–361, 1991.

On Interface Objects In Object-Oriented Databases

Norman W Paton, Ghassan al-Qaimari and Khoa Doan

Department of Computing and Electrical Engineering,
Heriot-Watt University
Riccarton, Edinburgh EH14 4AS, Scotland, UK
e-mail: < norm,ghassan,vibama>@cee.hw.ac.uk
phone: +44-31-449-5111 ; fax: +44-31-451-3431

Abstract. This paper describes an approach to the support of interface objects in an object-oriented database, and outlines some of the consequences of representing interface data as database objects. Existing architectures for implementing database interfaces are reviewed, and certain shortcomings identified, which essentially stem from an impedance mismatch between the database and its interface. It is shown how an existing graphical component set can be cleanly and transparently integrated with an existing object-oriented database, thereby removing the above impedance mismatch and providing persistent graphical data. This interface can then be used to implement generic, tailorable and application-specific interface concepts, each of which is exemplified in the paper.

1 Introduction

It has been recognised for some time that interfaces to databases lag behind certain other areas of database technology in terms of their maturity [1]. To remedy this situation it will be necessary for progress to be made in two distinct but complementary areas:

- The development of visual languages and systems which enhance the usability of database systems for all activities associated with an installation – querying, schema design, data modification, schema evolution, application development, data entry and database administration.

- The development of effective tools for the implementation of database interfaces, which as well as easing the implementation of the types of system mentioned above, facilitate the development of application-specific interfaces and the tailoring of system-supported tools.

Most recent research into database interfaces focuses upon the first of these areas, but the absence of effective, fully integrated tools for the development of database interfaces has limited the number of systems developed which embrace the full range of interface requirements associated with database systems.

This paper is concerned principally with the second of the areas identified above, namely the production of tools for database interface development. The particular focus of this paper is on using the database to implement its own interface – the close integration of tools for interface development with the database system is consistent with the long-term trend in database systems towards more of the functionality of an application being supported within the database system itself. For example, deductive databases integrate an inference mechanism with a relational data store, and persistent programming languages integrate imperative programming constructs with database storage managers. In each of these cases, the fully integrated approach is seen to be superior to the coupling of pre-existing components, as no impedance mismatch is introduced.

When interfaces to databases are developed, it is common for a new form of impedance mismatch to be introduced. The interface to the database is written using a user interface management system (UIMS) or graphical component set, in a program which subsequently calls out to the database system in order to access and store data. This leads to the following problems:

1. Graphical data manipulated by the interface cannot be stored directly in the database. This means that graphical information, such as a schema diagram which has been laid out by the user, must be mapped by the programmer onto the structures of the underlying data model. It also means that visualisations of database objects cannot be stored readily in the database for subsequent retrieval and display by the interface.

2. Development or modification of an interface to the database, or the implementation of an application-specific interface, requires knowledge of the two independently developed systems and the way in which they are linked.

3. Tools developed for the querying and manipulation of the database cannot be used on interface data, and vice-versa.

This paper describes an approach to the provision of a fully integrated database interface development system. The technique adopted is to integrate a graphical component set with an object-oriented database (OODB) in such a way that the original component set is completely transparent to users. This task has been eased by the facility to store both programs and data in the database, and by the presence of object-oriented mechanisms, such as inheritance and encapsulation.

The paper is organised as follows. Related work is summarised in section 2, to present a context for our architecture which is described in section 3. In section 4 it is shown how this fully integrated approach can be exploited to support uniform access to graphical data, application-specific interfaces, extensibility to support visualisations of advanced modelling constructs, and a multi-paradigm query interface. Section 5 presents some conclusions.

2 Related Work

This section reviews different approaches to the implementation of graphical interfaces to databases. No attempt is made to review the facilities which are provided by different interfaces, as that is not the focus of this paper.

It is standard for graphical interfaces to be constructed using general-purpose interface development systems, such as X-Windows toolkits or proprietary window managers [22, 7]. Such systems can then communicate with the database in the same way as other application programs, using an embedded query language, a procedure library, or inter-process communication.

It has long been recognised that object-oriented techniques are highly suitable for the implementation of graphical component sets [25]. However, in the case of OODBs, it is common for the database interface to be implemented using a system other than the database [25], even where the database is associated with a powerful programming language [5].

An alternative strategy is to use a UIMS to control dialog and to support direct manipulation of visual representations of database data [17]. In this approach, the high-level facilities of the UIMS do facilitate some modification of an interface without requiring detailed knowledge of two programming systems. However, there is no direct support for persistent interface data, and changes to the overall functionality of the interface rather than simply to the display component are likely to require significant programming effort.

More fully integrated techniques have, however, been proposed. In [18] a graphics programming environment for PS-algol is described. In this approach, a small number of primitive graphics types are built upon to yield a persistent graphics toolkit. A descendent of the original PS-algol system for Napier88, which provides a complete windowing environment, is described in [8]. There are two major differences between these systems and the one described in this paper: in these approaches the toolkit is implemented from a low level using the database language, and the database languages used do not support an object-oriented model of data.

More similar approaches to that presented in this paper are described by [24, 6], in which the on-screen representation of database objects is described using other database objects. However, these papers do not describe how the object-oriented model is associated with the underlying display manager or how interface extensibility can be achieved using overriding.

A combined approach, in which a UIMS is implemented using an object-oriented database, is described in [16]. This approach enables the interactive specification of interfaces, and overcomes the impedance mismatch associated with the use of a separate UIMS. The work described in this paper has a similar motivation to [16], but the focus of this paper is at a lower level. Rather than describing how a UIMS integrated with a database can be used, we present how a persistent graphical component set can be constructed, and show how the resulting architecture can be easily extended using object-oriented techniques. A more comprehensive description of integrated interface architectures is presented in [21].

3 Architecture

3.1 Options

This section describes the architecture of a system which integrates an existing graphical component set with the OODB ADAM [15]. The approach described here has been implemented in ADAM within the ECLiPSe [14] persistent Prolog system, which includes the PCE graphical component set. The approach is generally applicable, in that similar results could be obtained using different OODBs and graphical component sets. The ADAM graphical toolkit is known as EDEN, and the relationships between the major components of the interface are shown in Figure 1. EVE is a data browser and manipulation tool, and is described further in section 4.2.

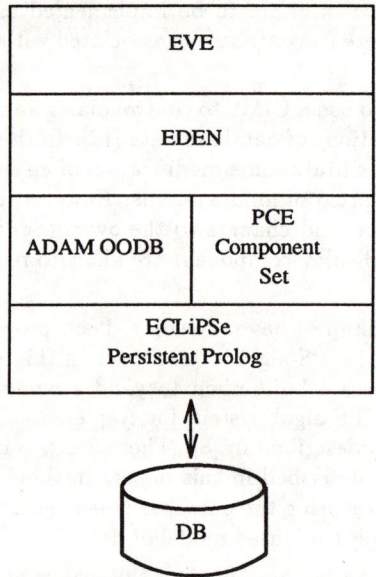

Figure 1: Components of system

The premise which led to the development of EDEN is that it would be useful to be able to implement ADAM graphical interfaces using ADAM itself. Two distinct architectures for such a system have since been used:

1. Implement a graphical component set in ADAM which provides an object-oriented view of a low-level window library.

2. Integrate ADAM with an existing graphical component set, in such a way that the component set selected is hidden from ADAM programmers.

An implementation was attempted using the first approach [26], which was built upon the Xlib library of X-Windows. However, this approach was subsequently abandoned as the resulting system proved to be prohibitively slow, and because substantial amounts of code were required to provide a toolkit at an appropriately high level. Performance problems in this case stemmed from the large amount of functionality which had to be supported using the (relatively slow) database language. When using the toolkit approach, a greater proportion of the interface functionality is handled outside the database, using routines written in C, although the nature of the back-end toolkit is hidden from the EDEN programmer.

As significant effort has been put into the provision of toolkits which support graphical objects such as windows, dialog boxes, sliders, menus and pictures, any technique which enables such a component set to be smoothly integrated with an OODB removes the need to start working at a lower level, and enables re-use of existing interface toolkit facilities.

A characteristic of existing toolkits is that they have an object-oriented style, even when they are programmed using conventional imperative languages, such as C. The approach taken in EDEN is to provide a 'view' of an existing toolkit using the constructs of the ADAM data model. Thus EDEN programs are standard ADAM programs – database objects are created, related to each other, updated and destroyed using standard ADAM operations. However, the sending of messages to objects which are part of EDEN can have the side-effect of placing the object on screen, changing its representation on screen, or removing it from the screen.

3.2 Menu Example

EDEN consists of a number of ADAM classes (50 at present), each of which represents an interface construct – a menu, a button, a picture, a slider, etc. The way in which each of these concepts is created and manipulated is very similar, which means that an integration of an OODB with a component set can be achieved in a modest period of time. This section describes the approach using the example of a menu.

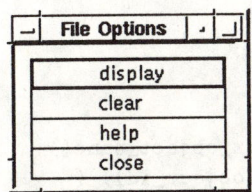

Figure 2: Sample EDEN menu.

A menu is a list of items displayed vertically on a screen, each of which can be selected using a pointing device, such as a mouse. For example, figure 2 depicts a simple EDEN menu:

Where such a menu is considered as an object, it is seen to have certain properties which can be specified as attributes on the class *menu*, including a *name* (File Options) and a number of *members* (display, clear, ...). It is also necessary to associate some behaviour with a *menu*, so that the system knows what to do when an item on the menu is selected. Furthermore, there is some functionality associated with a menu – it can be *opened, closed,* and even *destroyed.* This is achieved by defining a class *menu* as follows (the following examples do not use ADAM notation, but are intended to be as self explanatory as possible – for a more detailed description of the actual ADAM code, see [3]):

```
class menu is_a window {
    attributes {
        name: string;
        members: set of string;
    }
    methods {
        make_component() {...}
        ...
    }
}
```

In the above, it is assumed that the superclass of *menu* is *window,* which supports methods such as *open* and *close.* A *menu* object is created in the same way as any other database object:

```
m = menu();
m.put_name("File Options");
m.put_members({"display","clear",...});
...
```

The crucial architectural feature of the interface is that there is no interaction at all with the graphical toolkit during the creation of the *menu* object *m.* It is only when the menu is opened that it becomes necessary to call the graphical toolkit. Sending the message *open* to the object *m* leads to the invocation of the method *make_component* attached to the class *menu.*

```
class window {
    ...
    open() {
        x_object_id = self.x_object_name();
        if not (x_in_use(x_object_id)) {
            self.make_component();
            x_open(x_object_id);
        }
    }
}
```

It is the role of the *make_component* method, which is defined on every EDEN class, to construct the object in the toolkit which is equivalent to the EDEN object on which it is invoked. For the class *menu* the definition of *make_component* is as follows:

```
class menu is_a window {
    ...
    make_component() {
        x_menu_id = self.x_object_name();
        if not (x_in_use(x_menu_id)) {
            x_make_menu(x_menu_id,name);
            for each m in members do
                x_add_menu_item(x_menu_id,m);
            super.make_component()
        }
    }
    ...
}
```

In the above definition, *x_menu_id* is the name of the menu in the toolkit which corresponds to the EDEN menu object on which *make_component* has been invoked. The algorithm first checks to see if the object *x_menu_id* already exists in the current invocation of the toolkit. If so, the routine exists. If not, then calls are made to the toolkit which create the corresponding menu *(x_make_menu)*, and then add each of the members of the EDEN object to the toolkit object. Subsequently *make_component* is invoked on *super*, which leads to the invocation of the definition of *make_component* on the superclass of *menu*, namely *window*. This operation is responsible for handling features common to the creation of all windows, such as size and cursor shape. The relationship between the EDEN and toolkit objects is depicted graphically in figure 3.

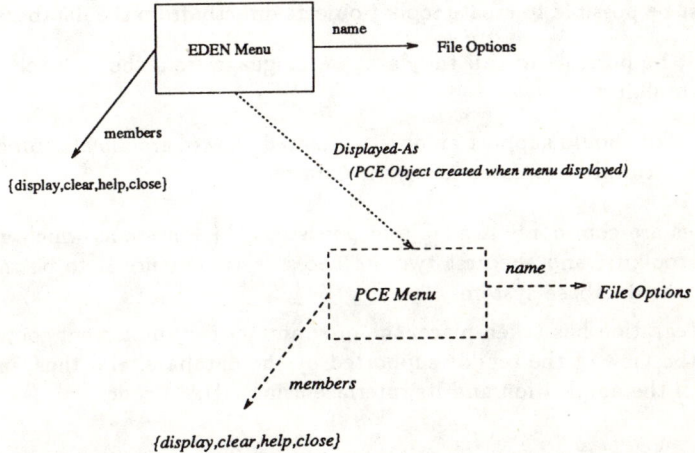

Figure 3: Relationship between EDEN/PCE objects. The ADAM object is represented using solid lines, its PCE counterpart using dashed lines, and the relationship between them using a dotted line. The presence of the PCE object is hidden from the user of the ADAM object.

The operations associated with an interface object such as a menu are implemented using callback routines. A callback routine is a procedure which is invoked automatically whenever an action is performed on the on-screen representation of an object. The crucial feature of callback behaviour is that it is instance specific, and thus cannot be implemented using a methods (which are used to represent class-specific behaviour).

In EDEN, callback behaviour is supported by storing the callback code of an instance in an attribute. It is then necessary to arrange that whenever the toolkit detects an action the code stored in the appropriate attribute is executed. This is achieved by attaching callback behaviour to every toolkit class, which retrieves the code attached to the corresponding database object and arranges for its invocation. This is clearly only possible where the database supports the storage of code, or a pointer to a piece of code, as the value of a attribute.

3.3 Summary

The crucial feature of the relationship between EDEN objects and toolkit objects is that every piece of information which appears on screen under the control of the toolkit is fully described by a standard ADAM object. Because of this, such objects can persist, be related to other objects, etc, without any changes being necessary to the ADAM storage manager. All the features of the toolkit can be made available through ADAM routines, and performance is comparable to that of the original toolkit, as only short sections of code need to be executed within the database system.

Integrating an interface in this way requires the following properties to be supported in the interface from the database system to the graphical toolkit:

1. It must be possible to create toolkit objects directly from the database language.

2. It must be possible to call the database language from the callback mechanism of the toolkit.

3. The toolkit should support an object-oriented view of graphical components that can be naturally expressed using the data model.

Such facilities are commonly available to persistent C++ systems which use links to X-Windows toolkits, and the first two are necessary if *any* use is to be made of the toolkit from the database system.

Once the integration has taken place, the programmer can implement complete interfaces using the view of the toolkit supported by the database, and thus, in this case, program both the application and its interface using ADAM code.

4 Exploitation

This section outlines certain benefits which follow from the architecture outlined in the previous section.

4.1 Uniformity

Certain advantages flow very directly from the fact that interface data is stored, accessed and manipulated using the facilities of the database:

- Persistent graphical data. In ADAM, every class which is an instance of a persistent metaclass persists along with its instances [15]. Thus, by explicitly making a small number of metaclasses persist, all EDEN data can be made to persist. Note that this is achieved without adding any new facilities to the ADAM storage manager – all EDEN data is represented using standard ADAM objects.

- Queries against interface data. For example, a query such as the following (expressed using the Daplex interface mentioned in section 4.3) will print the *name* of every *menu* in the database:

  ```
  for each m in menu
  print name(m);
  ```

- Wider applicability of database tools (e.g. an object browser can browse interface data). For example, figure 5 shows the use of the EVE browser [20] to browse the instances of the EDEN class *tree*, which is used to build hierarchically structured compound graphical objects).

- Simplified application development environment (i.e. only one language, no impedance mismatch, references from application objects to interface objects, etc).

This latter feature can be illustrated using a simple example from geographic information systems. An ADAM database was produced independently of the interface for storing low-level information on roads, junctions and other boundaries for subsequent analysis [2]. A simple application of the interface is to enable maps stored in the database to be drawn using the graphical interface. This can be achieved by attaching a method called *draw* to each of the geographical objects which have to be represented on the screen. For example, to draw the centre line of a road, it is only necessary to retrieve its start and end points, create a new EDEN *line* object, and then to draw that line in an EDEN *picture* object, as shown in figure 4.

The drawing of the figures on the map can then be achieved by creating a *picture* and iterating over all the objects which have to appear on the map, sending them the message *draw*.

A simple map-drawing program which draws streets, junctions and street names has been written in under 50 lines of EDEN code. Because the lines and text on the map are represented as database objects, the map can be stored in the database along with the objects from which it was constructed, and then redrawn simply by sending the associated *picture* the message *open*, which is quicker than drawing the map from scratch (in this case, it takes about 5 times as long to rebuild a display as it does to reopen it).

```
class road {
    attributes {
        name: string;
        start_junction: junction;
        end_junction  : junction;
        ...
    }
    methods {
        draw(p: picture) {
            l = line();
            l.put_start(start_junction.get_point());
            l.put_end(end_junction.get_point());
            p.draw_line(l);
        }
        ...
    }
}
```

Figure 4: Fragment of geographical database schema.

4.2 Extensibility

A principal feature of ADAM is that its data model can be extended with new constructs such as relationships and composite objects, as described in [9, 19]. This extensibility at the model level places new demands on direct manipulation database interfaces, which must provide effective visualisations for the different categories of object described by the model. In effect, an extensible data model requires an extensible interface [20]. This section outlines how the EDEN system has been used to implement an extensible browser and manipulation system for ADAM called EVE (Extensible Visual Environment).

EVE is itself an ADAM object, which contains references to a number of EDEN objects which are used to present information and to interact with the user. The initial EVE display, which is shown in Figure 5, is a collection of windows, which are represented by three EDEN objects for scrolling through lists of names, and an EDEN *picture* object which is used to display part of the schema as a graph. Each of the schema components drawn in the schema graph are drawn using EDEN objects. Further information is obtained by clicking on the names of items or on graphical visualisations using a mouse. For example, clicking on an item in the schema graph using the left mouse button leads to a form being displayed which is used to step through the instances of the class (e.g. the form used to describe *tree* in figure 5).

Extensibility is supported at the interface level by allowing changes to the way in which different categories of object are presented. For example, the way a relationship object is presented and interacted with should not be the same as a composite object, as these object classes have different roles and thus different semantics [4].

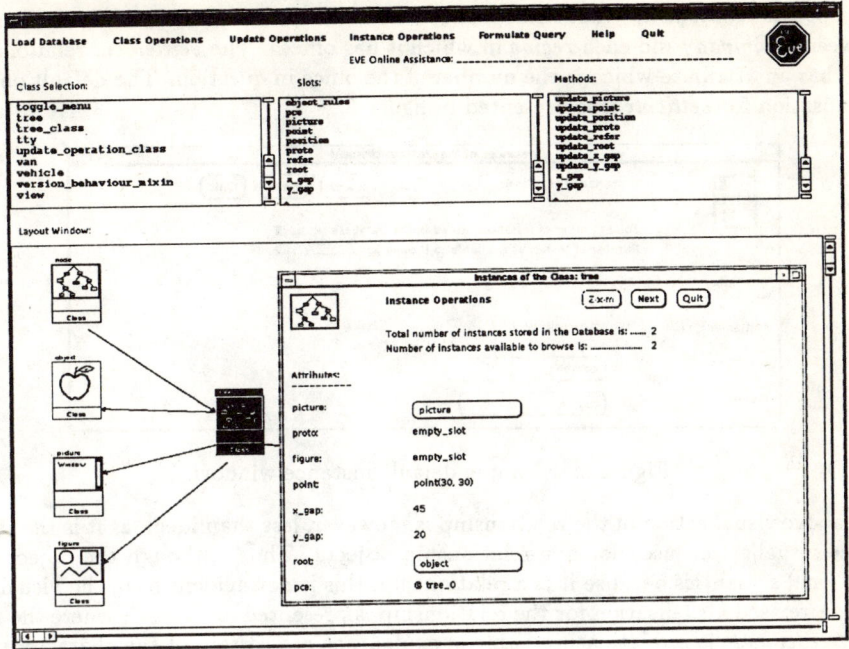

Figure 5: Layout of EVE browser.

Extensibility becomes practical at the interface level only if the designer of the interface has provided mechanisms which ease the modification of certain carefully identified parts of the interface. It is not necessary to facilitate wholesale reorganisation of the interface in this case. All that is required is that the ways in which different categories of objects are presented for direct manipulation are amenable to modification.

In ADAM, the data model can only be extended with new constructs by experienced users, and thus it can be assumed that the people who will need to develop new visualisations are competent programmers. The ADAM data model is extended by revising the ways in which objects are created by overriding default class creation operations at the metaclass level.[1] It thus seems reasonable to try to mirror the way in which extensions to the model are achieved when implementing extensions to the interface. As the interface is implemented using the same object-oriented techniques as the database system, this is also a practical approach to pursue.

For example, the standard way in which instances are displayed is shown in Figure 5, where an instance of the class *tree* is being browsed. In an application it might also be required to browse instances of classes which have been built using extensions to the basic model (e.g. ADAM has been extended to support *relationship* [9], *version* [11], *active-rule* [12] and *composite* [19] object types, each of which might reasonably be visualised using different techniques).

In what follows, it is assumed that the class *settlement* has been created as an instance

---

[1] A metaclass is an object which is used to specify the structure and behaviour of class objects [15].

of a special *relationship* metaclass. The class *settlement* represents the relationship between a *company* and each *region* in which it has offices. The *settlement* relationship itself has an attribute which is the number of the office in question. The default object visualisation for *settlement* is presented in figure 6.

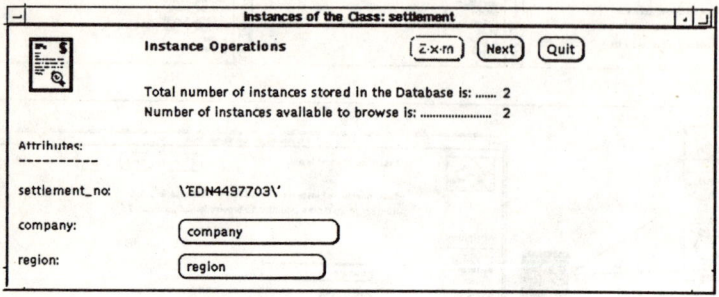

Figure 6: Example default instance window.

The above visualisation of the relationship is, however, less than ideal, as it is the same as the visualisation used for non-relationship objects. Thus, although the object has additional semantics because it is a relationship, this is not evident from the visualisation. A revised visualisation for the relationship is presented in figure 7, where the fact that *settlement* is a relationship is made explicit, as are certain of the characteristics of the relationship (e.g. cardinality and constraints [9]).

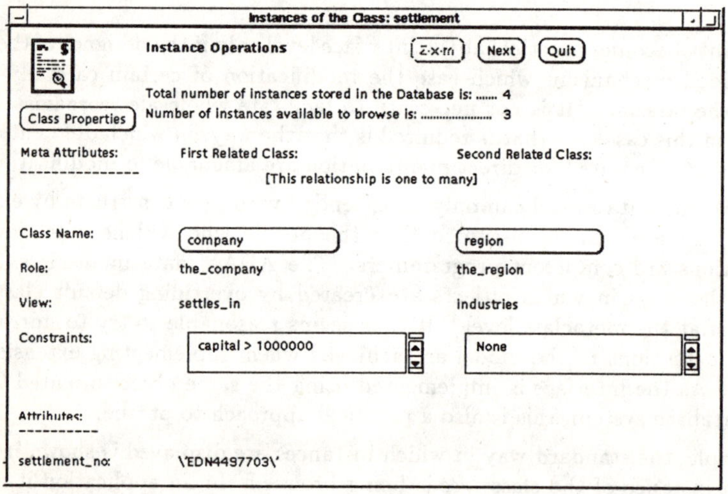

Figure 7: Extended visualisation for relationship objects.

This can be implemented using overriding and inheritance, as suggested above. The default visualisation of an instance is created by sending the message *new* to the class *eve_instance_form*. To achieve the alternative visualisation, a subclass of *eve_instance_form* is created with a revised definition of *new* which performs the following tasks:

1. Send *new* to *super*, thereby creating a standard instance visualisation form without attribute information.

2. Place the attributes on the form according to the revised layout.

3. Place additional information on the form which describes the meta-attributes of the relationship.

This approach enables the required change in visualisation to be achieved using a modest amount of additional code, as most of the functionality in *eve_instance_form* has been reused. Similar approaches can be used to modify other features of the display, such as the way in which the schema graph is drawn, or the iconic representation of particular classes. Extensions to the interface can thus be achieved within the context of a fixed overall framework, using techniques similar to those which were used to extend the data model.

4.3 Query Interface

EDEN has been used as the implementation platform for a multi-paradigm query interface [13], which allows users to express queries over ADAM databases using a textual query language (Daplex [23]), a form-based interface, or a graph-based interface. The interface also supports the translation of queries from one paradigm into another. This section outlines how the query interface has been implemented as an application of the EDEN toolkit.

The multi-paradigm interface is built around the four ADAM classes depicted in figure 8, namely *query_mixin, daplex_interface, graph_interface* and *form_interface*. This class hierarchy allows the functionality common to all the paradigms to be stored in *query_mixin* and then inherited by the specific interfaces. For example, all properties and operations relating to the generic internal representation of a query are defined in *query_mixin*.

The visual representations required by the three existing paradigms are very different – the Daplex interface requires an editor window into which the textual query can be typed; the form-based interface represents each class of interest to a query as a form; the graph-based interface is based around two picture windows, one depicting the database schema and the other the query. For example, figure 9 contains an example query expressed using the graph-based interface.

Information associated with the display of a particular query interface is stored as properties of the class used to model the corresponding paradigm. For example, in the case of the graph-based interface depicted in figure 9, the class *graph_interface* must reference the base window which contains the interface, the figures which represent the schema, and the the figures which represent the query. This is done by defining properties on *graph_interface* which reference the EDEN objects which are depicted on screen. As the EDEN objects are normal ADAM objects, their object-identifiers can be stored directly in the attributes of *graph_interface*. For example, the following code fragment shows part of the definitions of *query_mixin* and *graph_interface*:

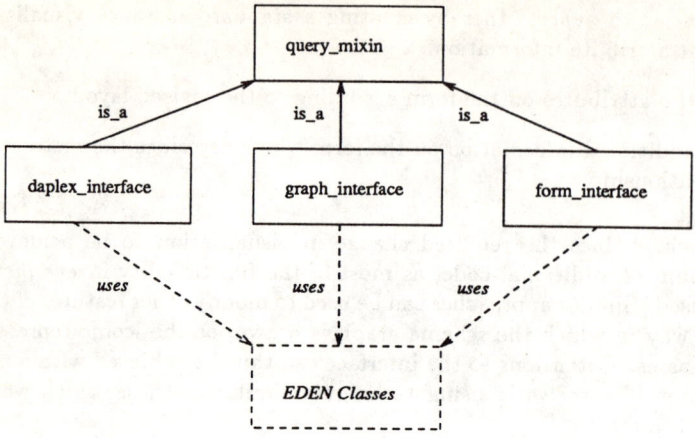

Figure 8: Overview of classes used in query interface.

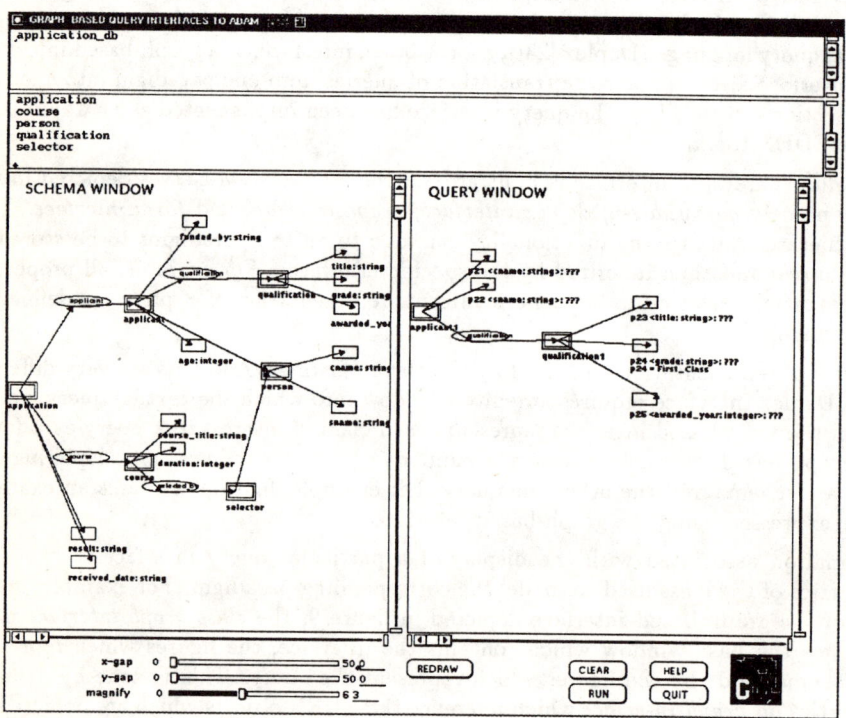

Figure 9: Example display from the graph-based interface.

```
class query_mixin {
    attributes {
        internal_form: set of query_component;
        ...
    }
    ...
}

class graph_interface is_a query_mixin {
    attributes {
        picture_window: picture;
        ...
    }
    ...
}
```

In the multi-paradigm interface, queries are represented internally using an object-oriented canonical form represented using ADAM objects accessed through the *internal_form* attribute of *query_mixin*. EDEN objects which represent the visual aspects of a particular interface are defined on paradigm-specific classes (e.g. the attribute *picture_window* on *graph_interface*). Furthermore, when the user interacts with the EDEN objects used to represent a query (for example, to extend the query graph), the callback behaviour associated with the interaction can directly invoke the methods of *graph_interface* or *query_mixin*, as both parts of the interface are implemented in ADAM.

5 Conclusions

This paper has shown how an object-oriented graphical toolkit can be fully integrated with an OODB, in such a way that the database language is used to implement higher-level interface functionality. Such a close integration of the interface with the database has a number of advantages over more conventional architectures – a single language is used for implementing the interface, the application, and entensions to the data model; interface data can be stored in the database, and accessed/manipulated using existing database facilities; the object-oriented facilities of the data model of the database can be used for sharing useful interface data and for extending interface functionality.

Several examples of such extended functionality have been presented in this paper – a simple map drawing program, an extensible direct-manipulation schema design tool/object browser and a multi-paradigm query interface. EDEN has also been used to develop a debugger for an active rule system [10]. The uniform representation of instances, classes, interface components and modelling constructs as objects has thus been exploited to provide a powerful environment for the development of advanced data-intensive applications.

Acknowledgements The second author is supported by a grant from the British Council and Arab Student Aid International and the third by the UK Science and Engineering Research Council. We are grateful to Alistair Kilgour, Oscar Diaz and Arturo Jaime for helpful discussions relating to the topic of this paper.

References

[1] Laguna Beach Participants, Future Directions In DBMS Research. *SIGMOD Record, 18(1)*, pages 17–26, 1989.

[2] A.I. Abdelmoty, M.H. Williams, and J.M.P Quinn. A Rule-Based Approach To Computerized Map Reading. *Information and Software Technology*, 35(10):587–602, October 1993.

[3] G. Al-Qaimari. *A Direct Manipulation Interface to an Extensible Object-Oriented Database*. PhD thesis, Computing and Electrical Engineering Department, Heriot-Watt University, Edinburgh, Scotland, 1994.

[4] G. Al-Qaimari and N. W. Paton. Design and Evaluation of Visualisations for Advanced Data Modelling Constructs. In C. Chrisment, editor, *Basque International Workshop on IT (BIWIT)*, pages 169–182. Cepadues Press, 1994.

[5] J. Almarode and T. Lougenia Anderson. GemStone Visual Interface Designer: A Tool for Object-Oriented Database Design. In *Object-Oriented Databases: Analysis, Design and Construction (DS-4)*, pages 73–94. North-Holland, 1991. W. Meersman et al (Eds).

[6] T. Lougeia Anderson, E. F. Ecklund, and D. Maier. PROTEUS: The DBMS User Interface as an Object. In *On Object-Oriented DB Systems*, pages 139–156. Springer-Verlag, 1991. K. R. Dittrich and U. Dayal (Eds).

[7] P.J. Barclay, C.M. Fraser, and J.B. Kennedy. Using a Persistent System to Construct a Customised Interface to an Ecological Database. In *The 1st International Workshop On Interfaces to Database Systems (IDS92), Glasgow*, pages 225–243. Springer-Verlag, 1992. R. Cooper (Ed).

[8] Q. Cutts, A. Dearle, and G. Kirby. WIN Programmers Manual. Technical Report CS/90/17, University of St. Andrews, 1990.

[9] O. Diaz and P.M.D. Gray. Semantic-rich user-defined relationship as a main constructor in object oriented databases. In W.Kent R.A. Meersman and S. Khosla, editors, *Object-Oriented Databases: Analysis, Design and Construction (DS-4)*, pages 207–224. North-Holland, 1991.

[10] O. Diaz, A. Jaime, and N.W. Paton. DEAR: A DEbugger for Active Rules in An Object-Oriented Context. In N.W. Paton and M.H. Williams, editors, *Rules In Database Systems: Proceedings of the 1st International Workshop*, pages 180–193. Springer-Verlag, 1994.

[11] O. Diaz and N. Paton. Sharing behaviour in an object oriented database using a rule-based mechanism. In M.S. Jackson and A.E. Robinson, editors, *Aspects of Databases - Proc. British National Conference on Databases (BNCOD 9)*, pages 17–37. Butterworth-Heinemann Publishers, 1991.

[12] O. Diaz, N. Paton, and P.M.D. Gray. Rule management in object oriented databases: a uniform approach. In R. Camps G.M. Lohman, A. Sernadas, editor, *17th Intl. Conf. on Very Large Data Bases, Barcelona*, pages 317–326. Morgan Kaufmann, 1991.

[13] D. K. Doan, N. W. Paton, A. C. Kilgour, and G. Al-Qaimari. A Multi-Paradigm Query Interface To An Object-Oriented Database. 1993. Submitted for publication.

[14] ECRC/ICL. *ECLiPSe, User Manual*, 1992.

[15] P.M.D. Gray, K.G. Kulkarni, and N.W. Paton. *Object-Oriented Databases: A Semantic Data Model Approach*. Prentice-Hall International(UK), Hertfordshire, 1992. ISBN 0-13-620203-3.

[16] R. King and M. Novak. Designing Database Interfaces with DBface. *ACM Trans. Information Systems*, 11:105–132, 1993.

[17] R. Marin, M. Taboada, R.P. Barreiro, J. Mira, and A. Delgado. Rapid Prototyping of Medical Graphic Interfaces. In *Proc DEXA*, pages 161–166, 1992.

[18] R. Morrison, A. Dearle, A. L. Brown, and M. P. Atkinson. An Integrated Graphics Programming Environment. *Computer Graphics Forum 5(2)*, pages 147–157, 1986.

[19] N. Paton, O. Diaz, and M.L. Barja. Combining active rules and metaclasses for enhanced extensibility in object-oriented systems. *Data and Knowledge Engineering*, 10:45–63, 1993.

[20] N. W. Paton, G. Al-Qaimari, and A. C. Kilgour. An Extensible Interface To An Extensible Object-Oriented Database System. In *The 1st International Workshop On Interfaces to Database Systems (IDS92), Glasgow*, pages 265–281. Springer-Verlag, 1992. R. Cooper (Ed).

[21] N. W. Paton, R. Cooper, D. England, G. Al-Qaimari, and A. C. Kilgour. Integrated Architecture For Database Interface Development. 1994. To be published in IEE Proceedings E, Special issue on HCI.

[22] M. Schoning. A Graphical Interface to an Complex-Object Database Management System. In *The 1st International Workshop on Interfaces to Database Systems (IDS92), Glasgow*. Springer-Verlag, 1992. R. Cooper (Ed).

[23] David W. Shipman. The Functional Data Model and the Data Language DAPLEX. *ACM Transactions on Database Systems*, 6(1):140–173, 1981.

[24] F. States, E. Laenens, D. Vermeir, and L. Tarantino. A Seamless Integration of Graphics and Dialogues within a Logic Based Object-Oriented Language. *Journal of Visual Languages and Computing, 1*, pages 313–332, 1990.

[25] C. T. Wu. Benefits of Object-Oriented Programming in Implementing Visual Database Interface. *JOOP*, pages 8–16, March/April 1990.

[26] Z. Zhao. A Graphical Component Set for Database Interface Design. Technical Report, Computer Science Department, Heriot-Watt University, Edinburgh, Scotland, 1990.

Efficient Access to FDM Objects Stored in a Relational Database

Graham J.L. Kemp, Jesus J. Iriarte and Peter M.D. Gray

Department of Computing Science, University of Aberdeen, King's College,
Aberdeen, Scotland, AB9 2UE

Abstract. The P/FDM object-oriented database is based on the functional data model and has a modular design, allowing alternative kinds of object storage to be used. This is achieved by implementing a small set of basic data access and update routines for each kind of storage module. In this work, a relational database management system has been used to provide object storage, and we describe how the data access routines have been implemented. The principal query language used with P/FDM is Daplex, which is normally translated to Prolog, including calls to the basic data access routines. The query is optimised to minimise the expected number of calls. This gives very general method execution and pattern matching search. However, much better performance can be achieved for simpler data-intensive Daplex queries against a relational storage module by translating these to a single SQL statement. We describe a program called DAPSTRA which performs this translation quickly in a fashion transparent to the user, and compare performance.

1 Introduction

We have built an object-oriented database system, P/FDM [2], which is based on the functional data model (FDM) [12]. Most of this system is written in Prolog, and hash file routines, written in C, are used to provide persistent object storage. The logic programming language Prolog and the functional query language Daplex can both be used to query P/FDM. The main application of this database so far has been storing and analysing protein structure data [3].

In our work with protein structure databases, we are collaborating with protein chemists to design a schema for a new protein database, extending the kind of information stored. Our partners in this project have experience in storing protein data in relational databases [6] [5], and in developing menu-based interfaces to these, tailored to the application. Relational organisation has been successful for queries that are answered by exhaustive scans of one or two tables, but the limited expressive power of SQL has been a drawback. In contrast, we have found the flexibility of Daplex and Prolog advantageous, and functional data model organisation has facilitated answering complex *ad hoc* queries e.g. looking for hydrophobic microdomains [9]. Further, a protein modelling system

---

* This work was supported by a grant from the EC.

has been implemented which uses this experimental structural data, and also uses the P/FDM database to store design data and versions of protein models which are generated during the modelling process [8].

Since our project partners intend using the SYBASE relational database management system, we are experimenting with using relational tables to provide object storage for P/FDM. This would allow us to share the same physical data format, without being limited to having a relational perspective of the data and using only SQL. P/FDM's modular design makes it easy for alternative kinds of storage module to be used. The minimum work that needs to be done is to implement a layer of primitive routines, conforming to a protocol. This gives a consistent interface between P/FDM and heterogeneous storage modules. Versions of these routines which operate on data stored in SYBASE have been implemented.

Further work can achieve storage-specific improvements. Simple Daplex queries against a relational storage module can be answered more efficiently if these can be translated to a single SQL statement equivalent to the original query and that SQL statement passed directly to the relational database server, bypassing the primitive P/FDM routines. This is because although we end up accessing the same tuples by both techniques we save the overhead of executing many small queries across the interface by performing one large query. We have implemented a program called DAPSTRA, in Prolog, which performs this translation.

In Sect. 2, we describe how entities and functions are mapped onto relational tables in this work, and the operation of primitive P/FDM routines which access data in relational modules. The DAPSTRA program, and the list comprehensions which are its input, are described in Sect. 3. In Sect. 4, we discuss the benefits of using the DAPSTRA program, and the features of Prolog and P/FDM which helped in its implementation. We also outline some directions for future work.

2 Relational Storage for FDM

The basic concepts in the P/FDM database are entities and functions. Entities are used to represent conceptual objects, while functions represent the properties of an object. Functions are used to model both scalar attributes and relationships, and may be single-valued or multi-valued. Entity classes can be arranged in subtype-hierarchies, with subclasses inheriting the properties of their superclass, as well as having their own specialised properties.

The Daplex language provides data definition statements for describing data according to the functional data model. Entity classes and functions are declared in a schema, and in P/FDM each section of schema has a header line stating what kind of storage module is used to store the data values described by the declarations. When a schema relating to data stored in a relational storage module is read in, the P/FDM system checks that the declarations are consistent with the FDM-relational mapping described below.

2.1 Mapping FDM onto Relational Tables

Each object class is stored in a table which has as its name the class name. In this table, each row represents an object instance, and each column stores the value of a single-valued function on the object, where the name of the column is also the name of the function. A vital point is that we add an additional column, called *oid*, which is used to store the object identifier, used internally to identify each instance. Thus it is necessary to reload existing relational data and to assign oid values, however, the original tables can be presented as views if necessary.

Consider the following Daplex data declaration statements which introduce a new entity class called *person* and two single-valued attributes (Fig. 1 shows the schema diagram corresponding to the declarations and queries given in this paper, and Fig. 2 shows the corresponding relational tables):

```
declare person ->> entity
declare forename(person) -> string
declare surname(person) -> string
```

In the corresponding relational module, we would have a table called person with three fields – *oid, forename* and *surname*.

Subclass-superclass relationships can also be modelled. For each subclass in a relational module, another table (or view) stores the values of single-valued attributes defined only on the subclass. Each row represents a subclass instance. Each subclass table also has an oid column, and the values stored in this column are a subset of the oid values in the superclass table. The following Daplex declaration introduces the class *student* as a subclass of *person*, and *undergrad* as a subclass of *student*. The *student* subclass has two specialised properties representing a student's year of study and faculty.

```
declare student ->> person
declare undergrad ->> student
declare year(student) -> integer
declare faculty(student) -> string
```

For these declarations, we would have a table called *student* with three fields – *oid, year* and *faculty*, and a table called *undergrad* with an *oid* field. If John Brown is a student, then there would be a row in the student table with oid value matching the oid value in the person table for John Brown. Additionally, if John Brown is an undergraduate, then there will also be an entry in the undergrad table with this oid value.

The values of single-valued relationships are stored in entity tables. Suppose we have classes called *course* and *section* which are related by a single-valued relationship called *has_course* defined on section.

```
declare has_course(section) -> course
```

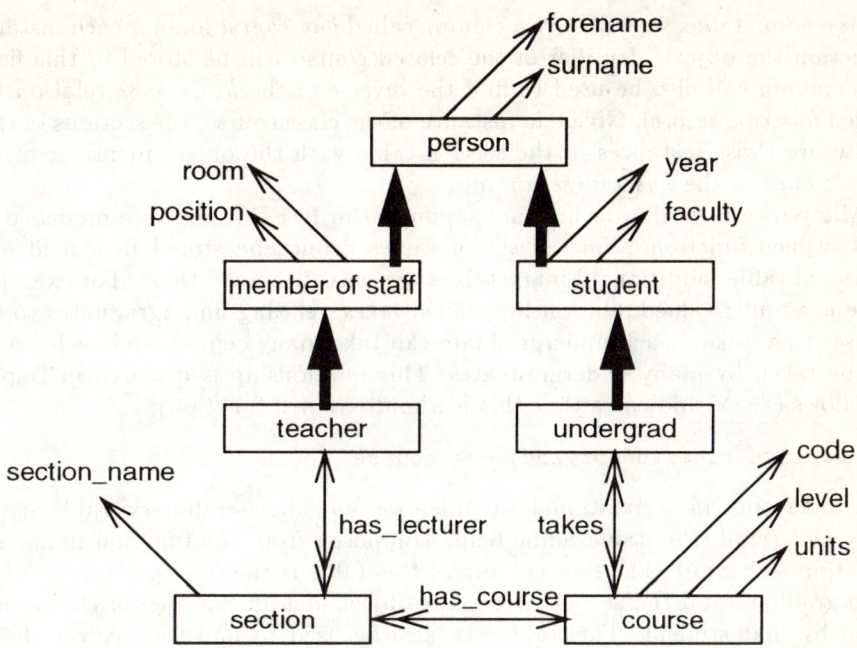

Fig. 1. Schema diagram. Object classes are represented by rectangular boxes. Labelled arrows represent relationships between objects. Thick arrows point from subclasses to their superclass.

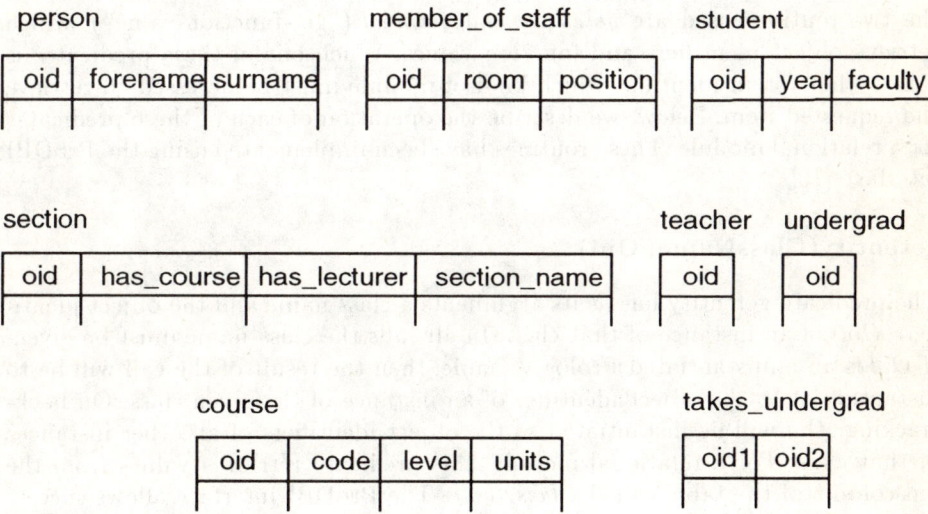

Fig. 2. Relational database tables corresponding to the schema shown in Fig. 1

In the *section* table, we will have a column called *has_course* and for each instance of section the object identifier of the related course will be stored in this field. This column can also be used to find the inverse of the *has_course* relationship (called *has_course_inv*). Given an instance of the class course, the sections of that course are those instances in the section table with the object identifier of the given course in the *has_course* column.

Many-to-many relationships are supported in P/FDM, and are modelled by multi-valued functions. Since a set of values cannot be stored in a field of a relational table, additional binary tables are used to model these. For example, there is a multi-valued relationship, called *takes*, relating undergraduates to the courses they take – each undergraduate can take many courses and each course can be taken by many undergraduates. This relationship is declared in Daplex as follows ("->>" indicates that this is a multi-valued function):

```
declare takes(undergrad) ->> course
```

To model this in a relational module, we introduce a binary table called *takes_undergrad* (this table name being composed from the function name and the argument type). The first column of this table is the object identifier of an undergraduate and the second stores the object identifier of one of the courses taken by that student. This table can also be used to find the inverse of this relationship.

2.2 Accessing Relational Storage Modules via P/FDM Primitives

The P/FDM database provides a small set of primitive routines implemented by Prolog predicates for performing data access and update. For data retrieval the two routines used are *getentity* and *getfnval* ("get-function-value"), which retrieve object identifiers and function values. When one of these predicates is called, the system identifies which kind of module must be accessed to retrieve the requested item. Below, we describe the operation of each of these predicates for a relational module. These routines have been implemented using the ProDBI interface [10].

getentity(ClassName, Oid)

The predicate getentity has as its arguments a class name and the object identifier (*Oid*) of an instance of that class. In all calls the class name must be given. If *Oid* is an uninstantiated Prolog variable, then the result of the call will be to instantiate it to the object identifier of an instance of the given class. On backtracking, *Oid* will be instantiated to the object identifiers of all other instances of that class. For a relational module, this predicate retrieves values from the oid column of the table called *ClassName*. The ProDBI interface allows successive tuples to be retrieved from the relational database on backtracking, thus all values in the oid column are retrieved in turn.

After we have retrieved an instance of a class, we usually want to access its properties (scalar attributes and/or relationships). Therefore, an additional action of the getentity routine is to retrieve the entire tuple and cache it in main memory so that an object's properties can be accessed without further calls to the database server. At first, this was done by asserting the tuple into Prolog's clause base, but this was found to be surprisingly slow. So instead, a cache has been implemented in C, and the code to manage this cache is dynamically linked into P/FDM when a relational module is opened. The cache is small, holding only one tuple from each entity table. However, this is satisfactory, suiting navigational queries. (This cache is not to be confused with the SYBASE server's cache).

If *Oid* is already instantiated when getentity is called, then getentity is used to test whether the given object belongs to the given class. This is most useful for testing subclass membership. When used in this way, the getentity routine first looks for the given instance in the cache, and only if it is not in the cache is the external relational database accessed.

getentity(ClassName, Key, Oid)

The second form of getentity takes as an argument a list containing the external key values of a particular object instance. P/FDM uses external key values as a fast way of finding object identifiers, and of ensuring there is only one internal object oid for any externally known object (and vice versa). External key values may change in the life of an object, but the oids never do. For example, suppose the attributes *forename* and *surname* form the external key of the class *person*. Then we can retrieve the object identifier of the person called John Brown with the call:

```
getentity(person,['John','Brown'],Oid)
```

This query is answered by retrieving the oid value from the tuple in the person table with 'John' in the forename field and 'Brown' in the surname field. Note that ProDBI will use an index on the table if one exists to locate tuples that have a field with a known value.

As well as scalar values, keys can include relationships. Suppose the external keys of classes *course* and *section* are declared as follows:

```
key_of course is code
key_of section is key_of(has_course), section_name
```

The external key of a section consists of the the section code and the key of the related course, which is that course's code. The following call will retrieve the object identifier of section a2 in course CS_4002:

```
getentity(section,['CS_4002','a2'],Oid)
```

To answer this query, the system first finds the object identifier of that tuple in the course table which has CS_4002 as its code. Then it finds the oid value from the tuple in the section table which has the object identifier (not the key!) of course CS_4002 in its *has_course* field and the value a2 in its *section_name* field.

Subclasses inherit the key of their superclass. For example,

```
getentity(student,['John','Brown'],Oid)
```

will first find the oid in the person table for the tuple with values 'John' and 'Brown' in the forename and surname fields, then test that there is a corresponding entry in the student table.

getfnval(Function, [Argument], Result)

A function name, representing an attribute or relationship, and an argument to which that function will be applied are given in a call to getfnval. The argument is given in a Prolog list because P/FDM supports multi-argument functions (not discussed in this paper).

Suppose getfnval is called with the function *forename* and the object identifier of a person as the argument. The result is found by retrieving the value in the *forename* field of the tuple in the person table with the given object identifier.

If *Result* is instantiated in the call, then getfnval is used as a test. For single-valued functions, getfnval first checks whether the tuple corresponding to the given argument is in the main memory cache. If it is, then the function value is immediately retrieved from that cached tuple. Otherwise, the database server is accessed via the ProDBI interface, and the entire tuple containing the requested value is retrieved and cached so that related attributes are available without requiring further database access.

Suppose in the above call, a student object identifier is given as an argument instead of a person object identifier. The forename function is not defined directly on *student*, but is inherited from the *person* superclass. In this case, the value of the inherited function would be retrieved from the corresponding entry in the *person* table (using the same oid value).

In addition to scalar attributes, getfnval is used to retrieve the values of relationship attributes. Consider the *has_course* relationship between *section* and *course*, shown in Fig. 1. This relationship is stored in the *section* table. The call

```
getfnval(has_course,[SectionOid],CourseOid)
```

will succeed where *CourseOid* matches the value in the *has_course* field of the tuple which has the given section identifier in the *oid* field. Values for the inverse relationship *has_course_inv* are found in a similar way. The call

```
getfnval(has_course_inv,[CourseOid],SectionOid)
```

will succeed where *SectionOid* matches the value in the *oid* field of a tuple which has the given course identifier in the *has_course* field. This inverse relationship is multi-valued, and the identifiers of all sections in the given course are found by backtracking.

A multi-valued function, such as that modelling the relationship between undergraduates and the courses they take is answered similarly by accessing the oids in the binary table *takes_undergrad* in Fig. 2.

2.3 Using Daplex to Access Data in a Relational Module

Data in P/FDM is accessed using the Daplex query language. Queries expressed in this high-level language are translated to Prolog for execution. This is done by first translating the query into a "list comprehension" (or "set expression") (see Sect. 3), and then optimising this before generating Prolog code to answer the query. This code includes calls to the P/FDM primitive routines (getentity and getfnval for data access), as well as ordinary Prolog goals. The translation process is outlined in Fig. 3.

Originally the P/FDM system had two kinds of storage module: main memory modules storing data in Prolog clauses, and hash file modules providing persistence. We have now developed a third kind using relational storage. Within a session, several different kinds of module can be open concurrently, but users access these in the same way, via the primitive routines. Daplex can also be used to query relational modules. Moreover, a single query can make reference to object classes stored in several different kinds of database module. This is because the database primitives that queries are translated into are independent of how the data they are to access is stored. It is only when these predicates are called that the system checks the actual argument types and the database meta-data [1] to identify what kind of storage module is to be accessed, and performs the necessary retrieval operation.

In the rest of this paper, we consider processing queries which only require access to relational modules. Such queries can be answered by translating these to Prolog, with calls to the basic access routines described in Sect. 2.2. Each of these calls may require the relational database to be accessed using the ProDBI interface. ProDBI itself works by sending SQL queries to the relational database server, since it doesn't have low-level access to SYBASE tables. Thus, a Daplex query is broken down into many small SQL queries, each answering only a small part of the original query. It is clear that the SQL server could often employ a more efficient query evaluation strategy if it were given the entire query at once, rather than being asked to answer sub-parts of the original query.

This drawback is illustrated by the following Daplex example, which finds the surnames of all people with forename "John".

```
for each p in person such that forename(p) = "John"
print(surname(p));
```

Translating this to Prolog with calls to P/FDM primitives, we have

```
getentity(person,P),
getfnval(forename,[P],'John'),
getfnval(surname,[P],S),
write(S),nl,
fail;
true.
```

Significantly, to answer this query, all tuples in the person table must be retrieved from the database server in turn, and for each tuple the value of the forename

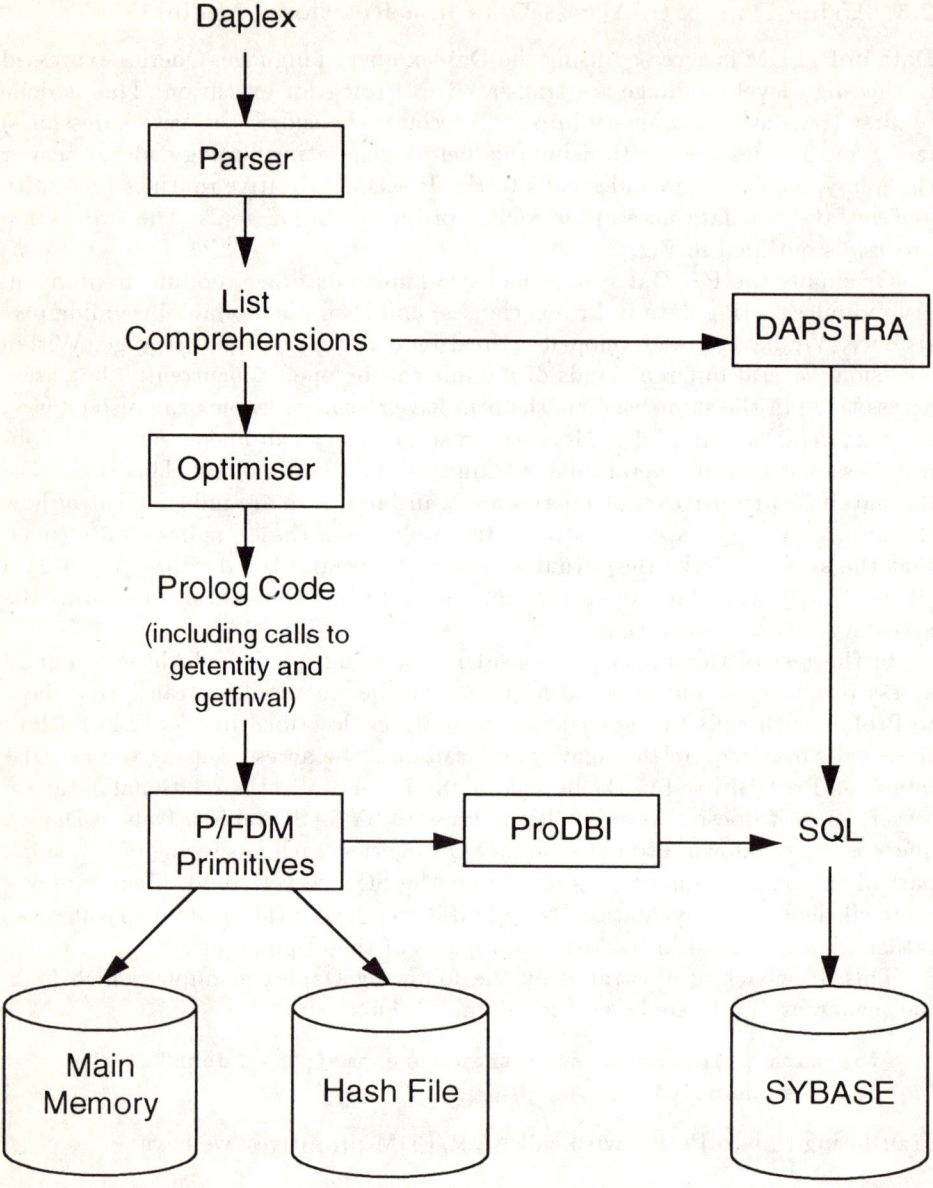

Fig. 3. Processing Daplex queries. Following the route on the left, any list comprehension can be translated to Prolog code accessing any kind of storage module. List comprehensions for simple Daplex queries against a relational module can be translated directly to SQL by the DAPSTRA program.

field is tested in Prolog. It would be better to give the constraint on the forename to the relational database server, thus letting the server filter the results to be returned. This query is equivalent to a single SQL statement:

```
SELECT   surname
FROM     person
WHERE    forename = "John"
```

If the Daplex query could be translated to an SQL query string, then this could be passed to a relational database server. The server could then find answers to the query and return only this data to the P/FDM system, reducing the amount of data transferred from the server, and performing tests on the data values as early as possible (i.e. on the SQL server). Additionally, if the relational table has an index on the forename column (even where this is not a unique identifier), then this can be used by the database server to improve performance further. This can be done by translating the list comprehensions into single SQL statements. A program called DAPSTRA (DAPlex-to-Sql TRAnslator) has been written in Prolog to perform this translation, and is described in the next section.

3 Translating List Comprehensions to SQL Using DAPSTRA

When a Daplex query is parsed, it is converted to Prolog terms containing the essential elements of the query, but in a simple form. These are equivalent to a list comprehension. For example, the query from the last section can be written as a list comprehension as follows:

$$[\ s\ |\ p \leftarrow \text{person};\ f \leftarrow \text{forename}(p);\ f = \text{``John''};\ s \leftarrow \text{surname}(p)\ ]$$

The variables whose values are to be printed are listed on the left of the vertical bar. The expressions on the right of the vertical bar are called *qualifiers*, and are either *filters* or *generators*. Each generator introduces one new variable, representing a scalar value or object instance drawn from the list given by the expression. At present, the expressions in generators which DAPSTRA can deal with are for class enumeration, function evaluation (i.e. accessing a stored attribute or relationship), class conversion (regarding an instance of one class as an instance of another in the same class hierarchy) and aggregate functions (like 'maximum'). Filters specify conditions that variables must satisfy. Filters that can be handled by DAPSTRA at present are comparisons, existentially quantified sub-expressions, conjunctions and disjunctions.

DAPSTRA processes the qualifiers one-at-a-time, and, as processing proceeds, two Prolog data structures are constructed. The first of these is a symbol table which contains term structures recording the variable name, table name, table identifier and column name of each variable in the list comprehension. If a variable is used as a join value between tables, then there will be more than one entry for this variable in the symbol table. The second data structure is a term representing the eventual SQL query, and this term contains three lists – a "select-list", a "from-list" and a "where-list", corresponding to the main clauses in an SQL "select" statement. The symbol table and the three query lists are implemented as incomplete lists. Each generator adds to the symbol table and/or one or more of the query lists, and each filter adds to the "where-list". When all qualifiers have been processed, the symbol table and query lists are used to generate the SQL query text.

Once the SQL text has been generated, it can be run by passing it to the database server using a routine provided by the ProDBI interface. A Prolog variable can be bound to the results retrieved and then further processing can be carried out in Prolog. Alternatively, if query just requires values to be printed then this can be done via a C interface routine without going back into Prolog.

The following example shows nested for-loops in Daplex. This query prints the course code of each second level course, together with the name of each section in that course and the surname of the teacher giving that section.

```
for each c in course such that level(c) = 2
   for each s in has_course_inv(c)
      print(code(c), section_name(s), surname(has_lecturer(s)));
```

The list comprehension for this query is:

$$[\ d,\ e,\ g\ |\ a \leftarrow \text{course};\ b \leftarrow \text{level}(a);\ b = 2;\ c \leftarrow \text{has\_course\_inv}(a);$$
$$d \leftarrow \text{code}(a);\ e \leftarrow \text{section\_name}(c);\ f \leftarrow \text{has\_lecturer}(c);$$
$$g \leftarrow \text{surname}(f)\ ]$$

This is translated to the following piece of SQL:

```
SELECT   t1.code, t2.section_name, t3.surname
FROM     course t1, section t2, person t3
WHERE    t1.level = 2 AND t2.has_course = t1.oid AND
         t2.has_lecturer = t3.oid
```

Queries which print the results of aggregate functions can be expressed in Daplex. For example, the following query prints the most units associated with any course.

```
print(maximum(units(course)));
```

The list comprehension for this is:

$$[\ m\ |\ m \leftarrow \text{maximum}(\ [\ u\ |\ c \leftarrow \text{course};\ u \leftarrow \text{units}(c)\ ]\ )\ ]$$

Note that the argument to "maximum" is a list comprehension, evaluating to the list of units, and m takes the value of the largest element in this list. The generated SQL query uses the built-in aggregate function "MAX".

```
SELECT   MAX(t1.units)
FROM     course t1
```

The results of aggregate functions can also be used as constraints. A query to find the codes of courses at the highest level can be expressed in Daplex:

```
for each c in course such that
   level(c) = maximum(level(course))
print(code(c));
```

Again, the list comprehension for this contains an inner comprehension as the argument to "maximum":

[code | c1 ← course; l1 ← level(c1);
       m ← maximum([l2 | c2 ← course; l2 ← level(c2)]);
       l1 = m; code ← code(c1)]

Aggregate functions cannot be used in an SQL where-clause, but a subquery can be used to provide a value for the test. Thus, the above query is translated to:

```
SELECT    t1.code
FROM      course t1
WHERE     t1.level = (SELECT MAX(t2.level) FROM course t2)
```

DAPSTRA can also deal with existentially quantified sub-queries. For example, the following piece of Daplex prints the codes of all courses which have some section taught by a senior lecturer:

```
for each c in course such that
   some t in has_lecturer(has_course_inv(c)) has
      position(t) = "SL"
print(code(c));
```

The list comprehension for this is:

[code | c ← course; code ← code(course);
       some([t | s ← has_course_inv(c); t ← has_lecturer(s);
       p ← position(t); p = "SL"])]

The SQL statement generated by the DAPSTRA program contains the keyword "EXISTS", followed by a sub-query. This subquery refers to the "global" table t1.

```
SELECT    t1.code
FROM      course t1
WHERE     EXISTS (SELECT  t2.has_lecturer
                  FROM    section t2, member_of_staff t3
                  WHERE   t2.has_course = t1.oid AND
                          t2.has_lecturer = t3.oid AND
                          t3.position = 'SL')
```

Attribute *position* is not stored in the teacher table, but has to be retrieved from the corresponding tuple in the member_of_staff table. Therefore, a join is performed between the section and member_of_staff tables in the sub-query, and the teacher table does not feature in the SQL query.

4 Discussion

Translating Daplex to SQL can achieve efficient query processing in a functional data model data base making use of relational storage modules for persistent data. Experiments with DAPSTRA show that translating queries directly to SQL can speed up queries by several orders of magnitude, compared with going via the P/FDM primitive routines. This better performance is achieved by passing all information in the original query to the relational database server, allowing it to filter results returned, rather than breaking a query into several SQL statements, passing each of these to the relational database server and testing variable values within Prolog. However, direct translation to a single SQL statement is not always possible. In these cases, Daplex queries can still be answered – Prolog backtracks if DAPSTRA fails to translate the query to a single SQL statement and the query is answered via the usual route. For example, this happens where the query uses derived functions (stored methods), recursive functions, or there is a complex navigation path with many joins that would slow down the SQL optimiser.

At present, the DAPSTRA program can deal with class enumeration, function evaluation (single-valued and multi-valued functions representing both scalar attributes and relationships, inverse relationships and inherited functions), class conversion, aggregate functions, comparisons, conjunctions, disjunctions and existentially quantified sub-expressions, These can be combined with arbitrary complexity. Currently it cannot handle multi-argument functions, enumerated sets and set operations (like 'union'). There are also extensions to Daplex for backtrackable updates (Embury and Gray, in preparation) which rely on Prolog backtracking, and thus cannot be translated to SQL. Daplex definitions for derived functions are not handled by DAPSTRA, however, SYBASE stored procedures could be generated from some of these.

List comprehensions are a useful and convenient intermediate form for queries. In this work, we have found it easy to translate these to SQL, for simple queries. Trinder and Wadler [13] use list comprehensions as a basis for deriving efficient query evaluation plans for relational databases. In our work with relational storage, we have just used them as a starting point for generating a text string containing a SQL query, leaving optimisation of this to the SQL server. However, in other work with P/FDM, list comprehensions have been optimised to give an efficient sequence of calls to basic data access routines [11] [7].

The DAPSTRA program makes extensive use of Prolog's unification mechanism and data structures. For example, the table identifier may not be known when an entry is added to the symbol table, but a Prolog variable can be put into that slot and that slot is instantiated when the variable is unified with a table identifier in some later statement. Incomplete lists are convenient data structures for representing the symbol table and query lists. The standard Prolog predicate *member* always succeeds when called with an item and an incomplete list, either because the item is present in the list, or because it can be added. This is particularly useful for adding items to a list only if they are not already in that list.

4.1 Evaluation of Performance

Table 1 shows performance figures for a selection of queries against a 2Mb database. The times were obtained by the single active user on a 16Mb Sun4 with some background disk I/O. The same data was loaded into both a hash file storage module and a relational module, and the same queries were run against each. Both of these storage modules were located on the same disk, which was directly attached to the Sun4. The SYBASE server was also running on this Sun4. All times (except SQL server CPU) include the time taken writing results to a file. The total elapsed time gives a rough but useful measure of the overall time taken to answer a query, particularly for the relational module tests where it covers client and server times and the time for inter-process communication and data transfer (however, we also measured CPU times for the SQL server). The relational module tests required hardly any physical reads and we would expect these to be slower with a bigger database, but note that in the worst case, assuming random physical reads taking 20ms, the upper limit for the multi-join query is only 160s, and in practice would normally be very much less. Thus, it is not a systematic test, but we think it is representative of realistic queries with a "warmed-up" database.

In the relational module tests, the elapsed time processing queries using the P/FDM primitives are roughly between 10 and several hundred times longer than the processing time using DAPSTRA. DAPSTRA was significantly faster for queries requiring joins because using the P/FDM primitives required lots of penny-packet processing, even though both accessed the same tuples via the same indexes. It was also spectacularly faster where it was able to use a merge-join strategy, since this takes $O(N \log N)$ time instead of $O(N^2)$.

If we consider just times using the P/FDM primitives (not DAPSTRA) and compare relational storage against hash files, then the use of client-server calls with SQL competes remarkably well with direct Prolog-C calls to an extensible hash file. In the case of the merge-join query, the small SQL queries generated cannot use the sort-merge technique, but it is able to use larger buffers than the hash file. The hash file module is more competitive on multi-join, as expected, since stored relationships and their inverses allow direct navigation.

The final queries in the table called derived functions and could not be translated to SQL, however, they were answered using a relational module by combining calculation steps with calls to the P/FDM primitives for data retrieval. Interestingly, the hash file module is significantly faster for these more complex queries.

Table 1. Performance figures for DAPSTRA and P/FDM primitives.

Query category	Number of results	Hash File Module		Relational Module			
		P/FDM primitives		P/FDM primitives	DAPSTRA		
		Total elapsed time	CPU time	Total elapsed time	Total elapsed time	SQL Server CPU time	Logical reads
Sequential scan of a single table	4530	85s	42s	56s	5s	0.20s	106
Sequential scan with non-key selection	32	65s	37s	52s	2s	0.10s	106
Navigational join on oid	32	65s	37s	67s	2s	0.32s	266
Existentially quantified query	8	15s	7s	9s	1s	0.06s	35
Merge-join query	5222	9293s	5348s	3100s	9s	2.18s	3164
Multi-join query	184	264s	166s	1400s	9s	3.34s	8173
Query calling derived function	32	32s	22s	53s	-	-	-
Query calling recursive derived function	5	27s	17s	110s	-	-	-

4.2 Future Directions

Leading on from this work, we intend looking at "mixed-model" optimisation, dealing with queries requiring some data to be retrieved from a relational database and some data from other kinds of module, or a calculation that cannot be performed using SQL. At present, such queries can be answered by translating the query to the Prolog including calls to the P/FDM primitives. However, as mentioned above, breaking a query into its most basic steps and executing these in sequence can be inefficient. We aim to identify sub-parts of a query that can be grouped and passed to the SQL server at the same time and then combine results of this search with other data retrieval operations and calculations.

So far, our work has focused on retrieval. The P/FDM system also provides primitive routines for adding new entity instances and adding new function values. Versions of these routines have been written which operate on relational modules, again by using the ProDBI package. Updates expressed in Daplex are translated into Prolog code including calls to these primitives. We have not yet tried translating Daplex update commands directly into SQL. This has not been a limitation for the protein structure application since that data is loaded in bulk and is not normally updated interactively. However, interactive updates are important in design applications, like modelling new protein structures by homology. If we were to extend the DAPSTRA program to deal with update commands, we could evaluate the use of relational modules for design storage, instead of the hash files that we use at present.

5 Conclusions

We have used a relational database to provide an alternative form of persistent storage for a functional data model database. Thus we have the benefits of using a robust commercial product for storing our large data sets, and sharing the same data format as our project partners who wish to develop customised interfaces to a relational database management system. We do not claim that our object/relational mapping is original, indeed others have mapped objects onto relational tables [4]. However, as far as we know, ours is the only system using Daplex with relational storage.

The DAPSTRA program can translate a subset of Daplex queries into single SQL statements by operating on an internal form of the query which resembles a list comprehension. Using DAPSTRA, performance for simple searches is close to that obtained by using SQL directly, i.e. the time to generate the SQL is not significant. The main efficiency improvement in translating simple list comprehensions to a single SQL statement, rather than to the equivalent Prolog, comes from two sources. First, it avoids the overhead of parsing and moving penny-packet queries with one result. Secondly, selection is done early on the server instead of in Prolog.

Daplex has greater expressive power than SQL, and other queries against the relational schema that cannot be translated to SQL can still be answered by translating these to Prolog code including calls to P/FDM retrieval routines. Still more demanding searches, combining calculation with data retrieval, can be written directly in Prolog.

Our objective was to present a functional data model view of protein structure data, exploiting a relational database's query optimiser and indexing where possible, while still being able to process any arbitrary Daplex query. We consider this to be a practical advance that is generally useful, and one that is necessary for our work with large volumes of protein data.

References

1. Embury, S.M., Jiao, Z. and Gray, P.M.D.: Using Prolog to Provide Access to Metadata in an Object-Oriented Database. In Proc. of The Practical Application of Prolog, London, 1st-3rd April (1992)
2. Gray, P.M.D., Kulkarni, K.G. and Paton, N.W.: Object-oriented databases: A semantic data model approach. Prentice Hall International (UK) Ltd., Hemel Hempstead (1992)
3. Gray, P.M.D., Paton, N.W., Kemp, G.J.L. and Fothergill, J.E.: An object-oriented database for protein structure analysis. Protein Engineering 3 (1990) 235-243
4. Hughes, J.G.: Object-oriented Databases. Prentice Hall International (UK) Ltd., Hemel Hempstead (1991)

5. Huysmans, M., Richelle, J. and Wodak, S.J.: SESAM: a relational database for structure and sequence of macromolecules. Proteins: Structure, Function and Genetics **11** (1991) 59–76
6. Islam, S.A. and Sternberg, M.J.E.: A relational database of protein structures designed for flexible enquiries about conformation. Protein Engineering **2** (1989) 431–442
7. Jiao, Z. and Gray, P.M.D.: Optimisation of methods in a navigational query language. In Delobel, C., Kifer, M. and Masunaga, Y. (eds.) Proc. 2nd International Conference on Deductive and Object-Oriented Databases, Springer-Verlag (1991) 22–42
8. Kemp, G.J.L.: Protein modelling: a design application of an object-oriented database. In Gero, J.S. (ed.) Artificial intelligence in design '91, Butterworth-Heinmann Ltd., (1991) 387–406
9. Kemp, G.J.L. and Gray, P.M.D.: Finding hydrophobic microdomains using an object-oriented database. CABIOS **6** (1990) 357–363
10. Keylink Computers Limited: ProDBI Quintus/Sybase Interface V3.0B User Manual (1992)
11. Paton, N.W. and Gray, P.M.D.: Optimising and Executing DAPLEX Queries using Prolog. The Computer Journal **33** (1990) 547–555
12. Shipman D.W.: The Functional Data Model and the Data Language DAPLEX. ACM Transactions on Database Systems **6** (1981) 140–173
13. Trinder, P. and Wadler, P.: Improving List Comprehension Database Queries. Proceedings of TENCON'89, Bombay, India (1989) 186–192

A Conceptual Language for Querying Object Oriented Data

Peter J Barclay and Jessie B Kennedy

Computer Studies Dept., Napier University
219 Colinton Road, Edinburgh EH14 1DJ

Abstract. A variety of languages have been proposed for object oriented database systems in order to provide facilities for *ad hoc* querying. However, in order to model at the conceptual level, an object oriented schema definition language must itself provide facilities for describing the behaviour of data. This paper demonstrates that with only modest extensions, such a schema definition language may serve as a query notation. These extensions are concerned solely with supporting the interactive nature of *ad hoc* querying, providing facilities for naming and displaying query operations and their results.

1 Overview

Section 2 reviews the background to this work; its objectives are outlined in section 3. Section 4 describes NOODL constructs which are used to define behaviour within schemata, and section 5 examines how these may be extended for interactive use. The resulting query notation is evaluated in section 6. Section 7 outlines some further work and section 8 concludes.

2 Background

NOM (the Napier Object Model) is a simple data model intended to allow object oriented modelling of data at a conceptual level; it was first presented in [BK91] and is described fully in [Bar93]. NOM has been used to model [BK92a] and to support the implementation [BFK92] of novel database applications, and also for the investigation of specific modelling issues such as declarative integrity constraints and activeness [BK92b] and the incorporation of views [BK93] in object oriented data models.

The data definition and manipulation language NOODL (Napier Object Oriented Data Language) may be used to specify enterprises modelled using NOM. A NOODL schema contains a list of class definitions, which show the name and ancestors of each class.

A class definition also includes the names, sorts, and definitions of the properties of each class. Property definitions may contain simple expressions showing how the value of the property is derived from those of other properties. The ability to specify such derived properties allows the capture of data's behaviour within the enterprise schema. A class definition may also contain operations, constraints, and triggers, which are not discussed in detail here (see [BK91] or [Bar93] for more details).

NOM supports a principle of context substitutability, demanding that where an instance of some class is required, an instance of one of its descendant classes may always be substituted; this requires strict inheritance.

An example NOODL schema is shown in shown in figure 1; the syntax of NOODL is described in [Bar93].

The GNOME system (Generic Napier Object Model Environment) is an implementation of NOM in the persistent programming language Napier88 [DCBM89], [MBCD89]. Although the query language described here has been successfully implemented and may be used to interrogate objects managed by GNOME, this exposition will not address implementation issues.

2.1 NOM's Query Model

The construction of schemata requires an implicit query model for the evaluation of derived properties. Here, objects exchange messages, in response to which the query expressions encoded in the definitions of their properties are evaluated; these evaluations may result in the sending of further messages to further objects. This approach maintains a strong correspondence between real world and model objects.

Specifically, and unlike many other models, NOM does not allow the creation of new objects as the result of a query (although new *collections* of existing objects may be formed). In addition to adherence to the conceptual model, this prevents query results from being detached from the class lattice. This dispenses with the need to classify result-objects in the preexistent hierarchy (*eg*, [DD91], [Kim89]). This principle also provides *closure* in the query model; since queries may return only collections of preexisting objects, these may certainly be the targets of further, cascaded messages. Since no new objects are created, problems of comparing identifiers of objects returned by queries do not arise.

3 Objectives of This Work

A variety of object oriented database query languages exist; some are languages supporting the logical model provided by a particular OODB (*eg*, [MSOP86]); others are implementations of the query languages of semantic data models (*eg*, [KA87]); some are attempts to add object oriented extensions to SQL (*eg*, [ont90], [RS87]). These languages are intended to allow users to perform *ad hoc* queries on a database, to embed these in application programs, or both. However, Kim has argued that many of these languages are inadequate since they are not based on an underlying object oriented model of querying [Kim89], which takes into account the different abstraction mechanisms used in the schema definition against which querying is performed.

However, since an object oriented data model must capture the behaviour of the objects described, a query notation is necessary simply to *describe* an enterprise. The only alternatives are either to use natural language comments to describe the behaviour of data objects (losing precision), or to describe this behaviour in a host programming language (losing the conceptual level of the data description). As Zicari *et al* have pointed out, in object oriented database systems, the query language and the method definition language are seldom the same [Zic91]. Efforts are underway to establish a standard object oriented data description language [Atw93], [Hol93]; such a task would be facilitated by establishing a standard data manipulation language.

Since a data description language (DDL) must necessarily describe how objects interact with each other, it must contain a data manipulation language (DML); hence it is not possible to maintain two separate notations for these functions.

3.1 Integration of the Schema Definition Language and the Query Language

In the course of developing NOODL it became apparent that a schema definition language required considerable behavioural capture in order to specify derived properties, as well as constraints and triggers. When desire to support *ad hoc* querying in GNOME necessitated a query specification language, it was decided to develop this language by the minimal reasonable extension of NOODL. This approach seemed to offer the best integration of modelling and query notations, and would be easiest to implement since a compiler already existed for NOODL as a schema definition language.

Further, since NOM was designed as a 'vanilla' model, supporting only those features agreed upon by the majority of object oriented data models, it seemed that this approach might give some insight into the ability of any object oriented data model notation to support *ad hoc* querying, provided only that it allows specification of behavioural aspects of the model without resorting to use of a 3GL.

The facilities of NOODL as a schema definition language, and then its adaptation to *ad hoc* querying, are discussed in subsequent sections.

4 NOODL as a Schema Definition Language

This section shows how, in schema definitions, behavioural expressions may require to be written. The names of properties defined in NOODL schemata can be used as gettors and settors for those properties; this already provides a basis for a navigational query notation. In order to increase behavioural expressivity, it is necessary also to have constructs to handle collections of objects, and to build up more complex query expressions. These are described in the succeeding sections. The examples are based on the schema shown in figure 1.

4.1 Basic Query Expressions

Basic queries are of two types, here called navigational-style and search-style queries.

4.2 Navigational-Style Expressions

A navigational-style query finds some information which is implicit in the enterprise model. For example, consider the schema in figure 1 describing people with spouses, who own coloured cars (assuming one car per person). The property spousesCarColour returns the colour of any Person's spouse's car. If LEIF is an object of class

```
                  schema Example

     domain Colour is ( "crimson", "aquamarine", "puce" )
     domain Money is { defined elsewhere }

  class Person                        class Employee
  properties                          ISA Person
     { stored properties }            properties
     name     : Text     ;;              salary  : Money   ;;
     city     : Text     ;;              company : Company
     age      : Number   ;;
     spouse   : Person   ;;
     car      : Car      ;;
     children : #Person  ;;
     { derived properties }
     grandchildren         : ##Person is
        self.children.children ;;
     spousesCarColour      : Text is
        self.spouse.car.colour ;;
     likeMindedCarOwners : #Person is
        Person where its.car.make = self.car.make


  class Car                           class Company
  properties                          properties
     make   : Text    ;;                 name : Text  ;;
     colour : Colour                     city : Text  { etc }

                  end_schema { Example }
```

Fig. 1. Example NOODL Schema

Person, then the expression `LEIF.spouse.car.colour` is a navigational-style query returning the colour of Leif's wife's car.

The tokens `spouse`, `car` and `colour` are messages which elicit the value of the property of the same name; the definition of the property, including whether the value is settable or derived, is found in the enterprise schema (strong encapsulation). The dot operator `.` sends the message on its right to the object returned by evaluating the expression on its left[1]. The general form of such a navigational style expression is:

   `<receiver>.<message_name>[.<message_name>]*`

In a property definition appearing in an enterprise schema, `<receiver>` will usually be the reserved word `self`, which denotes the instance receiving the message for the property being defined.

---

[1] Although statements involving expressions with one and more than one dot operator are respectively called 'simple' and 'complex' predicates by Kim [Kim89], there is no essential difference between these.

4.3 Search-Style Expressions

A search-style query finds all the objects in some collection which match a given selection criterion. This style of query is more usually associated with *ad hoc* querying of a database, but may reasonably be required also to allow definition of derived properties in an enterprise schema, where the value of that property is a set of instances meeting some condition.

For example, a property likeMindedCarOwners of class Person, which returns all Person instances owning the same kind of car as the instance in question, may be defined as follows:

```
Person where its.car.make = self.car.make
```

The general form of a search-style query expression is:

```
<collection> where <predicate>
```

In an enterprise schema, `<collection>` will usually be the name of a class in the schema, to whose full extent it is taken to refer. In `<predicate>` the reserved word `it` or `its` is taken to stand for an element of the collection, to allow formulation of the selection criterion, and the reserved word `self` refers to the instance of the class defined whose property is being evaluated.

Kim points out that the collection to which a query is posed may be either the direct extent of a class, or its full extent, including the instances of all descendant classes [Kim89]; Chan calls this issue *class qualification* [Cha92]. On account of the principle of context substitutability, the name of a class in a query expression in NOODL is always taken to refer to its full extent; however, at the cost of complicating the selection predicate, it is possible to define precisely which descendant classes are to be included in the search space, rather than just the two possibilities cited by Kim. For example, the following query will retrieve all persons called "Leif", but omitting any who are instances of the class Manager. Instances of all classes descended from Person, either above or below Manager in the class lattice, are to be included:

```
Person where its.name  = "Leif"
         and its.class <> Manager
```

4.4 Treatment of Set-Valued Properties

The value of a set-valued property is a set of objects or of primitive values. The following operations are available on sets; their names are NOODL reserved words: `union`, `intersection`, `difference`, `add`, `remove`, `member`, `cardinality`, `element` (and `contains`, described below). The first three perform the appropriate binary set operation and return a new set. The next three add an element, remove an element, or test for its prior inclusion. The operation `element` returns a random element of the set (but always the same element for a given set instance); this allows access to the element of a singleton set, and also permits computational recursion over sets.

Where any other message is sent to a set, this message is mapped over all the set's elements (and, where appropriate, the set of responses returned). This allows a very transparent treatment of sets, and also allows queries to return nested collections which preserve the association structure of the enterprise model. So for example, the expression `LEIF.children` returns the set of Leif's children, and the expression `LEIF.children.name` returns the set of names of Leif's children. Given the family tree shown in figure 2, various expressions and the objects they return are shown in table 1.

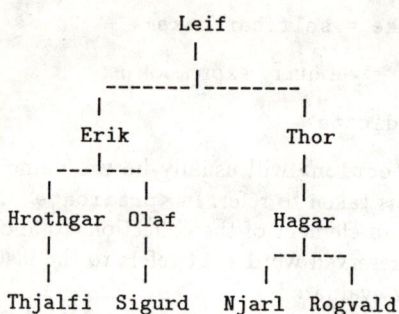

Fig. 2. Family Tree

expression	value
LEIF.children	{ERIK, THOR}
LEIF.children.children	{{HROTHGAR, OLAF}, {HAGAR}}
LEIF.children.children.children	{{{THJALFI}, {SIGURD}},{{NJARL, ROGVALD}}}

Table 1. Set-Valued Expressions from Family Tree

The `contains` operator determines whether a value is present anywhere within a nested collection. This allows the structure of the nested collections to be retained, unlike the 'flattening' operators provided in some object oriented query languages (*eg*, the `reunion` operator of LIFOO [BM81], or the `flatten` operator in ENCORE [SZ90]). If it *is* required to flatten a collection, this can still be done by using `contains` to select from the top level collection everything present in any nested subcollection. For example, {{HROTHGAR, OLAF}, {HAGAR}} can be flattened to {HROTHGAR, OLAF, HAGAR} by evaluating

`Person where LEIF.children.children contains it`

This expression picks out and returns all instances of class Person which are present (at any level) in the nested collection.

4.5 More Complex Expressions

More complex behavioural expressions may be built from sequences or compositions of simple query expressions; these may also contain conditional or update statements[2].

The target for a query is an object or collection of objects. Since the result of a query is also an object or collection of objects, the query model is *closed*; hence it is possible to compose, or nest, queries.

It has been proclaimed by Atkinson *et al* that the data model of an object oriented database system should be computationally complete [ABD+89]; if computational completeness is not to be relegated to a host programming language, it is necessary that is should be provided by the data language. For this purpose, NOODL has a conditional expression in the form of an `if` statement. Provision of a conditional expression, together with implicit iteration over sets and recursive function calls, allows the language to be considered computationally complete. Properties (and operations and triggers) may thus be defined which in principle perform arbitrary computations.

5 Adaptation to *Ad Hoc* Querying

Preceding sections have focused on the subset of NOODL dealing with what are traditionally considered data manipulation tasks. NOODL allows the construction of enterprise schemata where the behaviour of objects may be represented. In particular, it is possible to specify rules for the derivation of the values of properties.

NOODL allows the design of schemata for object oriented databases such as the GNOME system. However, one feature normally provided by a database management system is some form of *ad hoc* querying, allowing casual users to explore the data stored without resorting to writing programs. Persistent applications have included form-based [CMA87] or graphical [BFK92] interfaces, and also browsers for the persistent store [KD90]. Here, some simple extensions to NOODL are presented which allow it to be used as an *ad hoc* query language. Unlike forms and some graphical interfaces, NOODL is not application specific when used as a querying mechanism; it may be used for any enterprise describable within the object oriented modelling approach adopted here. Further, the data store is interrogated at the conceptual level of the enterprise model, rather than at the level of programming language constructs.

The following sections investigate what extensions to NOODL would be necessary in order for it to function as an *ad hoc* querying language.

5.1 Requirements for *Ad Hoc* Querying

Used as a tool for data description, NOODL provides facilities for retrieving and updating values or sets of values, and for selecting objects satisfying some criterion. Only modest extensions to these facilities are required for *ad hoc* querying.

---

[2] The semantics of *mixed* query and update statements may be problematical as discussed by Ghelli *et al* in [GOPT92].

Firstly, since there is no notion of 'display' in data definition, some means of showing what the user wants to know must be provided.

An enterprise schema is a complete conceptual description of an enterprise, serving as a 'definitive text' for applications serving the enterprise. *Ad hoc* querying, on the other hand, is an iterative, explorative procedure; facilities are required to incrementalise the construction of queries, and allow a feedback loop between formulating a query and seeing the result (query-building). The syntax of a query language should support these activities as naturally as possible.

Such support is provided by local names, which may be assigned to the (collections of) objects returned by a query, or to a query itself. Together with the display operation, these provide a sufficient basis for *ad hoc* querying. Displaying data and managing local names and definitions are facilities available during a query session; the NOODL constructs supporting these activities are not used within an enterprise schema.

Such locally defined query expressions may be viewed as 'behaviour constructors' ([YO91]); they may also be used to express join-like queries, retrieving together information not related through the relationships encoded in the enterprise schema ('coincidences in the data').

The following sections describe extensions to NOODL which support the necessary functionality; some examples of *ad hoc* queries executed using this system may be found in the appendix.

5.2 Conceptual *Ad Hoc* Query Model

A query model is implicit in the specification of derived properties. The concept of a *querier* extends this model to *ad hoc* use.[3] The querier is an object which straddles the interface between the real world and the data space. Its user interface allows a user to construct NOODL queries, which are syntax- and sort-checked, and could in principle be optimised; the corresponding sequence of messages are then sent into the data space, and a new collection of objects constructed in response to these. The querier then represents these objects to its human user in some intelligible format.

5.3 Local Definitions — Tags

The two approaches to querying supported are navigational-style and search-style queries. In constructing complex queries (especially nested queries), it is often useful to break the query down into distinct components. The user should be allowed to construct queries incrementally, rather than being forced to resubmit an entire query when only a component subquery requires modification.

To support this approach, the querier allows local definitions. Here, a local name, called a *tag*, is introduced to refer to an intermediate query result. This tag is known only within the query session, not within the enterprise schema. As a convention, such tags are written in upper case.

Earlier examples used the token LEIF to refer to the object representing the person Leif; this name is defined to the querier as a tag as shown, and prevents the need to embed the expression locating the object LEIF in queries which refer to it.

---

[3] GNOME's query facility is an implementation of this querier.

```
Person where its.name = "Leif" ;;
tag LEIF result.element
```

Here, `element` removes the object LEIF from the singleton set which is returned by the query; `result` is a NOODL reserved word providing a tag always bound to the result of the most recently executed query.

Tags are more useful where entire collections are retrieved, examined interactively to ensure that they do indeed contain the correct objects, and then used as building blocks for the construction of other more complex queries. The general form of a tag definition is:

```
tag <tag_name> <query_expression>
```

The concept of a local definition is further developed in a succeeding section on query methods, which are locally defined query expressions.

5.4 Seeing the Result

So far, queries which return (collections of) objects have been discussed, with no indication of how the result may be displayed. Here, the relational model has a clear advantage, since relations correspond closely to the concept of a table; tuples retrieved from relations may be displayed as tables, the relational `project` operator (*ie*, the SQL command `select`) being used to customise the contents of these tables.

The objects returned by NOODL queries are collections of objects, possibly with properties which are other objects, and possibly with properties which are collections. It is harder to display these as tables, since neither complex objects nor collections conveniently fit into a single slot. A further problem is that although a certain collection of objects is returned as a query result, we may wish to display information relating to several classes of object (*eg*, 'show the name and salary of all IBM employees, and the make and colour of the car they drive').

These difficulties constitute an under-estimated difficulty in arriving at a clear conceptual query model for object oriented data. This section demonstrates how the NOODL `show` command, (available in interactive mode only), can be used for the tabular visualisation of query results (including nested tabulation); object-valued properties and set-valued properties will be discussed, together with display of information from different but navigationally-linked classes; display of information from classes unrelated in the application schema will be treated in the following section.

The show Command The `show` command displays the requested information for each of a collection of objects, with the option of attaching textual headings to the resultant table. Tabularisation is automatically provided. The information requested may be the value of any property of the object, or of any other object to which it is navigationally linked. The example below shows the name and salary of all IBM employees, together with the make and colour of their car.

```
Employee where its.company.name = "IBM" ;;
show "name" result.name, "earns" result.salary,
     "car" result.car.make, "car colour" result.car.colour
```

```
name              earns    car     car colour
=============    =====    =====   ==========
Leif Svensson |  20000 |  Volvo | crimson
Erik Leifsson |  15000 |  Volvo | aquamarine
```

Where the value of a property is a collection, each value of the collection is shown nested in the table; nesting may in principle be to any depth. The query below shows all people together with their children and grandchildren.

```
show "person" Person.name,
     "children" Person.children.name,
     "grandchildren" Person.children.children.name
```

```
person            children              grandchildren
=============    =================    =====================
Leif Svensson |  Erik Leifsson      | Hrothgar Eriksson
                                    | Olaf Eriksson
              |  Thor Leifsson      | Hagar Thorsson
Erik Leifsson |  Hrothgar Eriksson  | Thjalfi Hrothgarsson
              |  Olaf Eriksson      | Sigurd Olafsson
Thor Leifsson |  Hagar Thorsson     | Njarl Hagarsson
                                    | Rogvald Hagarsson

- - - - - - - - - - - etc - - - - - - - - - - - -
```

An attempt to show the value of an object-valued (*ie*, non-lexical) property will show its object identifier as shown below.

```
Person where its.name = "Leif" ;;
tag LEIF result.element        ;;
show "Leif's wife" LEIF.spouse
```

```
Leif's wife
===========
o# 26473
```

```
Object where its.oid = 26473 ;;
show "Leif's wife's name" result.name
```

```
Leif's wife's name
=========================
Freyja Thorgrimssdottir
```

5.5 Local Definitions — Query Methods

Query methods are behaviour constructors, which locally name some query in the same way that tags locally name some object or collection of objects. Query methods are introduced by the NOODL reserved word **defun**, and after definition may be used within a query session as if they were properties defined for the relevant class in the enterprise schema.

Query methods may be used to incrementalise the construction of complex queries, and also to represent 'join-like' queries.

The join operator is highly used in the relational model. Often, the need for a join arises directly from the limitations of this model; since all attributes must be primitive, a query such as the example above must be expressed as something like:

```
SELECT PERSON.NAME, PERSON.WAGE, CAR.MAKE, CAR.COLOUR
FROM PERSON, CAR, COMPANY
WHERE PERSON.CAR_REG = CAR.REG_NO
  AND PERSON.COMPANY_NO = COMPANY.COMPANY_NO
  AND COMPANY.NAME = 'IBM'
```

Here, the joins really encode the navigational link between person, car, and company, inherent in the conceptual schema; this kind of join is never necessary in NOM since object-valued properties are permitted.

Sometimes, however, a join will be used in the relational model to search for a 'coincidence' in the data — some relationship not directly expressed in the enterprise schema. The need to retain the ability to express such queries in object oriented models has been pointed out by Shaw and Zdonik [SZ90], and by Yu and Osborn [YO91].

Consider a query to show the name of all companies located in the same city as each person, based on the schema in figure 1; this requires a join-like search. The query can be achieved by defining a query method[4] **same_city** which returns the colocated companies of its person argument as follows:

```
defun same_city ( Person ) : # Company is
    Company where its.city = self.city
```

This defines a query method which traverses the extent of class Company and returns all those instances whose city property matches that of its argument, an instance of class Person; this method may be applied to an instance of class Person as if it were a property defined in its schema. The class on which the query method is defined is shown in parentheses after its name; it is to an instance of this class (or its descendants) that the reserved variable **self** refers when it appears in the following definition.

In order to show the colocated cities of each person, **same_city** is mapped over the extent of class Person:

```
show "the person" Person.name,
     "colocated companies" Person.same_city.name
```

Further, the example shows that this approach may also be used to express queries which return properties of more than one object, without the need to create new objects or classes at query time.

---

[4] The syntax for the definition of query methods is similar to that for the definition of *operations* in NOODL schemata.

5.6 Treatment of Null Values

Zicari *et al* have pointed out that few object oriented query models have attempted a treatment of null values [Zic91]. Although problematical in the relational model, it is possible that approaches to nulls based on the criterion of identity (*eg*, that of Larner [Lar91]) may be well suited to an object oriented model where identity is a central concept ([KC86]). This is a topic for further research.

The current version of NOM, however, takes a simple, pragmatic approach to the treatment of null values. In the same way that a class Object is provided as the most general class (used to hold those definitions common to all classes) the class Bottom is provided as the most specific class. From the principle of context substitutability, this means that an instance `bottom` of class Bottom can appear in the context of an instance of any other class. `bottom` is a NOODL reserved word referring to such a (newly-generated) instance of class Bottom.

All the properties inherited by class Bottom are overridden by definitions which always return that same instance of class Bottom in response to any object-valued message, or suitable fail-values in response to any primitive-valued message. In this way, an instance `bottom` can cascade through a query expression of arbitrary depth.

For example, if evaluation of the expression `LEIF.spouse.car.colour` should fail because Leif has no wife, the following evaluation sequence will occur:

```
LEIF.spouse.car.colour
  -> bottom.car.colour
     -> bottom.colour
        -> ""
```

This pragmatic approach has desirable properties, described in [Bar93]. Particularly, the use of `bottom` as a null value fits into the conceptual framework of NOM, and the presence of a `bottom` cannot cause a message expression to fail to be evaluated; `bottom` may also be used to represent object deletion. Expressions which may involve `bottom` may be statically sort-checked ensuring semantic consistency. The approach has been implemented, and could also be extended to gather debugging information automatically for cases where unexpected null values are encountered.

6 An Evaluation of Query Models

Yu and Osborn [YO91] have evaluated the query models proposed by Manola and Dayal [MD86], Osborn [Osb88], Straube and Özsu [SO91], and Shaw and Zdonik [Sha87]. Table 2 is a summary of their results, together with an evaluation of NOODL (as a query notation) in the same framework. A 'Y' means that the criterion is met, a 'N' that it is not met, a dot that it is partially met, and a question mark that it is not clear from any available documentation whether it is met.

The criteria of the evaluation are explained in detail in [YO91]. Yu and Osborn state that the features checked in their evaluation, although at times somewhat mutually incompatible, are generally desirable. It is interesting to notice, that although not originally designed for *ad hoc* querying, NOODL compares favourably within this framework.

	Manola + Dayal	Osborn	Straube + Ozsu	Shaw + Zdonik	NOODL
OBJECT ORIENTEDNESS					
object identities	.	.	.	Y	.
encapsulation	Y	N	Y	Y	Y
inheritance	N	N	Y	N	Y
polymorphism	N	.	N	N	Y
classes + collections	N	Y	N	Y	Y
heterogeneous sets	?	Y	Y	Y	Y
EXPRESSIVENESS					
extends rel. alg.	Y	Y	N	Y	.
object constructors	.	Y	N	N	N
invocable behaviours	Y	N	Y	Y	Y
behaviour constructors	N	N	.	N	Y
dynamic type creation	Y	Y	N	Y	N
querying closures	Y	N	N	N	Y
behaviours as objects	N	N	N	N	N
FORMALNESS					
formal semantics	N	N	Y	.	N
closed	N	N	Y	Y	Y
PERFORMANCE					
strong typing	Y	N	Y	Y	Y
optimisable	Y	Y	Y	Y	Y
DATABASE ISSUES					
object lifetimes	N	.	N	?	.
schema evolution	N	.	N	N	Y
calculus	N	N	.	N	N

Table 2. Summary of Yu and Osborn's Evaluation (NOODL added)

7 Further Work

The version of NOODL described here has been used for investigation of various issues in object oriented data modelling. However, for practical use it requires some extensions, whether used for data definition (incorporation of query expressions in schemata), for embedding in programs, or for *ad hoc* querying. These extensions include a wider range of primitive sorts (including graphics sorts), a wider range of collection types, aggregate functions and collection literals. It is planned to pursue some case studies in the use of NOODL, and to experiment with, and perhaps automate, the mapping of NOODL onto the query languages provided by some proprietary object oriented database systems.

It is planned to map the querying constructs of NOODL onto a formal model such as list [Tri90] or object [CT94] comprehensions; this will enable the application of appropriate logical optimisation techniques (*eg*, [TW90], [JG91]). Addition of indexing structures also remains to be undertaken.

The tabular visualisation mechanism provided by the current version of NOODL is intended as a basic, minimum facility for the presentation of data. Work is ongoing to develop graphical tools which will integrate querying with schema management, and provide more comprehensive forms of data visualisation.

8 Conclusion

The use of NOODL to express queries over object oriented data arose, not from the intention to design a language for *ad hoc* querying, but from the recognition that if a data description language is to capture the behavioural aspects of the data, it must be capable of expressing data manipulation.

The notation presented has been based on a conceptual query model, which the authors believe is simple and natural. Provision of such a 'vanilla' query model, based on the features essential to the object oriented paradigm, makes it possible to construct enterprise schemata without losing the conceptual level by embedding in a host programming language.

Addition of some modest features have extended the notation sufficiently to allow construction of a wide class of *ad hoc* queries, including some that the query languages of many prototype OODBMSs are unable to express (see [BK93] and [CHT93]). The show command allows a tabular visualisation of object oriented data. Local definitions support the incremental construction of complex queries, and query functions support the incremental construction of join-like subqueries without the need to create new object identities. These added features do not extend the semantics of the notation; rather, they simply make it more convenient for interactive use.

NOODL provides simple but powerful constructs for querying. Although it has distinctive aspects, such as the transparent treatment of set-valued properties, it is proposed not so much as a novel query language, but rather as a demonstration of the integration of schema definition and querying notations.

When an *ad hoc* query notation is supported, these queries should be expressed in the same notation as the conceptual model. Failing to do this has two undesirable consequences: firstly, the number of notations the user must master may increase to as many as three; and secondly, cognitive dissonance may arise if the conceptual model, which is likely to be held up as a reference during the construction of queries, is expressed differently.

Appendix — Query Examples

This section presents two more substantial queries expressed in NOODL. (A more complete set of example queries, adapted from those used by Gray *et al* in [GKP92, chapter 2], may be found in [Bar93]). These examples are adapted from queries used in [CHT93], and refer to the following NOODL schema, adapted from Chan's paper:

```
                    schema Chans_Examples

    class Company                    class Financier
    properties
       name    : Text       ;;       class LoanGivingDealer
       models  : # CarModel          ISA Dealer, Financier

    class CarModel                   class Address
    properties                       properties
       facilities : # Text  ;;          street   : Text ;;
       dealers    : # Dealer            postcode : Text ;;
                                        city     : Text

    class Dealer                     class Garage
    properties                       properties
       name    : Text       ;;          name    : Text ;;
       address : Address                address : Address

                   end_schema { Chans_Examples }
```

(**Query 1**) Find names and prices of all non-Ford models that have an insurance group lower than 5; the answer should include only hatchbacks and saloons with radio and cassette player:

```
defun non_ford ( CarModel ) :  Boolean is    { determine whether this }
     Company where its.name <> 'Ford'   ;    { model is available     }
     result.models contains self        ;;   { from non Ford dealer   }

Carmodel where its.carType = 'Saloon'
         or its.carType = 'Hatchback'
        and its.facilities contains 'tapeplayer'
        and its.facilities contains 'radio'
        and its.non_ford                     ;;

show result.name, result.price               ;;
```

(**Query 2**) Show names of Ford models and Ford dealers that provide loan as a financial option for car purchase; the answer should include only dealers located in a city where there are at least two garages:

```
{ show number of garages in city where a dealer is located }

defun num_garages ( Dealer ) : Number is
     Garage where its.address.city = self.address.city    ;
     result.cardinality                                   ;;

defun ideal_dealer ( CarModel ) is
     LoanGivingDealer where self.dealers contains it
                     and its.num_garages >= 2             ;
     show result.name, result.address                     ;;


tag ford_companies Company where its.name = "Ford"       ;;
CarModel where ford_companies.models contains it         ;;
show result.name, result.ideal_dealer
```

References

[ABD+89] M Atkinson, F Bancilhon, D DeWitt, K Dittrich, D Maier, and S Zdonik. The Object Oriented Database System Manifesto: (a Political Pamphlet). In *Proceedings of DOOD*, Kyoto, Dec 1989.

[Atw93] Thomas Atwood. The Object DBMS Standard. *Object Magazine*, pages 37 – 44, September-October 1993.

[Bar93] Peter J Barclay. *Object Oriented Modelling of Complex Data with Automatic Generation of a Persistent Representation*. PhD thesis, Napier University, Edinburgh, 1993.

[BFK92] Peter J Barclay, Colin M Fraser, and Jessie B Kennedy. Using a Persistent System to Construct a Customised Interface to an Ecological Database. In Richard Cooper, editor, *Proceedings of the 1st International Workshop on Interfaces to Database Systems*, pages 225 – 243, Glasgow, 1992. Springer Verlag.

[BK91] Peter J Barclay and Jessie B Kennedy. Regaining the Conceptual Level in Object Oriented Data Modelling. In *Aspects of Databases (Proceedings of BNCOD-9)*, pages 269 – 305, Wolverhampton, Jun 1991. Butterworths.

[BK92a] Peter J Barclay and Jessie B Kennedy. Modelling Ecological Data. In *Proceedings of the 6th International Working Conference on Scientific and Statistical Database Management*, pages 77 – 93, Ascona, Switzerland, Jun 1992. Eidgenössische Technische Hochschule, Zurich.

[BK92b] Peter J Barclay and Jessie B Kennedy. Semantic Integrity for Persistent Objects. *Information and Software Technology*, 34(8):533 – 541, August 1992.

[BK93] Peter J Barclay and Jessie B Kennedy. Viewing Objects. In *Advances in Databases (Proceedings of BNCOD-11)*, pages 93 – 110. Springer Verlag (Lecture Notes in Computer Science Series), 1993.

[BM81] O Boucelma and JL Maitre. Querying Complex-Object Databases. Internal report, University of Marseilles, 1981.

[Cha92]   Daniel Chan. A Survey of Object Oriented Database Query Languages. Internal report, University of Glasgow, Feb 1992.
[CHT93]   Daniel KC Chan, David J Harper, and Philip W Trinder. A Case Study of Object Oriented Query Languages. In *Proceedings of the International Conference on Information Systems and the Management of Data*, pages 63 – 86. Indian National Scientific Documentation Centre (INSDOC), 1993.
[CMA87]   RL Cooper, DK MacFarlane, and S Ahmed. User Interface Tools in PS-algol. Technical report PPRR-56-87, Universities of Glasgow and St Andrews, Mar 1987.
[CT94]   Daniel KC Chan and Philip W Trinder. Object Comprehensions: A Query Notation for Object-Oriented Databases. In *Proceedings of BNCOD-12*, Guildford, Surrey, 1994. Springer Verlag.
[DCBM89]   Alan Dearle, Richard Connor, Fred Brown, and Ron Morrison. Napier88 - A Database Programming Language? In *Proceedings of DBPL-2*, pages 213 – 230, 1989.
[DD91]   KC Davis and LML Delcambre. Foundations for Object Oriented Query Processing. *Computer Standards and Interfaces*, 13:207 – 212, 1991.
[GKP92]   Peter MD Gray, Krishnarao G Kulkarni, and Norman W Paton. *Object Oriented Databases: A Semantic Data Model Approach*. Prentice Hall, 1992.
[GOPT92]   Giorgio Ghelli, Renzo Orsini, Alvaro Pereira Paz, and Phil Trinder. Design of an Integrated Query and Manipulation Notation for Database Languages. Technical report FIDE/92/41, Universities of Pisa, Salerno, Glasgow and Sviluppo Research Laboratory, 1992.
[Hol93]   Glenn Hollowell. *Handbook of Object Oriented Standards: the Object Model*. Addison Wesley, 1993.
[JG91]   Zhuoan Jiao and Peter MD Gray. Optimisation of Methods in a Navigational Query Language. In *Proceedings of DOOD-2*, pages 22 – 41, 1991.
[KA87]   KG Kulkarni and MP Atkinson. Implementing an Extended Functional Data Model in PS-algol. *Software Practice and Experience*, 17(3):171 – 185, 1987.
[KC86]   S Khoshafian and GC Copeland. Object Identity. In Norman Meyrowitz, editor, *Proceedings of OOPSLA*, pages 406 – 416, Portland, Oregon, September 1986.
[KD90]   Graham Kirby and Alan Dearle. An Adaptive Graphical Browser for Napier88. Technical report, University of St Andrews, 1990.
[Kim89]   Won Kim. A Model of Queries for Object Oriented Databases. In Peter MG Aspers and Gio Wiederhold, editors, *Proceedings of VLDB*, pages 423 – 431, Amsterdam, 1989. Morgan Kaufmann.
[Lar91]   Adrian Larner. On Nulls. Internal report, IBM, Warwick, 1991.
[MBCD89]   R Morrison, F Brown, R Connor, and A Dearle. The Napier88 Reference Manual. Technical report PPRR-77-89, Universities of Glasgow and St Andrews, Jul 1989.
[MD86]   F Manola and U Dayal. PDM: an Object Oriented Data Model. In *Proceedings of the International Workshop on Object Oriented Database Systems*, pages 18 – 25, Sep 1986.
[MSOP86]   D Maier, DJ Stein, A Otis, and A Purdy. Development of an Object Oriented DBMS. In *Proceedings of OOPLSA*, pages 472 – 482, 1986.
[ont90]   ONTOS SQL User's Guide. *(ONTOS documentation)*, Dec 1990.
[Osb88]   SL Osborn. Identity, Equality, and Query Optimisation. In KR Dittrich, editor, *Advances in Object Oriented Database Systems (Proceedings of the 2nd International Workshop on Object Oriented Database Systems)*, pages 346 – 354. Springer Verlag, Sep 1988.

[RS87]   LA Rowe and MR Stonebraker. The POSTGRES Data Model. In *Proceedings of VLDB-13*, pages 83 – 96, Brighton, Sep 1987.

[Sha87] GM Shaw. An Object Oriented Query Algebra. *Bulletin of the IEEE Technical Committee on Data Engineering*, 12(3):29 – 36, Sep 1987.

[SO91]   DD Straube and MT Özsu. Queries and Query Processing in Object Oriented Database Systems. *ACM Transactions on Information Systems*, pages 387 – 430, 1991.

[SZ90]   GM Shaw and SB Zdonik. A Query Algebra for Object Oriented Databases. In *Proceedings of the 6th International Conference on Data Engineering*, pages 154 – 162. IEEE Computer Society Press, 1990.

[Tri90] Phil Trinder. Comprehensions, a Query Notation for DBPLs. Technical report CSC90/R16, University of Glasgow, 1990.

[TW90]   Phil Trinder and Philip Wadler. Improving List Comprehension Database Queries. Technical report CSC90/R4, University of Glasgow, 1990.

[YO91]   L Yu and SL Osborn. An Evaluation Framework for Algebraic Object Oriented Query Models. In *Proceedings of the 7th International Conference on Data Engineering*, pages 670 – 677. IEEE Computer Society Press, 1991.

[Zic91] Roberto Zicari. A Framework for Schema Updates in an Object Oriented Database System. In *Proceedings of the 7th International Conference on Data Engineering*, pages 2 – 13. IEEE Computer Society Press, 1991.

The Jupiter System : A Prototype for Multidatabase Interoperability

John Murphy[1] and Jane Grimson[2]

[1] Dublin City University, Republic of Ireland.
[2] Trinity College Dublin, Republic of Ireland.

Abstract. The goal of the Jupiter system is to provide interoperability services to a federation of autonomous and possibly heterogeneous database systems. The participants are free to withdraw at any time with the result that global integration of the participant schemas is not seen as a feasible solution. Our solution is to provide a multidatabase layer and a suitable interoperator language to allow information providers to construct loosely-coupled interoperable autonomous information systems. The enormous problems faced by information system providers are compounded by the difficulty of integrating key applications which have been developed using traditional methods with applications developed using, for example, object-oriented technology. A goal of our research is to address the area of multidatabase interoperability and to this end we have constructed the Jupiter prototype.

1 The Need for Distributed Data Processing

It is a fact of life that todays enterprises are more and more in need of decentralised information systems. This is largely due to the fact that many businesses have evolved in such a way that it is natural to view their operations as distributed operations. The information systems which are required to support these operations should also be distributed. This makes sense as we would like information systems to model their real world counterparts as closely as possible. It is also a fact that many enterprises have heavily invested in business critical legacy systems [3]. These systems are massive by any scale (10^7 LOC) and are practically impossible to rewrite. Therefore, apart from interesting research issues, there is a fundamental business need for distribution and interoperability solutions.

Database Management Systems (DBMS) allow the corporate data resource to be viewed at a number of levels. In the past it was common for all data to be centralised for effective and efficient use and it was not unusual for the data to be stored on a single large–scale mainframe computer. Increasingly, there is a demand for the data resource to be available to users of workstations and personal computers; a parallel development is the need for distribution of the data resource. It makes sense that the the data should be available at the location where it is most urgently required and the interaction of database technology and network technology has made this goal feasible [2].

Data distribution causes many new problems which are not present in centralised systems, it is very difficult to maintain consistency between a centralised data resource and possibly decentralised local data resources without the aid of supporting software. The need for software to support data distribution has resulted in the development of distributed database management software which has itself been given impetus by the rapid developments in telecommunications and network technologies. An additional problem is that many old centralised systems use 'difficult' data models, i.e. *network and hierarchical*, an inherent disadvantage is that future decentralised local data sites often opt for a more usable model such as the relational model leading to to difficult data model integration problems. This is a fundamental problem and it has in many respects slowed down the take up of distributed systems technology. This is because the distributed systems approach probably works best in a green fields site [2].

A more realistic approach is the multidatabase (MDB) approach which allows existing systems to participate and interoperate with the data resource without the need for a totally homogeneous logically integrated Distributed Database (DDB). For technically mature organisations this approach necessitates substantial redevelopment of existing applications to fit in with the DDB. Redevelopments would include amending existing applications so that they use the new DDB DDL/DML for accessing data resource; possible redefinition and reloading of data so that it is compatible with the data model of the DDB; remodelling and respecifying the data of each existing application system in the data dictionary of the DDB.

The problem of heterogeneity can be viewed at a number of levels : there can be heterogeneity at the system level, i.e. hardware and operating system heterogeneity; at the data model level, i.e. relational, hierarchical, network, object-oriented; at the semantic level, semantic differences of data within the same model. In the face of this heterogeneity, it is surely the single greatest problem facing the database community to provide multidatabase systems which can provide a single system image to an enterprise data resource which may be distributed and consist of heterogeneous autonomous systems. The MDBS provides a homogenising layer on top of the existing database systems and applications [11]. The existing systems operate independently without centralised control. This autonomy can lead to structural and representational conflicts which must be homogenised so that MDBS users can access the underlying data resource with a single uniform database language as opposed to a separate language for each underlying independent database.

This presupposes that there is some higher level schema representation of the data stored in the component databases. It is quite common for the relational model of data to be used as the common data model (CDM). Although it is mentioned in the literature, few examples exist of CDM implementations in an object-oriented model. This is because there is not, as yet, widespread agreement as to what constitutes an object-oriented-data model. In this work we have based our Common Data Model (CDM) on a formal model of objects [13] which has been described in the Z notation [18].

In the discussion that follows many of the definitions are taken from [17]. A database system consists of one or more databases which are managed by a database management system (DBMS). A federated database system is a collection of autonomous cooperating component DBSs. The component DBSs are integrated to various degrees via software which allows controlled and coordinated manipulation of the data resource. This software is known as the Federated Database Management System (FDBS). A significant characteristic of an FDBS is that independent component DBSs can continue with local operations and at the same time participate in the federation.

Multidatabase Management Systems (MDBMS) have multiple DBMSs, possibly of different types, and multiple *pre-existing* databases. An important characteristic of these systems is the presence of both local and global users. MDBMSs may be further categorised into the relatively obscure class of systems known as *unfederated* MDBMSs which have no local users and the more common category of *federated* MDBMSs which have both local and local users.

1.1 The Research Goals of the Jupiter Project

This paper describes research relating to the formal specification, design and implementation of the Jupiter system. The principal goal of the Jupiter project is to formally specify and construct an interoperator prototype which will allow autonomous systems to cooperate and share information in a controlled manner. Our focus is specifically on *database* interoperability and to this end we describe an architecture for database interoperability which consists of a number of services and a multidatabase language JIL, which allows a multidatabase user to access these services. The semantics of the multidatabase language JIL is based on an extension to the relational algebra for multidatabases which is subject of a forthcoming paper. This paper concentrates on the interoperability capabilities as they apply to multi-relational databases. The schema and implementation architectures are also outlined.

The research is novel in a number of areas which will be outlined later in this paper. Briefly, an architecture is proposed for management of heterogeneous database systems. The distinguishing features of the Jupiter system are:

1. Jupiter is constructed using Orbix, which is an implementation of the Common Object Request Broker Architecture (CORBA).
2. A Common Data Model (CDM) is used and is specified formally. We have specified the model in a novel way using a denotational style of specification [16] and we have mapped the JIL language to this model. In this way complete specifications exist for relational, entity-relationship, functional and object-oriented subsets of the JIL language [14].
3. Unlike most multidatabase system languages, JIL makes explicit use of a modified version of Sheth and Larson's five-layer architecture. The additional mappings from export schemas to local conceptual schemas and from Federation schemas to export schemas, means that user queries on federated

schemas are better insulated from changes to the underlying export and conceptual schemas. The mappings are effected by the 'bind' statement of the JIL language.

1.2 Organisation of the Paper

There are five sections in this paper : Section one, the current section; Section two discusses the research goals of the Jupiter project and describes the schema and implementation architectures of Jupiter; Section three outlines the interoperability services provided by Jupiter and describes how a user interacts with Jupiter by way of an example; Section four describes the *negotiation* aspects of the Jupiter system, i.e. how users can request information from information providers and grant access to their own information; Section five concludes the paper with remarks relating to future and continuing research work.

2 The Jupiter Interoperator

Interoperability, the ability of heterogeneous information systems to work together cohesively has become an active research area in recent years. In this section the Jupiter system is outlined. The system is being implemented as a layer above the Orbix system which is an implementation of OMG's CORBA architecture [6] with value-added extensions. The overall goal of Jupiter is to support interoperability between heterogeneous database systems. The kernel of the Jupiter system is an advanced dictionary system and multidatabase language which provide a number of services above Orbix.

Jupiter can support a loosely coupled federation of databases, that is, it can support the management of a federation of database systems using its own multidatabase language. The users are allowed to specify the data which they will share with other users via export schemas. Other users can browse the export schemas and construct a number of federation schemas from them. Federation schemas containing information from possibly heterogeneous databases can be manipulated by the JIL multidatabase language.

Query and Data exchange protocols are designed as Jupiter 'methods' defined against the CDM. All participating DBMSs will have access to these methods through the JIL language. The user can request direct access to a data resource or opt to use a quasicopy. Jupiter and the JIL language support the negotiation protocol described in [1]. A user can request information which is *nearly up to date*. The user can specify time, version and arithmetic constraints on the information received via quasicopy, e.g. the information must be within two versions of the latest version; the information must be within ten percent of a particular value; a new quasicopy must be loaded within one hour if the information providers copy is updated. In Section four we outline the language support provided by JIL for this protocol. An important advantage of this protocol is that it allows the information provider, i.e. the publisher of an export schema to *automatically* decide whether to share information or not with a information requester. The decision is based on current load factors and the parameters provided by the information requester.

The schema architecture of Jupiter follows the five-level architecture for federated DBMSs proposed by Sheth and Larson. See Figure 1. The *local schema* is the conceptual schema of the participating DBMS expressed in the data model of the local DBMS. The *participation schema* is a description in the CDM of the subset of data the local database wishes to share, which may be the entire local schema. The *export schema* allows different subsets of the data a site wishes to share to be presented to prospective importers, i.e. it presents a *view* of the underlying participant schema. Jupiter will allow the definition of any number of export schemas to be defined over each participation schema. A *federated schema* represents the integration of multiple export schemas and includes information on data distribution that is generated when integrating export schemas, i.e. there are no separate distribution or allocation schemas. Commands on the federated schema are translated into commands on the export schemas and thus the federated schemas support distribution in Jupiter.

Our five-level architecture is based on the proposal by Sheth and Larson. However, we deviate from their proposal in one respect : the component schema (participation schema in Jupiter) of Sheth and Larson's original architecture is a full local data model to common data model translation, we feel that the participation schema (partial translation) approach is more pragmatic and reduces the amount of unnecessary translation to the common model in Jupiter. In the Sheth and Larson five-level architecture two reasons are given for defining the component schemas in the common data model (CDM). They are :

1. A single representation is used to describe the divergent local schemas
2. It is possible to add semantics that are missing from the local schema to the component schema.

For a tightly coupled FDBS, the Sheth and Larson's component schema facilitates integration and negotiation tasks and for a loosely coupled FDBS it facilitates multidatabase queries and views. The approach taken in the Jupiter architecture, is, we feel, more appropriate in that only those critical parts of a local schema are made available directly to an export schema via the participation schema.

Figure 2 in Section 2.2 shows the implementation architecture of the Jupiter system. Each participating site has two databases (at least) The first is the participant DB and is under the control of the local DBMS; the second is the Jupiter metadatabase, Jupiter/MDD which is under the control of the Jupiter Interoperator. The metadatabase is implemented as a distributed dictionary service built on Orbix. As the underlying common model is object-oriented the metadata is represented naturally as a set of distributed objects.

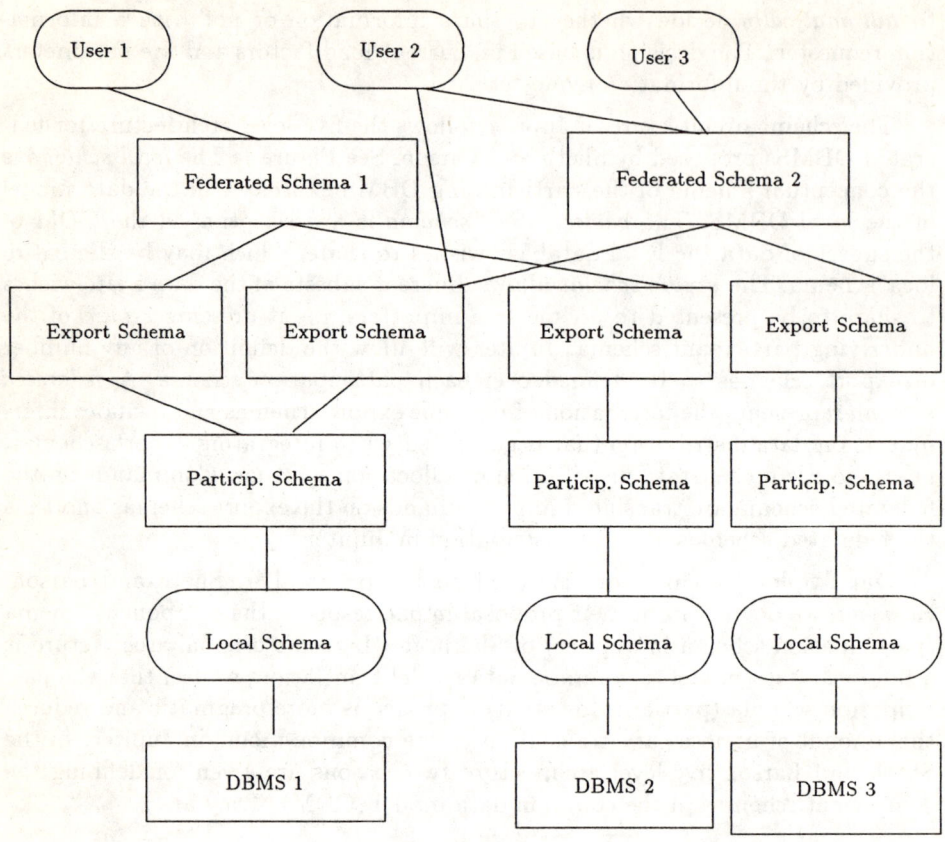

Fig. 1. Jupiter Schema Architecture

2.1 Implementation

Given the nature of the Jupiter interoperator (it is implemented on a distributed object system layer), we would like to support distribution and replication of the metadata. It is a desirable for security reasons to control the replication and distribution and to this end a security mechanism is implemented which can choose the nodes at which metadata can be stored and the nodes into which it can be read.

Each federated schema can be viewed as an object which provides a set of users with access to some federated set of participating DBs. These are known as Federated Database Objects (FDBOs).

There were two possibilities for implementing the Jupiter architecture. The first was to use an existing OODBMS to support persistence in Jupiter. This approach has limitations in that it would be difficult to prevent the creation of a federation object on an untrusted machine. An additional difficulty is that many OOPLs operate in a 'closed world' mode, i.e. they do not allow access to

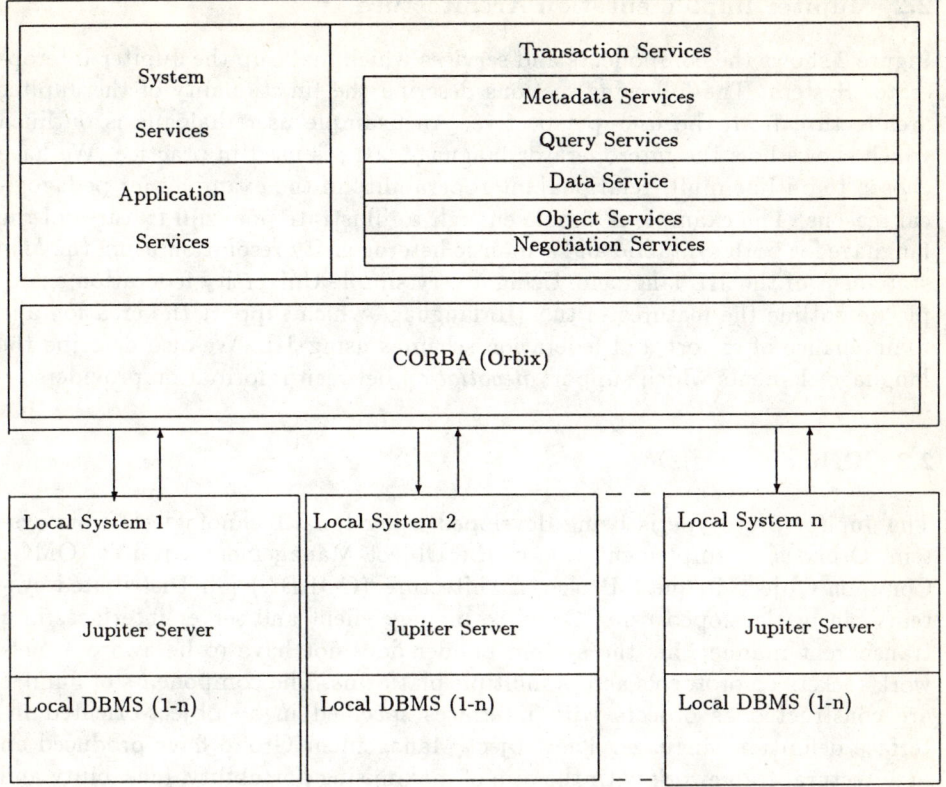

Fig. 2. Jupiter Implementation Architecture

resources outside their own environments. This would make it all but impossible to encapsulate the federations as objects. Also, a separate communications layer would have to be constructed to allow interoperation between remote sites. There is also the problem of the *particular* OO data model used in the OODBMS, there is no standard formal OO model and there can be significant differences between database using different competing models.

The second possibility was to use a distributed object management system, for example Orbix. The distributed objects can be accessed by the Jupiter/MDD component. The basic JIL primitives are implemented and encapsulated by Orbix objects which can be distributed throughout the system and be accessed transparently at other nodes. The Interoperator layer has a dual role in that it provides lightweight persistence for the metadata of the federation and it also provides for the distribution of that metadata as well as the distribution of Jupiter services to the remote nodes of the federation. Most accesses to metadata in Jupiter will be through pre-determined queries which can be supported by searches on simple data structures, this function is supported by Jupiter/MDD.

2.2 Jupiter Implementation Architecture

Figure 2 shows the components and services which make up the Jupiter Interoperator System. The following sections describe the functionality of the Jupiter architecture from the user perspective. An example user dialogue is outlined which shows how the interoperator language, JIL, is used in practice. We have chosen to outline multi-relational interoperability in the examples for pedagogical reasons. The example is simple enough to illustrate powerful features of the language for both syntactic and semantic heterogeneity resolution using the *bind* statement of the JIL language. Using a very simple University federation example we outline the features of the JIL language which support the creation and maintenance of export and federation schemas using JIL. We also describe the language elements which support *negotiation* between information providers.

2.3 Orbix

The Jupiter prototype is being developed using Iona Technologies' Orbix system. Orbix is an implementation of the Object Management Group's (OMG) Common Object Request Broker Architecture (CORBA) [6]. Distributed systems can be developed using Orbix to manage client and server interfaces in a transparent manner, i.e. the system builder does not have to be aware of network sockets or protocols across multiple platforms. The components of Jupiter are constructed as objects with interfaces specified in an object-oriented interface definition language. The Object Management Group have produced an architectural framework with the aim of maximising portability, reusability and interoperability. The OMG Reference Model describes the abstract structure of an application and the major interfaces it requires in order to operate, i.e. Application Programming Interface definitions and data exchange interfaces. Orbix is a full implementation of the OMG architecture and adds several extensions to the basic specification.

3 Interoperability : The User View

In this section, a method of interacting with Jupiter is shown. A goal for end-user interoperation is that a single system image is presented regardless of the number of participating heterogeneous database systems. The initial prototype supports command line interaction with the interoperator. The user is able to submit queries to a Jupiter server process at their local node using the Jupiter Interoperator Language (JIL), the local DBMS query language, or another participating DBMS's query language.

The Jupiter Interoperator will also allow the user to define an export schema and to create federation schemas. Definition and creation of these schemas is achieved through the DDL component of JIL. A query may be submitted at a federation node and Jupiter query services uses federation information stored in its distributed dictionary to decompose the query into sub-queries which can be addressed to component databases. The result of the sub-queries is merged by Jupiter data management services.

The Jupiter Interoperator Language (JIL) is introduced by way of an example. A simple federation of University databases is used. For simplicity and exposition of the language we assume that the four participants in the example federation use the same type of data model (relational). The example federation consists of four fictitious University databases. These are: Trinity College Dublin (TCD); Dublin City University (DCU); Limerick University (LU); and Maynooth University (MAY). Each of the Universities is assumed to have its own database for managing information of interest. The following sections describes possible schemas.

3.1 DCU DB Schema

DB DCU
    L(L#, Lname, tele)
    Stu(S#,Sname,
            Saddr1,Saddr2,Gavg)
    C(C#,Coursename)
    Faculty(F#,Fname)
    CourseFac(C#,F#)
    StuCourse(S#,C#)
    Prof(L#,F#)

3.2 LU DB Schema

DB LU
    Lect(L#, Lname, tel)
    Stu(Stuno,Sname,Saddr)
    C(C#,Coursename)
    Faculty(F#,Fname,L#)
    CourseF(C#,F#)
    StuC(Stuno,C#)

3.3 TCD DB Schema

DB TCD
    Lect(L#, Lname, tele)
    Stu(S#,Sname,Saddress)
    C(C#,Cname)
    Fac(F#,Fname)
    CFac(C#,F#)
    StuC(S#,C#)
    Prof(L#,F#)
    Head(L#,F#)

3.4 Maynooth DB Schema

DB MAY
    L(L#, Lname, telephone)
    Student(S#,Sname,Saddress,
               Nationality,Gradeavg)
    Course(Cno,Cname)
    Faculty(F#,Fname,location)
    CF(Cno,F#)
    SC(S#,Cno)
    Head(L#,F#)
    Prof(L#,F#)

3.5 An Example JIL Session

Using the above local schemas it is possible for the participants to define export schemas describing the data they are willing to share with others in the federation. A participant requests access to an export schema using JIL. The request may or may not be granted.

For example at the TCD node :

Jupiter
begin jil
create export exp1 from
      Lect(L#,Lname,Tele)
      Stu(S#,Sname,Saddress)
      Head(L#,F#)
      Fac(F#,Fname)

At the DCU node :

Jupiter
create export exp2 from
      L(L#,Lname,Tele)
      Stu(S#,Sname,Saddr1,Saddr2,gavg)
      Faculty(F#,Fname)
      Prof(L#,F#)

At LU :

Jupiter
create federation univ
      from (exp1) at TCD (exp2) at DCU

NOTE : a list of export schemas can be specified between the brackets for a particular site.

list export at global

$\Longrightarrow$ exp1 at TCD
$\Longrightarrow$ exp2 at DCU

list export at DCU

$\Longrightarrow$ exp2

list federation at local

$\Longrightarrow$ univ

list federation participant

$\Longrightarrow$ DCU Dublin City University
$\Longrightarrow$ LU Limerick University
$\Longrightarrow$ MAY Maynooth University
$\Longrightarrow$ TCD Trinity College Dublin

open federation univ
    bind(x to Stu)
    mselect x where x.Sname = 'Maguire'

$\Longrightarrow$ 9244 Maguire 40 Oakly Rd, Dublin 9 (DCU)
$\Longrightarrow$ 1000 Maguire St. Theresa Gardens, Dublin 8 (TCD)

close federation univ

open federation univ
    bind(x to Lect, L)
    mselect x where x.Lname = 'Jones'

$\Longrightarrow$ 7501 Jones 5363 (DCU)
$\Longrightarrow$ 20 Jones 5142 (TCD)

    At Maynooth :

Jupiter
create export exp3 from
    L(L#,Lname,Telephone)
    Faculty(F#,Facname,Location)
    Head(L#,F#)

    At LU :

open federation univ

update federation univ with export exp3 at may

close federation univ

open federation univ
        bind(x to L, Lect; y to Prof, Head)
        mselect x.Lname where x.L# = y.L#

⟹ Power
⟹ Smeaton
⟹ Grimson
⟹ Cardiff
⟹ Harris
⟹ Clapton

close federation univ

3.6 Optional and Dynamic Attributes

Not all attributes will be present for all tables in a federation schema. For example, the attribute *location* is present in the *Faculty* relation in export schema exp3 at Maynooth. Missing attributes can be specified in a multidatabase query as follows :

open federation univ
    bind(f to Fac* ; !Location)
    mselect f.*name, f.F#,   f.Location

⟹ Humanities 310 West Wing (MAY)
⟹ Engineering 410 East Wing (MAY)
⟹ Computing and Math. Science 1 (DCU)
⟹ Dublin Business School 2 (DCU)
⟹ Science 5 (TCD)
⟹ Arts 10 (TCD)

The optional attribute *Location* is simply specified in the bind list prefixed by an exclamation mark to show that this is an optional attribute and might not be present in all schemas.

The faculty *name* name attribute exhibits differences also. It is called *Facname* in the MAY export schema and *fname* in the DCU and TCD schemas. The name is resolved by using a partial attribute specification in the query, i.e. **name*. In the absence of an attribute in a schema, an optional attribute can be named. For example, in the *univ* federation schema there are three student tables. In MAY there is a *Nationality* attribute, consider the following query :

open federation univ
    bind(x to Stu)
    mselect x.S#,   x.Sname, x.Nationality or x.Saddr*
        where x.S#   between 1039 and 9248

⟹ 1040 Doyle Annamoe Park, Cabra. (TCD)
⟹ 5001 Thompson Irish (MAY)
⟹ 5010 Williams British (MAY)
⟹ 5020 DeBy Dutch (MAY)
⟹ 9244 Maguire 40 Oakly Rd, Dublin 9. (DCU)

Note also, that in the above example that the DCU schema for *Stu* contains an additional address line which is also retrieved.

The JIL language supports dynamic attributes, consider the the following query :

open federation univ
    bind(x to Stu ; y to gavg,gradeavg ;
        z to 'A1' 'A2' 'B1' 'B2'; w to 'A' 'A' 'B' 'B')
    dynamic grade(y) is map(z to w)
    mselect x.Sname where x.grade = 'A' or x.grade = 'B'

$\Longrightarrow$ Thompson (MAY)
$\Longrightarrow$ Williams (MAY)
$\Longrightarrow$ Maguire (DCU)
$\Longrightarrow$ Kelly (DCU)
$\Longrightarrow$ Brady (DCU)

A formula can also be applied to an attribute value dynamically. Imagine that a salary field exists for each lecturer in the *univ* federation. Furthermore, we wish to apply a salary increase to staff at Maynooth only. The following query allows a user to dynamically apply a formula to the value of the salary attribute for Maynooth staff :

open federation univ
    bind(x to L, Lect) dynamic sal is map(MAY.L.sal * 1.1)
    mselect x.Lname, x.Tele* where x.sal > 26000

$\Longrightarrow$ Grimson 5142 (TCD)
$\Longrightarrow$ Clapton 5144 (MAY)

4 Negotiation in Jupiter

The example sessions illustrate some of the features of JIL. What has not been shown is the negotiation protocol. The JIL language supports negotiation for federation resources using the negotiation protocol described in [1]. The protocol allows an importer of information to specify constraints relating to how timely the information is required to be. The importer requests the information and supplies parameters with the request to allow the exporter to assess the impact of granting the request on the exporters system. The exporter is free to reject any request.

The basic idea of the protocol is that a user can request direct access to federation data or can opt to have a local quasicopy of the required information. In the case of a quasicopy request the importer uses the JIL language to specify a *selection condition* and a *coherency* condition. Selection conditions specify the set of objects the importer wishes to import. Coherency conditions specify constraints relating to how often the quasicopy is updated. The JIL language support three types of coherency condition : *delay conditions* which state the maximum time lag between a copy and its original; *version conditions* specify the maximum version difference between the quasicopy and the original; *arithmetic conditions* specify the maximum numeric difference between quasicopy column or instance variable numeric values and original numeric values, the difference can be a numeric amount or a percentage deviation.

A user requests access to a published export schema via the *request* statement. For example, the following is a possible negotiation sequence prior to the previous transactions :
At LU :

Jupiter
request quasicopy on export exp2 at DCU
    with (time 10) or (version 3) or (diff percent 10 on gavg)
list request

$\Longrightarrow$ exp2 at DCU with (time 10)
    or (version 3) or (diff percent 10 on gavg)

At DCU :
Jupiter

$\Longrightarrow$ LU : request for quasicopy export exp1
    with (time 10) or (version 3) or (diff percent 10 on gavg)

grant quasicopy on export exp2 to LU
    with (time 10) or (version 3) or (diff percent 10 on gavg)

Granting the request is preceded by a calculation of the cost of meeting the request. If the cost exceeds a maximum value the request is refused otherwise the request is granted. The reader is referred to [1] for a treatment of cost estimation for a quasicopy request.

Assuming the request has been granted. The next Jupiter session at LU is:

Jupiter

$\Longrightarrow$ Request quasicopy on export exp2 at DCU
    granted with (time 10) or (version 3) or (diff percent 10 on gavg)

To revoke access to an export schema :
At DCU :

Jupiter

revoke quasicopy on export exp1 from LU

    At LU :

$\Longrightarrow$ Access to export exp1 at TCD revoked

It is of primary importance for interoperable systems that negotiation for shareable resources between autonomous sites be automated as far as possible and that the negotiation protocol should have a minimal impact on the operation and interoperation of the federation participants.

5 Conclusion

In this paper we have outlined a novel approach to the design and construction of interoperability services for use in a heterogeneous environment. The architecture of Jupiter was described and a description of the multi-relational component of the interoperator language JIL was provided. An approach to supporting heterogeneous DBMS interoperability was outlined which utilises the Orbix CORBA implementation to support interoperability in a novel way. Orbix provides a distributed object management services layer underneath Jupiter, and we believe that this is a promising approach to the problem of providing object distribution and interoperability in a heterogeneous environment. Also, the JIL language allows a user to define and manipulate data and mappings using a variant of Sheth and Larson's five layer architecture. To the best of our knowledge this approach has not been tried before. The language support for negotiation is, we believe, a critical feature of interoperable systems. There must be an effective and automatic method for a site to calculate the cost of sharing its information in the interests of maintaining a specific level of autonomy. There is no reference we know of in the literature to any multidatabase language which supports a negotiation protocol.

We are currently completing work on the development of formal language specifications for JIL. We have already completed the specification of the relational and multi-relation subcomponents in the denotational style. The multi-relational semantics has been developed and has equivalent expressive power to the multi-relational calculus defined by Grant et al. [9]. The implementation is at the prototype stage, an early version using the Amadeus system [5, 8] was used instead of Orbix to construct a prototype interoperator between the ORACLE and GemStone DBMSs. Our future plans are to complete the formal language specifications and to continue the implementation of the Jupiter system and language from these.

References

1. R. Alonso and D. Barbara. Negotiating data access in federated database systems. Technical Report CS-TR-160-88, Princeton University, Dept. of Computer Science, June 1988.
2. D. Bell and J. Grimson. *Distributed Database Systems*. Addison–Wesley Publishing Company, 1992.
3. M. Brodie. The promise of distributed computing and the challenges of legacy information systems. In *Proceedings of IFIP DS5 Semantics of Interoperable Database Systems*, pages 1–25, Lorne, Victoria, Australia, November 1992.
4. A. Diller. *Z : An Introduction to Formal Methods*. John Wiley, 1990.
5. Distributed Systems Group. An overview of the amadeus project, version 2.0. Technical Report TCD-CS-92-01, Trinity College Dublin, Dept. of Computer Science, January 1992.
6. The Object Management Group. *The OMG Object Model*. Object Management Group, 1992.
7. I. Hayes, editor. *Specification Case Studies, Second Edition*. Prentice Hall, 1993.
8. C. Horn and V. Cahill. Supporting distributed applications in the amadeus environment. *Computer Communications*, 14(6):358–365, 1991.
9. N. Roussopulos J. Grant, W. Litwin and T. Sellis. Query languages for relational multidatabases. *VLDB Journal*, 2:153–171, 1993.
10. J. Cardiff J. Grimson, S. Baker. Jupiter - a system for supporting database interoparability using a persistent object store. Dept. of Computer Science, Trinity College Dublin, Ireland, 1992.
11. W. Kim and J. Seo. Classifying schematic and data heterogeneity in multidatabase systems. *IEEE Computer*, December 1991.
12. W. Litwin. The future of heterogeneous databases. In *Proceedings of the Fall Joint Computer Conference*, Dallas, Texas, October 1987.
13. J.P. Murphy and J.B. Grimson. An Object Model in Z. *Database Technology*, 4(4):297–304, 1992.
14. J.P. Murphy and J.B. Grimson. The denotational semantics of a relational subset of the jil multidatabase language. Technical Report 99, Dublin City University, January 1993.
15. J.P. Murphy and J.B. Grimson. JIL/MDD : The jupiter interoperator dictionary for heterogeneous database systems. Technical Report 97, Dublin City University, August 1993.
16. David A. Schmidt. *Denotational Semantics — A Methodology for Language Development*. Wm. C. Brown Publishers, 1988.
17. A. Sheth and J. Larson. Federated database sytems for managing distributed, heterogeneous, and autonomous database systems. *ACM Computing Surveys*, 22(3):183–236, 1990.
18. J. Spivey. *The Z Notation : A Reference Manual, Second Edition*. Prentice Hall International, 1992.
19. J.B. Wordsworth. *Software Development with Z : A Practical Approach to Formal Methods in Software Engineering*. Addison–Wesley, 1992.

A MODEL FOR HETEROGENEOUS DISTRIBUTED DATABASE SYSTEMS

Keith G Jeffery, Liz Hutchinson, John Kalmus, Michael Wilson,
Wernher Behrendt, Colin Macnee

Systems Engineering Division, Rutherford Appleton Laboratory
Chilton, Didcot, OXON OX1 0QX UK

<kgj, ekh, jrk, mdw, wb, cam @inf.rl.ac.uk>

Abstract. The provision of access to autonomous heterogeneous distributed information sources (including databases) is becoming of increasing importance in most aspects of daily life. It has been the subject of intensive research for at least a decade, yet the solutions published to date have addressed only parts of the problem and have, in general, failed to provide an acceptable solution. We believe the problem can be rendered tractable by reconciliation of equivalent layers of information in the sources. We propose a new 5-layer model representing information richness or expressivity to assist in the integration of heterogeneous distributed database systems. The model has been used in a current ESPRIT project (MIPS), which utilises an embedded KBS to assist in query reformulation and answer construction when accessing heterogeneous distributed information sources, and shown to be useful.

1. Introduction

It can be argued that the provision of easy access to heterogeneous distributed databases is the key problem in information systems today. Databases built for specialised information system purposes can continue to fulfil those requirements, but increasingly the end-user requirements demand access not only to databases built for preconceived purposes, but also to a range of databases, built for different purposes, in order to provide the required information.

Application examples are numerous in engineering, finance, healthcare, travel and tourism, manufacturing, publishing and broadcasting, environmental protection - in fact in all aspects of modern life. The requirement for access to heterogeneous information sources can arise as a result of organisation takeovers (and thus acquisition of heterogeneous systems), organisation evolution (newer systems need to interoperate with heterogeneous legacy systems) or organisation interactions (requiring shared access to heterogeneous information sources to solve a common problem). The recent explosive growth in usage of WWW (World-Wide Web), which provides somewhat simplistic access to heterogeneous information sources, demonstrates the end-user need in the academic environment.

The paper is organised as follows: previous relevant work is reviewed in section 2. The existing models and the new proposed model are presented in section 3. Section 4 describes a realisation of the model in a current project and section 5 concludes.

2. Previous Work

2.1 Introduction

The problem solution mechanisms that have been proposed to provide integrated access to heterogeneous distributed information sources draw on pre-existing technologies and provide novel utilisations or integrations. In particular, they use previous work from one or more of the topics distributed systems, distributed databases (BeGr92), multidatabases (LiMaRo90), federated databases (ShLa90), view integration (HaRa91), schema integration (BaLeNa86), interoperability (Br92) and legacy systems (Br92).

2.2 Mechanisms

2.2.1 Introduction
Early work on the topic indicated the need to provide integration mechanisms for schemas and processes. Most of the work to date has concentrated on schema integration. The major techniques are reviewed, in order to acknowledge how the new proposed technique draws on the best features of those techniques.

2.2.2 Global Schema Technique
The aim of this technique is to produce, from an initial set of heterogeneous logical schemas built for different information systems requirements, one global homogeneous logical schema which is the superset of all the schemas, but with elimination of duplication of attributes. As such the usual technique is to find the common subset of attributes, and use them as the common core of the global schema with non-subset attributes being added. In a similar way, process integration aims to transform procedure calls against a local schema to procedure calls against the global schema. However, there are many problems which need resolution. Tools have been produced in some research projects to assist a database administrator in identifying possible common domains among attributes from different DBSs - for example (HaRa91).

2.2.3 Catalogue Technique
One technique that has been used with success in the IDEAS project (JeLaMiZaNaVa89) (and the subsequent EXIRPTS project) involves the following steps. Identification of attributes common to all the DBSs to be integrated, define a subset which is sufficient for identification of useful instances (records) but also a small subset of available information on that instance. For all instances, in all DBSs, this common subset is replicated in a catalog database available at each node, and maintained automatically using an advanced protocol (NaJeBoLaVa92). A query then consists of:
(a) an access to the common catalog at one node, selection of 'hits', storing of the primary keys of 'hits', partitioning the 'hits' file by node followed by :
(b) retrieval of all relevant attributes of the chosen instances from the distributed heterogeneous DBS.
The key point of this technique is that the intelligent system to perform schema reconciliation is human and static (it is done offline) before queries are allowed into the system!

The EXIRPTS project has investigated a more advanced technique using a dynamic multilingual thesaurus and attempts at dynamic (within query) schema reconciliation. The conclusion was that a sophisticated KBS (knowledge-based system) was required.

2.2.4 Hyperstructure Technique
Hyperstructures are becoming more common in text, graphics and image bases as well as in bases handling more conventional data. The hyperstructures have links which may imply rich semantics, and are thus richer than the simple semantics of, say, referential integrity in a relational DBMS. The technique proposed is to reduce the hyperstructure in its environment to a simpler structure with impoverished semantics associated with the structural links so as to permit the catalogue technique (described in 2.2.3) to be used - although in existing implementations (eg WWW) the catalogue is reduced even further to a 'table of contents' function.

2.2.5 Meta-Translation
This technique (HoFiGr87) involves translation of queries at a meta-level, i.e. at a level above that of the logical schemas. The technique needs to handle synonyms, homonyms and some structural relations. There is process integration by means of translated queries in relational systems.

Meta translation uses the principle of reverse engineering from logical to conceptual level (i.e. the proposition of a conceptual level model from a logical level schema)(SaCaGa91), (SiMa91). The extension of this work to the confederated data model (OmFiGr89) and beyond relational to object-oriented systems (RaFiGr91) demonstrated heterogeneous schema reconciliation by translation (essentially query re-writing) and (OmFiGr89) indicates the use of inferencing to assist integration as a future research area. The extended work to use domain constraints for query optimisation (FoGr92) demonstrates the need for such information to be available to the integration process for access to heterogeneous distributed databases.

2.2.6 Object Equivalencing
Object equivalencing is a powerful technique which allows integration of heterogeneous O-O DBSs (MaHeGe92). Object equivalencing relies on the premise that the logical level representation is a faithful reflection of the conceptual level (basic principle of O-O design) and has been demonstrated for integration (KiBaGaWo91). The O-O approach ensures that data structures are represented clearly and unambiguously, together with associated methods. Thus, there is much implied semantic knowledge which should make integration easier. However, unless the objects are exactly equivalent in attributes (not necessarily name), structure, domain constraints and methods, then integration will be extremely difficult. The encapsulation which so neatly provides a clean atomic unit of information with associated processing, at the same time prohibits integration at any level other than the encapsulation interface.

2.2.7 Mediation
Mediation (BaWi93) relies on the mediator accepting the logical level information and deducing or inducing a global logical level model (or more usually a global conceptual level model) within which to cooperate via actions at the re-engineered

logical level. However, the mediator requires much additional domain knowledge - gained from agents outside the immediate scope of the mediator - to be effective, and this problem is not yet resolved.

2.2.8 Intelligent Cooperating Systems
Intelligent Cooperative Systems (PaLaSe92), (WoLo92) require much knowledge outside of each independent system to allow real integration, including domain and tactical knowledge for provision of access to the required information. In particular, there is a lack of knowledge of semantics, constraints, rules in active databases, trigger and processing conditions.

2.2.9 KBS assist
The use of an embedded KBS assist for schema reconciliation has been attempted in an O-O environment, (QuFiGr92) building on the earlier meta-translation work (OmFiGr89),(RaFiGr91). More general work on the use of a KBS assist for data model, query and user requirement reconciliation in the MIPS project (Je92) exposes clearly the layered structure of the information and process model (and, as an aside, associated constraints and triggers expressed as rules) which leads to the proposed model in section 3. The use of a KBS with epistemic knowledge, tactical knowledge and domain knowledge provides a multilevel model, mappings between and within model levels, and a mechanism for reconciliation - not only of schemas but also of processes, constraints and user interaction.

We have discovered recently a project (ArChHsKn93) with similar aims to MIPS. It is currently documented in an internal research report (April 1993) of the USC Information Sciences Institute. It uses LOOM as the KBS and 9 ORACLE databases as the distributed environment - which, by use of a single proprietary DBMS based on a single data model, reduces some of the complexity. Furthermore, its main concern is query reformulation; the answer construction aspects are more-or-less ignored. However, it provides a parallel example to MIPS in the use of a KBS assist and in some ways validates the technique.

2.3 Problems

It is worth considering the problems facing a heterogeneous DB system integrator, if only to expose the slow progress towards their solution in the previous work until the use of KBS assists (2.2.9) and to demonstrate the need for a layered and contained approach to the solution as proposed in section 3. The problems have been catalogued (ShLa90), (Je92) but concern briefly :

(a) attribute names: degree of similarity of attribute described, syntax and semantics - see also (YuSuDa91);

(b) domains expressed differently in different DBSs, especially in range and precision of representation;

(c) constraints - see (CoQi92) for a classification. Work on representing such constraints in a rule-base (JeLaCu89) and constraint enforcement (DaWi89) have shown what is possible in a single DBS. Work on constraints has been extended

(GoGlJe93) to include semantic constraints, which will be of particular interest in integrated DBSs;

(d) calibration - especially of time-series scientific data;

(e) units of measurement - and automated conversion, including translation of text;

(f) nulls including the representation of 'not collected', 'not detected' or 'detected but not measurable'. Similar problems surround the representation of uncertainty and probability;

(g) keys - an attribute may form, or form part of, a key - and thus imply some structural relationship to other attributes;

(h) textbases: not only are there the language and character representation problems but also the interpretation of semantics. In many cases, the structure of the textbase is sufficiently well-defined for appropriate granules of text to be incorporated in the output result of the integrated DBS;

(i) graphics and images: if a particular graphic or image is regarded as a granule of information, and only output ion the result of the integrated DBS when referenced by some other attribute in the result, then the problem is reduced to a concern for representation. Any deeper structural equivalencing requires more semantic knowledge;

(j) structure: the major problem concerns the recognition of structure. The entity identified at data analysis time in the system development lifecycle could be implemented in many different ways, depending on the type of DBMS and the choice of representations. In a relational DBMS, typically an entity is split as tuples across relations linked by referential integrity constraints over foreign keys. In an O-O DBMS the implementation is totally different (as an encapsulated object).

An entity can change its properties and characteristics dependent on its role in an application. Thus, selection of the requisite attributes for a particular role is important. Substructures within entities in different DBSs within the integrated DBS are likely to be equivalent in that they represent a similar concept. However, matching of those substructures (i.e. identifying them and using them in an integrated way) requires a level of semantic knowledge currently unavailable in DBMSs. Few query systems permit recursive processing, and thus there is an immediate incompatibility of structure between DBSs within an integrated DBS.

Text structures - sentences, paragraphs, sections, chapters - have a structural relationship within any one document (entity) but their structural relationships to other entity substructures is unclear. The problem with graphics or image structures is even greater than that of text structures, because of the greater diversity of possible structures and their inter-relationships.

2.4 Summary

The key problem is the identification of equivalent (or can be transformed to equivalent) entity structures and attributes, to be manipulated by equivalent (or can be tranformed to equivalent) queries (including updates if required). Unfortunately, this identification requires - in addition to the information in the logical schemas - knowledge either encoded in the application code, (as procedures or rules) or stored in design documents (at conceptual or higher levels of abstraction and covering data, processes and rules, including constraints and triggers). In either case the required information for integration is unavailable to automated reconciliation in existing DBMS schemas at logical level. While data or system dictionaries have provided some of this information, they are not yet used widely and the IRDS standard (Gr90) does not provide all the required information. In addition, the information may not exist at all (and thus require inferencing to produce it) or may only be available in the intention of the end-user, and so require elicitation during dialogue with the system. Thus, the use of KBS assists to add knowledge, or higher level information, to the integration process is required.

3. The Proposed Model

3.1 The Existing Model

The basis for most database system architectures, whether centralised or distributed, homogenous or heterogeneous is the 3-layer (physical, logical, conceptual) model, representing respectively the physical realisation of the data model, the logical description (schema) of the data model and the conceptual representation (eg by E-R diagrams) of the data model. This model reflects essentially 3 layers or levels of information richness or expressivity, and is not to be confused with the topological model (ANSI75) of internal, conceptual and external layers.

However, this model fails to provide for the representation of more advanced database constructs, such as constraints and triggers which lie (in terms of expressivity) between the logical and conceptual layers and are concerned with process-data interaction. Constraints - especially domain and inter-attribute constraints - are of paramount importance when reconciling heterogeneous DBSs, yet are not recorded in DBS schemas based on the existing model. Event processing (triggers) can also be represented conveniently by constraints so providing some uniformity of representation between data and process - yet the existing model does not support this. Non-functional requirements at the conceptual level (performance, security, privacy) can also be represented as constraints, yet this is not possible in the existing model. The lack of facilities to represent temporal data in the existing model is well-known. Similarly, active database components are not represented. In summary, there is clearly a need for a modelling level to contain a level of expressivity represented by constraints (commonly expressed in an extension of FOPL (first order predicate logic). We propose the intensional level for this purpose.

Furthermore, the conceptual layer is usually represented - in design documents - by some kind of entity-relation diagram (for data) and some kind of dataflow diagram (for processing). This - even with extensions to EER (Extended Entity-Relation) providing sub-entities and labelled relations or ERT (Entity-Relation-Time) providing timestamped entities and relations between them - is insufficient to express the rich semantics of the end-user requirements, and also fails to record, at conceptual level, data - process interactions (Je93). Already identified are the need for data model independence (SpPaDu92) and for higher-level models (SaCaGa91). Thus, there is a need for a layer of the model which has a level of expressivity higher than that of the conceptual level, to contain the rich semantics of end-user and domain requirements expressed in descriptions of entities and relations that include role, temporal, and other evolutionary or time-v ariant properties. We propose the semantic level for this purpose.

Before considering the proposed 5-layer model extending the 3-layer model, it should be noted that a different 5-layer model has already been proposed (ShLa90). Their model does not follow the concept of layers of information richness or expressivity, but rather extends work on distributed database architectures by using layers which relate to configuration of the system or topology (ANSI75). Their layers are local, component, export, federal, external. The authors themselves point out that their model does not overcome the problems of redundancy between layers, semantics to ensure safe schema translation, integration or interpretation, efficiency or consistency of transaction management.

3.2 The Proposed Model

The proposed 5-layer model adds two layers to the 3-layer model (Fig 1). At the top a semantic layer is added, while an intensional layer is inserted between conceptual and logical. These two layers accommodate the required information analysed above. The proposed model thus has the layers in ascending order: physical, logical, intensional, conceptual, semantic.

The physical, logical and conceptual layers retain their purpose as in the existing 3-layer model. The semantic layer is used to record - by means of semantic graphs or similar constructs - the rich information obtainable from the end-user requirements, including both functional and non-functional requirements. The intensional layer records - in an extended first-order logic representation - constraints of all kinds (data, processing, functional and non-functional) so formalising at least some of the information from the semantic layer after it has been refined in the conceptual layer to conceptual models for the major entities and processes. It may be concluded that the proposed 5-layer model extends the 3-layer model to allow for greater complexity and richness of representation of entities, their relationships and the dynamics of data-process interactions including functional and non-functional constraints. That these richer representations require an embedded KBS for manipulation is unsurprising in view of the work on advanced databases (including deductive, deductive object-oriented and active databases) over the last decade or so.

This model has many advantages; it retains the clearly layered structure so allowing for independence of implementation, model and design method as provided by the existing model. However, it provides for the description and integration of data and process interaction information and thus paves the way for easier integration of heterogeneous distributed systems.

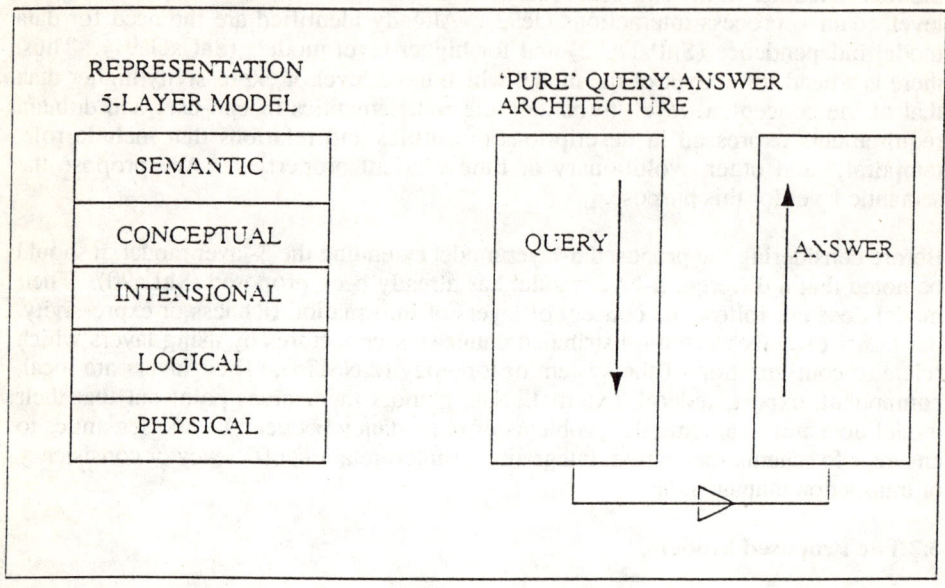

Fig. 1. The Proposed 5-Layer Model

4. The Model in an Application

4.1 The MIPS Project

The MIPS (Multimedia Information Presentation System) project is an ESPRIT III project (number 6542) started in May 1992. The application domain chosen for the demonstrator or proof of concept is tourism; the major standards concern SGML, HyTime, SQL, RDA and various representation standards for graphics and image. A KBS provides the reconciliation facilities, the system accesses heterogeneous distributed DBSs and the end-user utilises a multimedia workstation. The project thus investigates many of the problems discussed above.

4.2 The MIPS Architecture

Queries are initiable in one of two ways:
(a) from within a HyTime document - by instantiation of a query skeleton stored within the document structure - this implies a predetermined query ;
(b) from a query window, where the user can utilise a query-by-forms or a raw SQL-style interface.

The query in each case is handled by an interaction between the query processing module and the KBS which chooses appropriate target DBSs, sets up the communications required, partitions the query into fragments, makes any semantic changes required in each fragment (eg attribute name change), adds any required constraints and despatches the query fragments.

The responses to the query are screened by interaction between the answer construction module and the KBS for consistency and accuracy, and then amalgamated into a single HyTime document structure, to allow hyperlinked browsing of a multimedia document (or group of documents).

Perhaps one of the most interesting features of this system is the utilisation of several advanced technologies together. The utilisation of an advanced HCI (Human-Computer Interface) - with a KBS assist to the query processing module for user query disambiguation and explanation - is novel, although will utilise some of the concepts from ESPRIT II project MMI2 (WiFa91). The use of a KBS assist to the query processing module to refine, fragment and optimise queries in a heterogeneous distributed DBS environment is innovative. The use of a KBS assist to the answer construction module to assemble a consolidated answer ready for instantiation into a HyTime web (a graph with empty nodes constructed by the query processing module with the KBS during query breakdown and clarification) is novel. The use of a proposed standard (HyTime) to provide a framework for information presentation in an end-user workstation environment is also novel.

It will be noted that the integration technique used in MIPS draws on the best features of many of the pre-existing technologies, especially meta-translation (for query rewriting), hyperstructures (for answer presentation) and KBS assists in all parts of the system. However, the novelty lies in the integration of these techniques into a single system and the very great extension of previous work on KBS assists to encompass all aspects of the system. Both of these advances were only possible given the proposed 5-layer model.

4.3 The Mapping of the MIPS Architecture to the Model

The processes of the MIPS architecture can be mapped onto the 5 - layer model of representation illustrated in Figure 1, which is an extension of the 3-layer model.

The semantic layer aims to represent the user's purpose; the conceptual layer carries a representation in terms of an entity-relationship-attribute model of the particular application domain; at the next level, intensional representations of the databases about which the MIPS application has information are applied to the processes to constrain further the set of subqueries generated; the logical representations are equivalent to expressions in external query languages; physical representations are expressed in the external query languages themselves. At each level, some richness of representation is lost, but is stored to allow its recovery when the answer satisfying the original query is constructed. The five layers apply in reverse order to the processes involved in answer construction.

Figure 2 illustrates how the `pure' query-answer architecture has been integrated with the HyTime and presentation aspects of MIPS. The five layers are represented through the query-processing modules and the answer construction and presentation modules.

A single language, IRL (Internal Representation Language), is used for communication across the MIPS internal interfaces which will support a common protocol. The specification of the language is based on:

(a) application communications protocol (ACP) constraints - requirements placed on the language in its message passing role;

(b) the functionality of the processes which the IRL is intended to support; viz:
(1) breakdown and clarification of queries into sets of subqueries;
(2) interpretation and manipulation of retrieved data;
(3) the server role of the KBS throughout the architecture.

As outlined above, the richness of representation required across the MIPS interfaces varies throughout the architecture. The IRL is sufficiently rich and flexible to reflect these different levels of representational expressiveness, corresponding to the 5-layer model. This flexibility is included in the IRL by separating the ACP information from the message content in IRL expressions. The ACP remains constant across the architecture and provides an envelope for carrying messages in different forms, appropriate for different areas of functionality within the architecture. Dialects of the IRL have been defined to reflect the different functionality which will be supported across the architecture, and the varying level of representational richness required. The MIPS module interfaces are being implemented using the European Software Bus standard which provides suitable facilities to carry the IRL into and out of the various modules. Figure 2 uses a simplified view of the MIPS architecture to illustrate the levels of representation required across the MIPS internal interfaces.

5. Conclusions

The proposed 5-layer model, based on an extension of the classical 3-layer model and retaining the layering by information richness or expressivity has proved helpful in understanding and classifying heterogeneity in a distributed information source environment. The model provides a layered and thus contained (layer-by-layer) basis for integration technologies, and in particular works well with a KBS assist which provides the additional information to assist in integration which is lacking in logical level distributed database schemas. The model has been demonstrated to work as the basis for the detailed architectural design within the MIPS system.

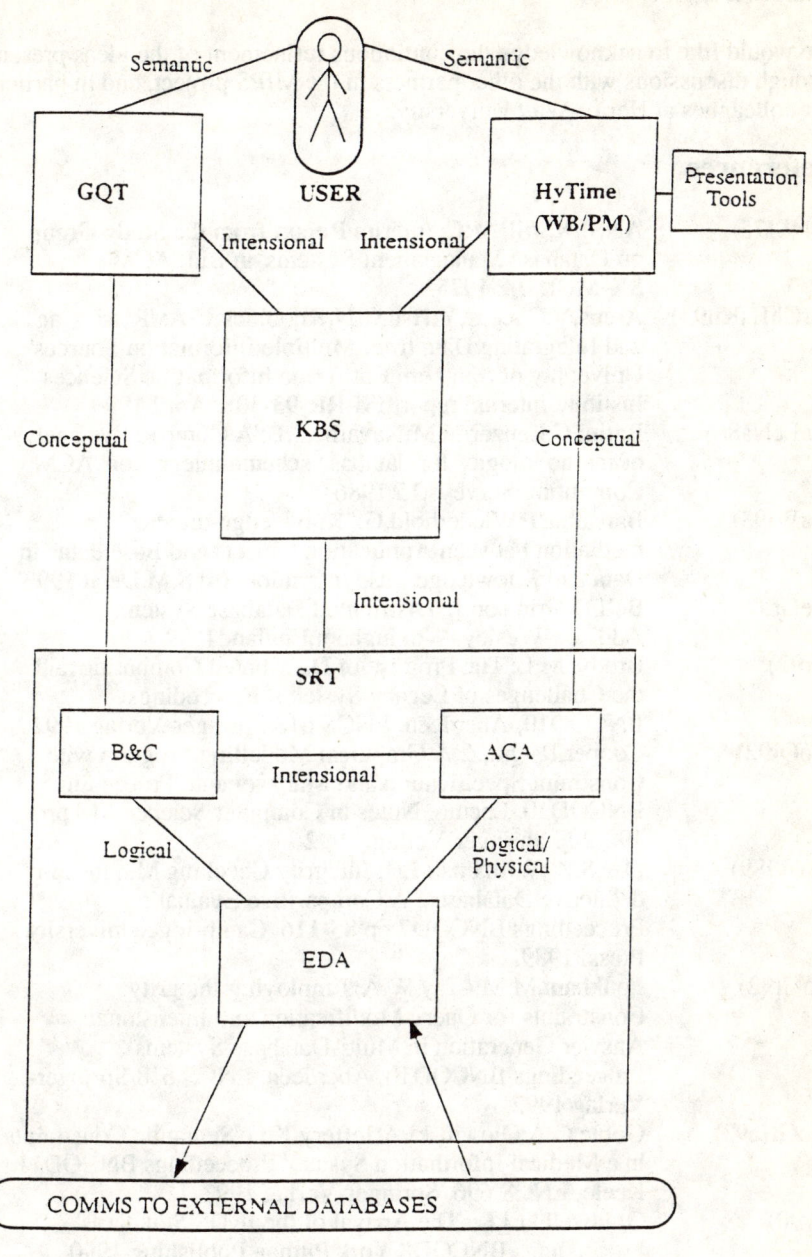

Fig. 2. Representation level (of the 5-layer model) and MIPS interfaces

Acknowledgements

We would like to acknowledge the continuous refinement of the ideas presented here through discussions with the other partners in the MIPS project, and in particular with our colleagues at Heriot-Watt University.

References

(ANSI75)	ANSI/XS/SPARC:'Interim Report from the Study Group on Database Management Systems' in Bull ACM SIGMOD 7,2 1975
(ArChHsKn93)	Arens,Y;Chee,C.Y;Hsu,C-N;Knoblock,C.A: 'Retrieving and Integrating Data from Multiple Information Sources' University of Southern California Information Sciences Institute Internal report ISI-RR-93-308, April 1993
(BaLeNa86)	Batini,C;Lenzerini,M;Navathe,S.B:'A Comparative analyi of methodologies for database schema integration' ACM Computing Surveys,15,1986
(BaWi93)	Barsalou,T;Wiederhold,G:"Knowledge-directed mediation between Application Objects and Base data' in Data and Knowledge Base Intgration, Ed S.M Deen 1993
(BeGr92)	Bell,D;Grimson,J: 'Distributed Database Systems' Addison-Wesley, Wokingham,England1992
(Br92)	Brodie,M.L:'The Promise of Distributed Computing and the Challenges of Legacy Systems' Proceedings BNCOD10, Aberdeen. LNCS 618 Springer-Verlag 1992
(CoQi92)	Cooper,R-Qin,Z: A Graphical Modelling Program with Constraint Specification and Management. Proceedings BNCOD10, Lecture Notes in Computer Science 618 pp 192-208 Springer-Verlag. 1992
(DaWi89)	Das,S.K.;Williams,M.H: Integrity Checking Methods in deductive Databases: A Comparitive Evaluation. Proceedings BNCOD7 pp 85-116. Cambridge University Press. 1989.
(FoGr92)	Fonkham,M.M;Gray,W.A:'Employing Integrity Constraints for Query Modification and Intensional Answer Generation in Multi-Database Systems' Proceedings BNCOD10, Aberdeen. LNCS 618 Springer-Verlag 1992
(GoGlJe93)	Goble,C.A;Glowinski,A;Jeffery,K.G:'Semantic Constraints in a Medical Information System' Proceedings BNCOD11 Keele, LNCS 696, Springer-Verlag 1993
(Gr90)	Gradwell,D.J.L: 'The Arrival of the IRDS Standards' Proceedings BNCOD8 York Pitman Publishing 1990
(HaRa91)	Hayne,S;Ram,S:'Multi-User View Integration System (MUVIS): An Expert System for View Integration' Proc 6th International Conference on Data Engineering 1986

(HoFiGr87)   Howells,D.I;Fiddian,N.J;Graw,W.A:'A Source-to-Source
                 Meta-Translation System for Relational Query
                 Languages' Proceedings VLDB13 Brighton 1987
(Je92)   Jeffery,K.G:'Database Integration' Proceedings
                 SOFSEM92 Conference, Ed. M Bartosek, Masaryk
                 University Brno, Czech Republic
(Je93)   Jeffery,K.G;'Extended Transition Networks for Systems
                 Development' Proceedings SOFSEM93 Conference, Ed.
                 M Bartosek, Masaryk University Brno, Czech Republic
(JeLaCu89)   Jeffery,K.G.-Lay,J.O.-Curtis,T:'A Logic-Based System for
                 Data Validation'. Proceedings BNCOD7 pp 71-84.
                 Cambridge University Press. 1989.
(JeLaMiZaNaPa89)Jeffery,K.G.;Lay,J.O.;Miquel,J.F.;Zardan,S.;Naldi, F.;
                 Vannini Parenti,I.: 'IDEAS: A System for International
                 Data Exchange and Access for Science'. Information
                 Processing and management 25(6) pp 703-711. 1989.
(KiBaGaWo91)   Kim,W;Ballou,N;Garza,J.F;Woelk,D:'A Distributed Object
                 Oriented Database System supporting Shared and
                 Private Databases' ACM Trans on Information Systems
                 9,1 1991
(LiMaRo90)   Litwin,W;Mark,L;Roussopoulos,N:'Interoperability of
                 Multiple Autonomous Databases' ACM Computing
                 Surveys 22,3 1990
(MaHeGe92)   Manola,F;Heiler,S;Georgakopoulos,D:'Distributed Object
                 Management' International Journal of Intelligent and
                 Cooperative Information Systems 1,1 1992
(NaJeBoLaVa92)Naldi,F.-Jeffery,K.G.-Bordogna,G.-Lay,J.O.-Vannini
                 Parenti,I.: 'A Distributed Architecture to Provide Uniform
                 Access to Pre-Existing, Independent, Heterogeneous
                 Information Systems'. RAL Report 92-003. 1992.
(OmFiGr89)   Omololu,A.O;Fiddian,N.J;Gray,W.A: 'Confederated
                 Database Management Systems' Proceedings BNCOD7,
                 Heriot-Watt University, Edinburgh, Cambridge
                 University Press 1989
(PaLaSe92)   Papazoglou,M.P;Laufmann,S.C;Selis,T.K:'An
                 Organzational Framework for Cooperative Intelligent
                 Information Systems' International Journal of Intelligent
                 and Cooperative Information Systems 1,1 1992
(QuFiGr92)   Qutaishat,M.A;Fiddian,M.J;Gray,W.A:'Association
                 Merging in a Schema Meta-Integration System for a
                 Heterogeneous Object-Oriented Environment'
                 Proceedings BNCOD10, Aberdeen. LNCS 618 Springer-
                 Verlag 1992
(RaFiGr91)   Ramfos,A;Fiddian,N.J;Gray,W.A: 'A Meta-translation
                 System for Object-Oriented to relational Schema
                 Translations' Proceedings BNCOD9 Wolverhampton,
                 Butterworth-Heinemann, 1991

(SaCaGa91)   Saltor,F;Castalanos,M;Garcia-Solaco,M:'Suitability of data models as canonical models for federated databas' SIGMOD Record 20,4 1991

(ShLa90)   Sheth,A.P;Larson,J:'Federated Databae Systems for managing heterogeneous, distributed and autonomous databases' ACM Computing Surveys 22,3 1992

(SiMa91)   Siegel,M;madnick,S.E:'A Metadata Approach to reslving Semantic Conflicts' Proc 17th VLDB, Barcelona, 1991

(SpPaDu92)   Spacciapetra,S;parent,C;Dupont,Y:'Model Independent Assertions or Integration of Heterogeneous Schemes' VLDB Journal 1 1992

(WiFa91)   Wilson,M.D.-Falzon,P.: Multimedia and Multimodal Systems: Architectures for Cooperative Dialogue. Proceedings ERCIM Workshop on Multimedia. Lisbon, November 1991.

(WoLo92)   Woo,C,C;Lochosvky,F:'Knowledge Commnication in Intelligent Information Systems' International Journal of Intelligent & Cooperative Information Systems 1,1 1992

(YuSuDa91)   Yu,C;Sun,W;Dao,S:'Determining Relationships amond names in heterogneous Databases' SIGMOD Record 20,4 1991

Springer-Verlag and the Environment

We at Springer-Verlag firmly believe that an international science publisher has a special obligation to the environment, and our corporate policies consistently reflect this conviction.

We also expect our business partners – paper mills, printers, packaging manufacturers, etc. – to commit themselves to using environmentally friendly materials and production processes.

The paper in this book is made from low- or no-chlorine pulp and is acid free, in conformance with international standards for paper permanency.

Lecture Notes in Computer Science

For information about Vols. 1–745
please contact your bookseller or Springer-Verlag

Vol. 746: A. S. Tanguiane, Artificial Perception and Music Recognition. XV, 210 pages. 1993. (Subseries LNAI).

Vol. 747: M. Clarke, R. Kruse, S. Moral (Eds.), Symbolic and Quantitative Approaches to Reasoning and Uncertainty. Proceedings, 1993. X, 390 pages. 1993.

Vol. 748: R. H. Halstead Jr., T. Ito (Eds.), Parallel Symbolic Computing: Languages, Systems, and Applications. Proceedings, 1992. X, 419 pages. 1993.

Vol. 749: P. A. Fritzson (Ed.), Automated and Algorithmic Debugging. Proceedings, 1993. VIII, 369 pages. 1993.

Vol. 750: J. L. Díaz-Herrera (Ed.), Software Engineering Education. Proceedings, 1994. XII, 601 pages. 1994.

Vol. 751: B. Jähne, Spatio-Temporal Image Processing. XII, 208 pages. 1993.

Vol. 752: T. W. Finin, C. K. Nicholas, Y. Yesha (Eds.), Information and Knowledge Management. Proceedings, 1992. VII, 142 pages. 1993.

Vol. 753: L. J. Bass, J. Gornostaev, C. Unger (Eds.), Human-Computer Interaction. Proceedings, 1993. X, 388 pages. 1993.

Vol. 754: H. D. Pfeiffer, T. E. Nagle (Eds.), Conceptual Structures: Theory and Implementation. Proceedings, 1992. IX, 327 pages. 1993. (Subseries LNAI).

Vol. 755: B. Möller, H. Partsch, S. Schuman (Eds.), Formal Program Development. Proceedings. VII, 371 pages. 1993.

Vol. 756: J. Pieprzyk, B. Sadeghiyan, Design of Hashing Algorithms. XV, 194 pages. 1993.

Vol. 757: U. Banerjee, D. Gelernter, A. Nicolau, D. Padua (Eds.), Languages and Compilers for Parallel Computing. Proceedings, 1992. X, 576 pages. 1993.

Vol. 758: M. Teillaud, Towards Dynamic Randomized Algorithms in Computational Geometry. IX, 157 pages. 1993.

Vol. 759: N. R. Adam, B. K. Bhargava (Eds.), Advanced Database Systems. XV, 451 pages. 1993.

Vol. 760: S. Ceri, K. Tanaka, S. Tsur (Eds.), Deductive and Object-Oriented Databases. Proceedings, 1993. XII, 488 pages. 1993.

Vol. 761: R. K. Shyamasundar (Ed.), Foundations of Software Technology and Theoretical Computer Science. Proceedings, 1993. XIV, 456 pages. 1993.

Vol. 762: K. W. Ng, P. Raghavan, N. V. Balasubramanian, F. Y. L. Chin (Eds.), Algorithms and Computation. Proceedings, 1993. XIII, 542 pages. 1993.

Vol. 763: F. Pichler, R. Moreno Díaz (Eds.), Computer Aided Systems Theory – EUROCAST '93. Proceedings, 1993. IX, 451 pages. 1994.

Vol. 764: G. Wagner, Vivid Logic. XII, 148 pages. 1994. (Subseries LNAI).

Vol. 765: T. Helleseth (Ed.), Advances in Cryptology – EUROCRYPT '93. Proceedings, 1993. X, 467 pages. 1994.

Vol. 766: P. R. Van Loocke, The Dynamics of Concepts. XI, 340 pages. 1994. (Subseries LNAI).

Vol. 767: M. Gogolla, An Extended Entity-Relationship Model. X, 136 pages. 1994.

Vol. 768: U. Banerjee, D. Gelernter, A. Nicolau, D. Padua (Eds.), Languages and Compilers for Parallel Computing. Proceedings, 1993. XI, 655 pages. 1994.

Vol. 769: J. L. Nazareth, The Newton-Cauchy Framework. XII, 101 pages. 1994.

Vol. 770: P. Haddawy (Representing Plans Under Uncertainty. X, 129 pages. 1994. (Subseries LNAI).

Vol. 771: G. Tomas, C. W. Ueberhuber, Visualization of Scientific Parallel Programs. XI, 310 pages. 1994.

Vol. 772: B. C. Warboys (Ed.),Software Process Technology. Proceedings, 1994. IX, 275 pages. 1994.

Vol. 773: D. R. Stinson (Ed.), Advances in Cryptology – CRYPTO '93. Proceedings, 1993. X, 492 pages. 1994.

Vol. 774: M. Banâtre, P. A. Lee (Eds.), Hardware and Software Architectures for Fault Tolerance. XIII, 311 pages. 1994.

Vol. 775: P. Enjalbert, E. W. Mayr, K. W. Wagner (Eds.), STACS 94. Proceedings, 1994. XIV, 782 pages. 1994.

Vol. 776: H. J. Schneider, H. Ehrig (Eds.), Graph Transformations in Computer Science. Proceedings, 1993. VIII, 395 pages. 1994.

Vol. 777: K. von Luck, H. Marburger (Eds.), Management and Processing of Complex Data Structures. Proceedings, 1994. VII, 220 pages. 1994.

Vol. 778: M. Bonuccelli, P. Crescenzi, R. Petreschi (Eds.), Algorithms and Complexity. Proceedings, 1994. VIII, 222 pages. 1994.

Vol. 779: M. Jarke, J. Bubenko, K. Jeffery (Eds.), Advances in Database Technology — EDBT '94. Proceedings, 1994. XII, 406 pages. 1994.

Vol. 780: J. J. Joyce, C.-J. H. Seger (Eds.), Higher Order Logic Theorem Proving and Its Applications. Proceedings, 1993. X, 518 pages. 1994.

Vol. 781: G. Cohen, S. Litsyn, A. Lobstein, G. Zémor (Eds.), Algebraic Coding. Proceedings, 1993. XII, 326 pages. 1994.

Vol. 782: J. Gutknecht (Ed.), Programming Languages and System Architectures. Proceedings, 1994. X, 344 pages. 1994.

Vol. 783: C. G. Günther (Ed.), Mobile Communications. Proceedings, 1994. XVI, 564 pages. 1994.

Vol. 784: F. Bergadano, L. De Raedt (Eds.), Machine Learning: ECML-94. Proceedings, 1994. XI, 439 pages. 1994. (Subseries LNAI).

Vol. 785: H. Ehrig, F. Orejas (Eds.), Recent Trends in Data Type Specification. Proceedings, 1992. VIII, 350 pages. 1994.

Vol. 786: P. A. Fritzson (Ed.), Compiler Construction. Proceedings, 1994. XI, 451 pages. 1994.

Vol. 787: S. Tison (Ed.), Trees in Algebra and Programming – CAAP '94. Proceedings, 1994. X, 351 pages. 1994.

Vol. 788: D. Sannella (Ed.), Programming Languages and Systems – ESOP '94. Proceedings, 1994. VIII, 516 pages. 1994.

Vol. 789: M. Hagiya, J. C. Mitchell (Eds.), Theoretical Aspects of Computer Software. Proceedings, 1994. XI, 887 pages. 1994.

Vol. 790: J. van Leeuwen (Ed.), Graph-Theoretic Concepts in Computer Science. Proceedings, 1993. IX, 431 pages. 1994.

Vol. 791: R. Guerraoui, O. Nierstrasz, M. Riveill (Eds.), Object-Based Distributed Programming. Proceedings, 1993. VII, 262 pages. 1994.

Vol. 792: N. D. Jones, M. Hagiya, M. Sato (Eds.), Logic, Language and Computation. XII, 269 pages. 1994.

Vol. 793: T. A. Gulliver, N. P. Secord (Eds.), Information Theory and Applications. Proceedings, 1993. XI, 394 pages. 1994.

Vol. 794: G. Haring, G. Kotsis (Eds.), Computer Performance Evaluation. Proceedings, 1994. X, 464 pages. 1994.

Vol. 795: W. A. Hunt, Jr., FM8501: A Verified Microprocessor. XIII, 333 pages. 1994.

Vol. 796: W. Gentzsch, U. Harms (Eds.), High-Performance Computing and Networking. Proceedings, 1994, Vol. I. XXI, 453 pages. 1994.

Vol. 797: W. Gentzsch, U. Harms (Eds.), High-Performance Computing and Networking. Proceedings, 1994, Vol. II. XXII, 519 pages. 1994.

Vol. 798: R. Dyckhoff (Ed.), Extensions of Logic Programming. Proceedings, 1993. VIII, 362 pages. 1994.

Vol. 799: M. P. Singh, Multiagent Systems. XXIII, 168 pages. 1994. (Subseries LNAI).

Vol. 800: J.-O. Eklundh (Ed.), Computer Vision – ECCV '94. Proceedings 1994, Vol. I. XVIII, 603 pages. 1994.

Vol. 801: J.-O. Eklundh (Ed.), Computer Vision – ECCV '94. Proceedings 1994, Vol. II. XV, 485 pages. 1994.

Vol. 802: S. Brookes, M. Main, A. Melton, M. Mislove, D. Schmidt (Eds.), Mathematical Foundations of Programming Semantics. Proceedings, 1993. IX, 647 pages. 1994.

Vol. 803: J. W. de Bakker, W.-P. de Roever, G. Rozenberg (Eds.), A Decade of Concurrency. Proceedings, 1993. VII, 683 pages. 1994.

Vol. 804: D. Hernández, Qualitative Representation of Spatial Knowledge. IX, 202 pages. 1994. (Subseries LNAI).

Vol. 805: M. Cosnard, A. Ferreira, J. Peters (Eds.), Parallel and Distributed Computing. Proceedings, 1994. X, 280 pages. 1994.

Vol. 806: H. Barendregt, T. Nipkow (Eds.), Types for Proofs and Programs. VIII, 383 pages. 1994.

Vol. 807: M. Crochemore, D. Gusfield (Eds.), Combinatorial Pattern Matching. Proceedings, 1994. VIII, 326 pages. 1994.

Vol. 808: M. Masuch, L. Pólos (Eds.), Knowledge Representation and Reasoning Under Uncertainty. VII, 237 pages. 1994. (Subseries LNAI).

Vol. 809: R. Anderson (Ed.), Fast Software Encryption. Proceedings, 1993. IX, 223 pages. 1994.

Vol. 810: G. Lakemeyer, B. Nebel (Eds.), Foundations of Knowledge Representation and Reasoning. VIII, 355 pages. 1994. (Subseries LNAI).

Vol. 811: G. Wijers, S. Brinkkemper, T. Wasserman (Eds.), Advanced Information Systems Engineering. Proceedings, 1994. XI, 420 pages. 1994.

Vol. 812: J. Karhumäki, H. Maurer, G. Rozenberg (Eds.), Results and Trends in Theoretical Computer Science. Proceedings, 1994. X, 445 pages. 1994.

Vol. 813: A. Nerode, Yu. N. Matiyasevich (Eds.), Logical Foundations of Computer Science. Proceedings, 1994. IX, 392 pages. 1994.

Vol. 814: A. Bundy (Ed.), Automated Deduction—CADE-12. Proceedings, 1994. XVI, 848 pages. 1994. (Subseries LNAI).

Vol. 815: R. Valette (Ed.), Application and Theory of Petri Nets 1994. Proceedings. IX, 587 pages. 1994.

Vol. 816: J. Heering, K. Meinke, B. Möller, T. Nipkow (Eds.), Higher-Order Algebra, Logic, and Term Rewriting. Proceedings, 1993. VII, 344 pages. 1994.

Vol. 817: C. Halatsis, D. Maritsas, G. Philokyprou, S. Theodoridis (Eds.), PARLE '94. Parallel Architectures and Languages Europe. Proceedings, 1994. XV, 837 pages. 1994.

Vol. 818: D. L. Dill (Ed.), Computer Aided Verification. Proceedings, 1994. IX, 480 pages. 1994.

Vol. 819: W. Litwin, T. Risch (Eds.), Applications of Databases. Proceedings, 1994. XII, 471 pages. 1994.

Vol. 820: S. Abiteboul, E. Shamir (Eds.), Automata, Languages and Programming. Proceedings, 1994. XIII, 644 pages. 1994.

Vol. 821: M. Tokoro, R. Pareschi (Eds.), Object-Oriented Programming. Proceedings, 1994. XI, 535 pages. 1994.

Vol. 822: F. Pfenning (Ed.), Logic Programming and Automated Reasoning. Proceedings, 1994. X, 345 pages. 1994. (Subseries LNAI).

Vol. 823: R. A. Elmasri, V. Kouramajian, B. Thalheim (Eds.), Entity-Relationship Approach — ER '93. Proceedings, 1993. X, 531 pages. 1994.

Vol. 824: E. M. Schmidt, S. Skyum (Eds.), Algorithm Theory - SWAT '94. Proceedings. IX, 383 pages. 1994.

Vol. 826: D. S. Bowers (Ed.), Directions in Databases. Proceedings, 1994. X, 234 pages. 1994.

Vol. 827: D. M. Gabbay, H. J. Ohlbach (Eds.), Temporal Logic. Proceedings, 1994. XI, 546 pages. 1994.

Vol. 828: L. C. Paulson, Isabelle. XVII, 321 pages. 1994.